Promoting the Colonial Idea

Propaganda and Visions of Empire in France

Edited by

Tony Chafer
Principal Lecturer in French and African Studies
University of Portsmouth

and

Amanda Sackur
Senior Lecturer in International History
London Guildhall University

palgrave

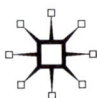

First published 2002 by
PALGRAVE
Houndmills, Basingstoke, Hampshire RG21 6XS and
175 Fifth Avenue, New York, N.Y. 10010
Companies and representatives throughout the world

PALGRAVE is the new global academic imprint of
St. Martin's Press LLC Scholarly and Reference Division and
Palgrave Publishers Ltd (formerly Macmillan Press Ltd).

ISBN 0–333–79180–0

Library of Congress Cataloging-in-Publication Data
Promoting the colonial idea : propaganda and visions of empire in France / [edited by] Tony Chafer and Amanda Sackur.
    p. cm.
    Includes bibliographical references and index.
    ISBN 0–333–79180–0
    1. France—Colonies—Public opinion—History. 2. Public opinion––France—History. 3. Propaganda, French—History. 4. France––Colonies—Race relations—Historiography. 5. Racism—France. I. Chafer, Tony. II. Sackur, Amanda.
JV1811 .P76 2001
325'.344—dc21
                                                    2001032731

10   9   8   7   6   5   4   3   2   1
11   10   09   08   07   06   05   04   03   02

Printed and bound in Great Britain by
Antony Rowe Ltd, Chippenham, Wiltshire

Promoting the Colonial Idea

Contents

List of Tables and Figures

List of Abbreviations

ANS	Archives Nationales du Sénégal, Dakar
ANSOM	Archives Nationales Section Outre-Mer, Aix-en-Provence (contains files from the former Ministry of Colonies, Rue Oudinot)
AOF	Afrique Occidentale Française
AOM	Archives d'Outre-Mer, Aix-en-Provence (contains files repatriated from France's former overseas territories)
CGTU	Confédération Générale du Travail Unifié
CVIA	Comité de Vigilance des Intellectuels Antifascistes
ENA	Etoile Nord-Africaine
FIDES	Fonds d'Investissement pour le Développement Economique et Social (Investment Fund for Economic and Social Development)
FLN	Front de Libération Nationale
FN	Front National
ILO	International Labor Organization
IOM	Indépendants d'Outre Mer
JOAOF	Journal Officiel de l'Afrique Occidentale Française
LAI	League Against Imperialism
LDH	Ligue des Droits de l'Homme
OAS	Organisation de l'Armée Secrète
PCF	Parti Communiste Français
RDA	Rassemblement Démocratique Africain
RPR	Rassemblement pour la République
SAINA	Services de Surveillance et Assistance des Indigènes Nord-Africaines
SFIO	Section Française de l'Internationale Ouvrière
SPMIC	Society for Protection of Mothers and Infants of Cambodia
UPC	Union des Populations du Cameroun

Acknowledgements

This book arises from a conference on 'Propaganda and Empire', organised by the Francophone Area Studies Research Group at the University of Portsmouth. The conference took place at the Institut Français, London, in September 1997. The group is undertaking a long-term research project on colonialism, decolonisation and postcolonialism in France, the primary focus of which is to study the ways in which empire has shaped contemporary France and French national identity. This book is one of a series on the theme of French imperialism which is currently being published by members of the research group. Particular thanks are due to Martin Evans, whose support for the project has been crucial to its success.

The editors wish to thank the Institut Français for providing such a congenial conference venue in the heart of London and René Lacombe, Cultural Attaché at the French Embassy in London, for his help in getting the conference off the ground. They would also like to acknowledge the generous financial support of the French Embassy, the Centre for European Studies Research at the University of Portsmouth and the Association for the Study of Modern and Contemporary France, without which the conference and this book would not have been possible.

TONY CHAFER
AMANDA SACKUR

Notes on the Contributors

Robert Aldrich is Associate Professor in Economic History at the University of Sydney. He is the author of several works on France in the South Pacific and of *Greater France: A History of French Overseas Expansion*. He is also the co-author of a study of France's present-day overseas *départements* and territories.

Catherine Atlan is a lecturer at the University of Poitiers and a researcher at the Centre d'Etudes Africaines (Ecole des Hautes Etudes en Sciences Sociales, Paris). She is currently working on a doctoral thesis in African History entitled 'Political Society in Senegal at the Time of Independence (1945–1968)'.

Tony Chafer is Principal Lecturer in French and African History at the University of Portsmouth. He is a specialist on decolonisation in French West Africa and on Franco-African relations, on which he has written widely. He has recently published an article on 'French African Policy in Historical Context' and has just completed a book entitled *France's 'Successful Decolonization'? The End of Empire in French West Africa, 1936–60*.

Alice L. Conklin is Associate Professor of History at the University of Rochester, NY. She is the author of *A Mission to Civilize: The French Republican Idea of Empire in France and West Africa, 1895–1930* (winner of the 1998 Berkshire Prize), and has recently coedited a reader on modern colonialism, entitled *European Imperialism, 1830–1930: Climax and Contradictions*. She is currently researching the emergence of a new discourse of cultural relativism in colonial and metropolitan France in the inter-war years.

Jonathan Derrick is a journalist and historian specialising in twentieth-century francophone Africa. Having prepared a PhD thesis on 'Douala under the French Mandate, 1916–1936' (School of Oriental and African Studies, London, 1979), he worked with *West Africa* magazine and reference book publishers Africa Books, and taught History at the University of Ilorin, Nigeria. Publications include *Middlemen of the Cameroons Rivers* (co-author with Ralph A. Austen).

Véronique Dimier is a Research Fellow at St Antony's College, Oxford. Her thesis was on 'The Training of Colonial Administrators in France and Britain, 1930–50: The Development of a Science of Colonial Administration'. Her publications include *Controverse autour de comparaisons Franco-Britanniques sur l'administration coloniale.*

Penny Edwards is a Postdoctoral Fellow at the Centre for Cross-Cultural Research, Australian National University, where she is conducting a comparative study of British and French colonialism in Burma and Cambodia. Her publications include *Cambodge: The Cultivation of a Nation, 1860–1945.*

Chris Flood is Head of European Studies at the University of Surrey. He is the author of *Pensée politique et imagination historique dans l'oeuvre de Paul Claudel* and *Political Myth: A Theoretical Introduction.* He co-edited *Political Ideologies in Contemporary France* and two collections on the politics of French intellectuals.

Hugo Frey recently completed a doctoral thesis on history writing under the Fourth Republic in France. He has a research interest on the culture of the French extreme right and has published articles in *Contemporary French Civilization*, the *Journal of European Studies* and *Modern & Contemporary France.*

Gilles de Gantès is a researcher at the Institut de Recherches sur le Sud-Est Asiatique, Marseilles. His research focus is on colonial theories and practices in the legal, cultural, social and economic fields in Indochina from the 1860s to 1920.

Odile Goerg is Professor of Modern History at Marc Bloch University, Strasbourg, and a member of the Institut Universitaire de France. She has published various works on the economic and social history of West Africa, including *Commerce et colonisation en Guinée, 1850–1913* and *Pouvoir colonial, municipalités et espaces urbains. Conakry et Freetown, des années 1880 à 1914.* She is also the coeditor of various works on youth and towns in Africa, notably *Fêtes urbaines en Afrique. Espaces, identités et pouvoirs.*

Jean-Hervé Jézéquel is a researcher at the Centre d'Études Africaines, Ecole des Hautes Etudes en Sciences Sociales, Paris. He was awarded a doctoral fellowship at the University of Chicago and is currently working on a doctoral thesis in African History entitled 'African Schoolteachers in French West Africa, 1903–1939'.

William Kidd is Reader in French at the University of Stirling. He has published extensively on twentieth-century French literature and ideology, war and memory, psychocriticism and iconography. He has recently published *Les Monuments aux morts mosellans de 1870 à nos jours: Etude historique et iconographique.*

Neil Macmaster is Senior Lecturer in Contemporary European Studies at the University of East Anglia. His latest book is *Colonial Migrants and Racism: Algerians in France, 1900–1962.* He is currently writing a book on *Racism in Twentieth Century Europe* and carrying out research on perceptions of Islam in contemporary France.

Isabelle Merle is a researcher at the Centre National de la Recherche Scientifique (CNRS). She is a specialist on the colonisation of the South Pacific and has published a work on the origins of colonial society in Nouvelle-Calédonie. She is currently working on a comparative history of French and British settler colonisation in the South Pacific, focusing on Australia, New Zealand and Nouvelle-Calédonie.

Amanda Sackur is Senior Lecturer in International History at London Guildhall University. Her research interests are in gender and cultural change in francophone West Africa and she has written widely on interactions between French and Africans in pre-colonial and colonial Senegal.

Emmanuelle Sibeud is Professeur Agrégé in History at the Ecole des Hautes Etudes en Sciences Sociales, Paris. Her thesis was on 'La naissance du savoir africaniste en France, 1878–1930'. Her publications include: with Anne Piriou, ed., *L'Africanisme en questions*, and with Jean-Loup Amselle, ed., *Entre Orientalisme et ethnographie: l'itinéraire africaniste de Maurice Delafosse (1870–1926).*

Pascal Venier is Lecturer in French History and Politics at the University of Salford and a specialist in French colonial history and international history. He is author of *Lyautey avant Lyautey* and is currently working on a book on Théophile Delcassé and Franco-British relations from Fashoda to the Entente Cordiale, 1898–1904.

Owen White is Associate Professor in the History of France and the French Empire at the University of Delaware. He was previously British Academy Research Fellow at University College, Oxford. His book *Children of the French Empire. Miscegenation and Colonial Society in French West Africa, 1895–1960* has recently been published by Oxford University Press.

Introduction

Until relatively recently, it was widely accepted that, with brief exceptions, late-nineteenth- and twentieth-century empire enjoyed little popular support and generated no great mass enthusiasm in Europe. Thus, it is argued, imperial issues had little impact on domestic politics. As a result, the study of imperial history has been that of elite activity or of particular interest groups such as missionaries or traders. Historians could stress that in Britain, for example, after a flush of jingoistic fervour in the late nineteenth century,

> [i]mperialism as a sophisticated concept, had been, and remained, the preserve of an elite, and a fractured elite at that. The public's lack of ideological commitment was matched by almost complete ignorance of the territories of Empire, the principles of its government, or the economic dimensions of the imperial connection. It was this combination of indifference and ignorance which ensured that the Empire was never a significant electoral issue and that decolonisation was accomplished without any of the national trauma experienced by France.[1]

Equally, in Germany, Nazi propaganda describing the loss of colonies in 1919 was markedly less successful than that which highlighted continental losses or which focused on anti-semitism. On the other hand, it was recognised that circumstances could modify popular apathy for imperial affairs. The Boer War is perhaps the most significant example of mass interest and involvement in the course of overseas expansion but at other times imperial issues could become significant too. It has also been argued that some politicians appealed to this well of potential support for British expansion as a counter to demands for reform and democratic participation at home. Certainly, in the 1890s particularly, Chamberlain, Rhodes and others in their circles believed firmly that imperialism offered an alternative to growing class conflict or significant political change.[2] Wehler has argued that the German search for colonies owed much to similar motives.[3] Yet mass support for imperial adventure was rarely sustained; once a crisis was resolved or territory seized, the public rapidly lost interest.[4]

French empire was even more of an elite affair, appealing only to a limited number of interested parties. In the nineteenth century a significant proportion of French expansion resulted not from policy decided in Paris but from the actions of over-enthusiastic or self-interested men on the spot.[5] Kanya-Forstner has shown how army officers in West Africa tended to dictate not only the pace of French conquests there but also the direction of French policy.[6] In Indochina, naval officers played a similar role. In other words, the seizure of territory was not a popular issue, and at times even parliament was hostile to further expansion. Indeed, in July 1885 Jules Ferry was forced to resign over intervention in Indochina. Even as the 'new imperialism' was supposedly taking form in the 1880s, French political attitudes were either largely apathetic or even actively hostile to colonial expansion. For the right, overseas activity was merely a distraction from the vital business of revenging the humiliating defeat of 1870–1 and, most important of all, regaining the 'French' territories of Alsace and Lorraine. For the left, on the other hand, colonialism was either irrelevant or an attempt to prevent social and political change within France.

Yet France apparently had a much more organised imperial lobby than Britain or Germany, a paradox which has attracted significant attention, especially in the anglophone world.[7] Research on the *parti colonial* has shown, however, that advocates of empire formed only a small bloc throughout the period of the Third Republic.[8] Their success owed more to the nature of parliamentary politics in France than to any constituency, let alone to mass support. In effect, a small bloc of pro-imperial politicians and civil servants used the weakness of the Third Republic to their own advantage, exploiting both the instability of French governments and the relative longevity of civil servants compared with Colonial Ministers.[9] That they could do so, however, was a sign that imperial expansion and development were of little political importance in France. Had these issues excited widespread interest, it is unlikely that they would have been suitable for political horse-trading. Thus the consensus of historical opinion has emphasised the importance of individuals – politicians, 'men on the spot', civil servants – in determining the course of European expansion. Most historians agreed that once the period of colonial scrambles was over, popular interest in empire was very difficult to maintain, another sign that it had never been fundamentally engaged by the process in the first place.

However, this picture has been transformed by a new generation of historians whose work has often straddled the boundaries of imperial, social and cultural history and who have been prepared to look at other disciplines such as sociology and anthropology in seeking to develop a broader picture of 'imperialism'. Led in particular by John MacKenzie, these historians have forced a revision in our perceptions of popular attitudes towards empire and thus in nineteenth- and twentieth-century imperial history. Although they do not argue that the empire necessarily loomed large in domestic politics for more than brief periods, in looking at popular culture, rather than focusing on political campaigns, such historians have shown that empire has played a far more significant role in shaping modern Britain than has hitherto been believed. Literature, for adults and for children, music hall, cinema, newspapers, popular songs, exhibitions, missionary pamphlets, advertising and a myriad of other aspects, projected images of race, empire and jingoistic nationalism which contributed to British perceptions of their place in the world. Membership of organisations such as the Boy Scouts and the Boys' Brigade offered yet more opportunities for absorbing pro-imperial messages. At the same time, carefully stage-managed pageants such as Victoria's Diamond Jubilee and annual Empire Day celebrations directed popular attention to the importance of Britain's imperial role.[10]

What is more, John MacKenzie has shown that this popular enthusiasm was more than a passive response to the rapid expansion of British territorial conquests in the late nineteenth century. Certainly, the most obvious forms of imperial celebration postdate the beginning of the so-called 'new imperialism'. Nonetheless, public attitudes did affect colonial policy-making and popular imperialism had an impact on both the course of British expansion and on British culture. In demonstrating this, MacKenzie's work has revolutionised the understanding of imperial history. From the 1980s on, a variety of historians have taken up the challenge, broadening our understanding of the relationship of the British to their empire.

This revolution has taken longer to affect the historiography of the French empire. Nonetheless, a variety of studies have begun to suggest that the elite nature of French imperialism requires significant qualification. William Schneider's examination of the popular press in the late nineteenth century shows that the arguments in favour of 'social imperialism' were aired in France just as they were in Britain and Germany, and at a relatively early date.[11] 'Penny papers' such as the *Petit Journal* and later the *Petit Parisien* enjoyed massive circulations and exerted a strong influence on public opinion, so it was significant that they were, on the whole, enthusiastic about empire.[12] Another study, comparing British and French imperial propaganda, concludes that the French effort was, if anything, more sustained than the British.[13] More recently, a variety of studies of advertising, literature, exhibitions and museology, the performing arts and other aspects of popular culture have emphasised the impact of empire on France itself.[14]

However, these studies do not merely substitute an emphasis on popular imperialism for the old stress on the 'official mind'.[15] Once again, the historiography of British imperialism offers some pointers to the significance of this effort to make the colonial empire popular. MacKenzie points out that the fact of widespread, pervasive, pro-imperial propaganda was not sufficient to create mass enthusiasm for empire, at least not on a sustained basis. Indeed, he maintains that the 'conventional historical wisdom' – that the British were largely indifferent to empire, ignorant of it and lacking a common experience which might give it definition – is '[i]n some respects ... unassailable.'[16] The importance of his approach lies more in understanding a new dimension of British social history and in a richer, more nuanced, appreciation of the interplay of imperial expansion and domestic politics.

The more studies of this kind are published, the more it becomes clear that imperialism was central to the British experience. One theme that has been of major importance is the role of imperialism in recasting national identities. Linda Colley, for example, argues that trade and empire were crucial to the emergence of a specifically British identity from the eighteenth century.[17] MacKenzie stresses that, rather than generating explicitly pro-imperial sentiments in the population at large, propaganda – official and unofficial – was most successful in remoulding British perceptions of themselves. The key was an 'ideological cluster' of renewed militarism and monarchism, social Darwinism and its associated racial theories, and a cult of national heroes. 'Together these constituted a new type of patriotism, which derived a special significance from Britain's unique imperial mission.'[18] Indeed, MacKenzie argues, the incorporation of such perceptions into British world views was so successful that imperialism could be considered a 'core ideology in British society' for at least seventy years.[19] By the end of the First World War, '[m]uch of the landscape of a defensive, nationalist popular imperialism had become so familiar as to be barely noticed', thus explaining why the British appeared to be indifferent to empire in comparison with earlier periods.[20]

The issue of identity was, if anything, of even greater importance in France at this time. The Third Republic was established in the wake of serious defeat by Prussia in 1870 and the divisive effects of the Paris Commune. Yet it lacked a firm base; the first parliament in fact contained a *royalist* majority. What is more, the Republic itself continued to be threatened from the radical right for more than a generation. Under these circumstances, it is not surprising that the Republic should mount a significant and concerted effort to generate a new French identity which could unite these disparate and often alienated groups.[21] In this respect, there were differences between Britain and France yet the results were remarkably similar. Like Britain (but unlike Germany and Italy, where claims to territory took on a different ideological complexion), France had a long history as a colonial power in the nineteenth century. Thus the empire was easily available as a symbolic unifying force. As Jenkins points out, 'between 1870 and 1914 the ideological and class character of nationalism under[went] a profound transformation'.[22] If French nationalism was republican rather than monarchical, it was a republic without revolution, based on militarism and heroic sacrifice, which harked back to former royal glories and emphasised race.

The relationship between this new nationalism and imperialism was less straightforward than in Britain, however. For many, imperial expansion was a distraction from the major task of *la revanche*: revenging their defeat at the hands of Germany, regaining the lost territories of Alsace and Lorraine and purging the humiliation of 1870–1. It took some time before the idea that the acquisition of new territories and carving out trading zones in the face of potential rivalry would strengthen France (and thus aid '*revanchism*') gained acceptance. Although protectionism and concerns about French economic weakness tended to strengthen the case of those arguing for expansion, governments vacillated about such moves well into the 1880s. It is here that the work of the various geographical societies and groups which coalesced into the *parti colonial* was so important. Not only did they provide a stream of learned and semi-learned papers advocating expansion but they also appear to have exerted an influence both on business and on the 'penny press' and thus, indirectly, on government and official thinking.[23] Indeed, their importance is shown by the fact that, as Venier points out in his chapter, in 1900 Lyautey focused much of his informal campaign on the various geographical societies. What is more, increasing stress on the military and the desire to strengthen the armed forces made it difficult to criticise the actions of individual officers whose actions were responsible for much French territorial expansion. Thus the domestic context of imperial propaganda, with which this volume is concerned, was significantly different from that of Britain, even if historians can perceive many similarities.

Unlike in Britain, the empire continued to play an integrative and unifying role in France long after the main scrambles were over. In part this can be explained by the greater need for unification given the enormity of the task in front of the Third Republic in 1870. However, it was also a result of the need to reintegrate territories restored to France after the First World War. As Goerg shows in her contribution to this volume, knowledge of the empire was used explicitly to foster a sense of belonging to France and a pride in its achievements. More generally, the alliance of social Darwinism, racism and the cult of military victory which lay behind enthusiasm for empire helped counter memories of defeat in Europe. Imperial propaganda conveyed a strong sense of French cultural, political and indeed 'racial' superiority, over both conquered peoples and, implicitly, over less successful colonial powers. This proved an attractive message to all Europeans but appealed particularly to the French in the aftermath of defeat and political upheavals which dominated the early years of the Republic. At the same time, the emphasis on France's (secular) civilising mission in the colonies – stressed repeatedly in unrealistic discussions of assimilation – reinforced the message of the superiority of the French Republic which dated back to the Revolution. In Britain, assumptions of superiority and international leadership were so taken for granted in the twentieth century that repetition was scarcely necessary. In contrast, France enjoyed no such consensus and the continued hostility of the right to republican ideology ensured that imperial propaganda was vital throughout the colonial period in order to create some common ground.

It is, however, necessary to remember that imperial 'propaganda' was generated by a variety of bodies for a myriad of different reasons. While the societies and political groups organised themselves into an overtly political lobby – with great success in the years before 1914 – many other forms of propaganda presented themselves as more neutral. Film-makers, exhibition organisers, authors of textbooks and academics or colonial officials debating the best way to approach colonial rule claimed to be offering an educational service or providing entertainment. Yet their work had a highly ideological component which was designed to sway its audience. A third group exploited popular perceptions of the empire for private ends; the construction of and use of such images in advertising is an obvious example.[24]

This highlights an important methodological point: to what extent were such uses of images promoting particular views of empire and to what extent were they merely reflecting prevailing perceptions? It is not always easy to distinguish the two. John MacKenzie suggests that the main criterion should be the deliberate attempt to influence public opinion. Thus, efforts to 'educate' the public about the empire were just as much propaganda and indeed were far more successful as campaigns to encourage expansion itself. Textbooks, newspaper articles, films and exhibitions were designed to influence the public and ensured the dissemination of particular images of the colonies, even if some of those images were themselves already part of popular culture.

It is also worth remembering the fact that the audiences for imperial propaganda were as varied as the vehicles employed. Some material was deliberately aimed at the elite: politicians, civil servants and people who might now be called opinion-formers. Venier's article, for example, shows the effective use of such means by Lyautey in his campaign to maintain the Madagascar policy instituted by Gallieni. The debates over the nature of colonial rule in West Africa and over race and citizenship discussed in the chapters by Sibeud, Conklin and Dimier also fit into this category. Other campaigns were aimed at a wider audience: the efforts to promote colonisation in New Caledonia (and also, less overtly, in Indochina) examined by Merle and de Gantès and the colonial exhibitions analysed by Goerg are clear examples. Equally, as Derrick shows, critics of empire needed to counter this propaganda by reaching as wide an audience as possible. Their failure to do so indicates the success of pro-imperial propaganda. Other campaigns were designed to foster imperial pride in children or young people.[25] However, even the distinction between mass propaganda and that aimed at an élite is, to a certain extent, artificial. In a world of mass media and mass participation in politics, public opinion was an effective ally in high politics.

Nor was propaganda necessarily aimed exclusively at the French population. Increasingly, as the twentieth century wore on, it became necessary to justify colonial rule to an international audience. In the first place, populations of the colonies had to be incorporated into the colonial state and then persuaded to remain within its purview. Assimilation, the French *mission civilisatrice*, provided a powerful ideology for colonial subjects as well as for French citizens. Edwards examines one such effort to rework gender relations in Cambodia. As with other sporadic efforts to remodel dependent societies from the Napoleonic era on, the implicit message – that French civilisation was both superior and attainable – was, perhaps, more significant than the results. This message reinforced the images and attitudes current in France, bolstering French faith in their superiority. However, it also offered a powerful attraction to some of those deemed 'inferior'. Elites within the colonies continued to demand assimilation long after French commitment to the idea had waned. Indeed, Atlan and Jezequel show how African representatives defended French policy, thus encouraging Africans to see the colonial state as the legitimate focus of their aspirations. Later they also played an important role in justifying French colonial policy to a different international audience. This second audience was composed of the community of colonial powers, whom it was also necessary to persuade of French fitness for imperial responsibilities. Especially after the First World War, competition for stewardship of Germany's colonies and of Ottoman territories, American and Soviet dislike of colonialism and, in the 1930s, German propaganda, made this form of discourse an important part of diplomacy. MacMaster discusses one clear example of French insistence on its stewardship of Muslim affairs with an eye to international opinion. Equally, the government's recourse to African spokesmen for colonial policy was designed to counter potential criticism of its rule in Africa.

It is, of course, difficult to tell exactly what effect colonial propaganda had on its audience. There are indications that although popular enthusiasm for empire was limited to times of crisis, in general terms such propaganda was very effective.[26] Both de Gantès and Merle show how immigration could be affected by campaigns – official and unofficial – in France, even if many immigrants were later deterred by what they found on arrival. On the other hand, White discusses the variety of responses to the prospect of inter-racial relationships. His conclusion should act as a reminder to be careful in discussing the effects of propaganda. Despite the relentless nature of colonial propaganda, creating stereotyped images of race and fostering a sense of French identity which depended in part on opposition to the subordinated – and inferior – subjects of the colonies, the audience still responded individually. It is unwise for historians to assume that the material disseminated is automatically reflected in public opinion.

Even more telling, perhaps, is the continuing importance of France's empire. Aldrich discusses the traces of the imperial past in Paris street names and monuments, and highlights the question of whether this has a significant impact on perceptions of the past. However, two other contributions also highlight the importance of such a legacy. Kidd addresses the issue of war memorials and points out their highly political nature, while Flood and Frey examine the ways in which the extreme right continues to use the imperial past. These articles demonstrate the similarities (and the differences) between the British and French cases. As in Britain, the impact of imperial propaganda was very general; it did not succeed in developing an enduring knowledge of or enthusiasm for '*les colonies*' but instead fostered a particular sense of French identity based on '*grandeur*' and racism. As a result, the loss of empire was problematic for both Britain and France. The importance of empire in countering defeat in Europe made decolonisation all the more difficult for France and the importance of the armed forces in both generating and encouraging expansion and colonial rule ensured that it was particularly traumatic for them.

The chapters in this collection – and in the volume on empire and culture, which accompanies it – underline the importance of France's colonial role in the development of French society and culture after 1870. Whether it was as a unifying factor or as a foil for the development of a sense of French identity, the empire was crucial to popular culture. To a large extent then, the propaganda which conveyed images of the empire to the populations of both the colonies and the metropole was vital to the creation of a French 'people' and to the consolidation of the Republic. What these books show is that popular imperialism must be taken into account if historians are to develop a nuanced and sophisticated understanding of their subject. Thus they act as both an early contribution to the debate and a call for further research.

Notes and references

1. J. M. MacKenzie, *Propaganda and Empire: The Manipulation of British Public Opinion 1880–1960* (Manchester University Press, 1984), p. 1.
2. B. Semmel, *Imperialism and Social Reform: English Social-Imperial Thought, 1895–1914* (Allen & Unwin, 1960).
3. H.-U. Wehler, *The German Empire, 1871–1918* (Berg, 1985); H.-U. Wehler, 'Industrial Growth and Early German Imperialism', in R. Owen and B. Sutcliffe, eds, *Studies in the Theory of Imperialism* (Longman, 1972); but see P. Kennedy, 'German Colonial Expansion: has the "Manipulated Social Imperialism" been Ante-dated?', *Past and Present*, no. 54, 1972, pp. 134–41.
4. This is perhaps not surprising; the Falklands/Malvinas war offers a very close recent parallel, as John MacKenzie has also pointed out; MacKenzie, *Propaganda and Empire*, p. 11.
5. A. S. Kanya-Forstner, *The Conquest of the Western Sudan: A Study in French Military Imperialism* (Cambridge University Press, 1969); R. Aldrich, *Greater France: A History of French Overseas Expansion* (Macmillan, 1996), pp. 75–82, 132.
6. Kanya-Forstner, *The Conquest of the Western Sudan*.
7. See for example, S. M. Persell, *The French Colonial Lobby, 1889–1938* (Hoover Institution, 1983); C. M. Andrew and A. S. Kanya-Forstner, 'The French

"Colonial Party": Its Composition, Aims and Influence, 1885–1914', *Historical Journal*, vol. 17, no. 1, 1974, pp. 99–128; C. M. Andrew and A. S. Kanya-Forstner, 'The *Groupe colonial* in the French Chamber of Deputies, 1892–1932', *Historical Journal*, vol. 17, no. 4, 1974, pp. 837–66; L. Abrams and D. J. Miller, 'Who were the French Colonialists? A Reassessment of the *parti colonial*, 1890–1914', *Historical Journal*, vol. 19, no. 3 (1976), pp. 685–725; M. Lagana, *Le Parti colonial français: éléments d'histoire*, Sillery, Québec, 1990; J. F. Laffey, 'Municipal Imperialism in France: The Lyon Chamber of Commerce, 1900–1914', *Proceedings of the American Philosophical Society*, no. 119 (1975), pp. 8–23; J. Cooke, *The New French Imperialism, 1880–1910: The Third Republic and Colonial Expansion* (David & Charles, 1973).

8. R. Girardet, *L'Idée coloniale en France, 1871–1962* (La Table Ronde, 1972), p. 110; Aldrich, *Greater France*, p. 100.

9. C. M. Andrew and A. S. Kanya-Forstner, 'Centre and Periphery in the Making of the Second French Colonial Empire, 1815–1920', *Journal of Imperial and Commonwealth History*, vol. 16, no. 3 (1988), pp. 9–34.

10. This literature is now far too extensive to discuss here. However, for critical, early contributions to this debate, see J. M. MacKenzie, *Propaganda and Empire*; J. M. MacKenzie, ed., *Imperialism and Popular Culture* (Manchester University Press, 1986); E. Hobsbawm and T. Ranger, eds, *The Invention of Tradition* (Cambridge University Press, 1983); G. Arnold, *Hold Fast for England: G. A. Henty, Imperialist Boys' Writer* (Hamish Hamilton, 1980); P. Brantlinger, *Rule of Darkness. British Literature and Imperialism, 1830–1914* (Cornell University Press, 1988); J. Rowbotham, *Good Girls Make Good Wives: Guidance for Girls in Victorian Fiction* (Blackwell, 1989), especially pp. 180–220.

11. W. Schneider, *An Empire for the Masses: The French Popular Image of Africa, 1870–1900* (Greenwood Press, 1982).

12. Schneider, *An Empire for the Masses*; see especially pp. 6–8.

13. T. G. August, *The Selling of Empire: British and French Imperialist Propaganda 1890–1940*, Westport, CT, 1985. See also S. Lemaire, 'L'Agence économique des colonies. Instrument de propagande on creuset de l'idéologie coloniale en France (1870–1960)', unpublished PhD thesis, European University Institute, Florence, 2000.

14. R. Bachollet, ed., Bibliothèque Forney, ed., *Négripub. L'image des Noirs dans la publicité depuis un siècle* (Somogy, 1992); C. Hodeir and P. Michel, *L'Exposition coloniale* (Complexe, 1991); C.-R. Ageron, 'L'exposition coloniale de 1931: mythe républicain ou mythe impérial?' in P. Nora, ed., *Les Lieux de Mémoire, vol. I: La République* (Gallimard, 1984); P. Blachard and A. Chatelier, eds, *Images et colonies: Nature, discours et influence de l'iconographe coloniale liée à la propagande coloniale et à la représentation des Africans et de l'Afrique en France, de 1920 aux Indépendances* (Syros, 1993). See also M. Evans and A. Sackur, eds, *French Popular Culture and the Imperial Idea, 1870–1960*, Palgrave, forthcoming.

15. This term is borrowed from R. Robinson and J. Gallager with A. Denny, *Africa and the Victorians: The Official Mind of Imperialism* (Macmillan, 1961; 2nd edn, 1981).

16. MacKenzie, *Propaganda and Empire*, p. 1.

17. L. Colley, *Britons: Forging the nation, 1707–1837* (Yale University Press, 1992), pp. 55–71.

18. MacKenzie, *Propaganda and Empire*, pp. 2,7.

19. MacKenzie, *Propaganda and Empire*, p. 11.

20. MacKenzie, *Propaganda and Empire*, p. 10.

21. See for example, E. Weber, *Peasants into Frenchmen: The Modernisation of Rural France, 1870–1914* (Chatto & Windus, 1977), B. Jenkins, *Nationalism in France: Class and Nation Since 1789* (Routledge, 1990), pp. 75–102; R. Gildea, *The Past in French History* (Yale University Press, 1994), pp. 112–13, 118–23.

22. Jenkins, *Nationalism in France*, p. 75.

23. Schneider, *An Empire for the Masses*, pp. 21–32.

24. See for example, Bachollet, Negripub; J. P. Nederveen Pieterse, *White on Black: Images of Africa and Blacks in Western Popular Culture* (Yale University Press, 1992).

25. See N. Cooper, 'Rewriting Indochina: Metropolitan Colonial Historiography and Representations of Indochina in Metropolitan School Manuals, 1905–1955' in Evans and Sackur, *French Popular Culture*; Y. Holo, *'L'imaginaire coloniale dans la bande desinée'*, in Blanchard and Chatelier, eds, *Images et Colonies*. This is a significant theme in discussions of British popular imperialism as well. See, for example, J. Mangan, *'Benefits Bestowed'? Education and British Imperialism* (Manchester University Press, 1988); G. Arnold, *Hold Fast for England*; J. Rowbotham, *Good Girls Make Good Wives*, pp. 180–220.

26. Lemaire, *'L'Agence économique des colonies'*, pp. 727–34.

Part I
The Empire and Public Opinion

1
Migration to Indochina: Proof of the Popularity of Colonial Empire?

Gilles de Gantès

Even at its apogee, the colonial empire was only a secondary concern in French public opinion. This was particularly true for Indochina. If we refer to the first sample surveys after 1945,[1] the French seemed to be uninterested in, or even hostile, to the empire. However, it is very difficult to measure how far this indifference ran, since to this day most historians have tended to study colonial propaganda rather than its impact. The speeches of colonial propagandists are well known, as is the vision of the colonial world transmitted via school books, literature and art.[2] Yet, the influence of this propaganda on French public opinion remains unclear because of the difficulty of testing its impact. Studying colonial migrations may help us to understand the popularity of Indochina from the point of view of the average French person rather than that of the pro-colonial elite. Which groups felt concerned? What led French people to migrate to the Far East? How significant was the role of government agencies and colonial associations in this? All these questions may be considered by observing the men and women who made the difficult choice to emigrate and establish themselves in the Far East.

Indochina was far away, with a poor climate and poor health conditions. It was heavily populated compared with African colonies. Indochina did not need any 'white proletariat'. Yet thousands of Frenchmen went there to settle and this exodus is remarkable, at least for the period before 1920. Following the First World War, Indochina was fully equipped with hospitals, theatres, schools, colleges and even a university. It had roads, railways and so on. Moreover, the security situation seemed to be much the same as in France. For the 1920s and 1930s, we can thus understand why many Frenchmen looked to this colony as a wonderful place, where they could aspire to a higher standard of living, with paid holidays every three years and double pay when they were in the colony. Before 1914 it was not as easy, and this is one important reason why the presence of almost 20 000 French people in Indochina in 1914 seems so remarkable.

The beginnings of Cochinchina: a new opportunity reserved for the 'happy few' already living in the Far East

Colonial historians, who proudly repeated that France had conquered Cochinchina in 1859 and Cambodia in 1863, remained silent about the fact that this conquest had been contested for a long time, perhaps more in France than in Asia. At the end of the Second Empire, many French politicians thought that the new colony offered nothing of interest to France and promoted the idea that it should be returned to the Dai-Nam empire.[3] Debates were heated and, in the end, Cochinchina seems to have remained French only by chance. After the 1870–1 Franco-Prussian War, French governments had other priorities than the development of '*la France d'Asie*'. When a naval officer, Francis Garnier, tried to take Tonkin in 1873 and was killed in a battle, the French government did not seek revenge, but gave orders for a conciliatory approach to be adopted in negotiations with the Dai-Nam court. In fact, taking over Cochinchina seemed unnecessary. When supporters of Cochinchina wrote and said that its potential for exporting rice was very promising, most French politicians noted that France's needs were already supplied by Italy at a better price. The only advantage of occupying Cochinchina was the opportunity to control a good harbour near China's southern shores. In the 1860s, the occupation of Cochinchina appeared to be a chimera, as had been the other overseas expeditions of the Second Empire, such as the Crimean War and the Mexican adventure. And yet, in spite of this lack of encouragement, 1200 Frenchmen (not including military personnel) lived in Saigon in 1873 and, more amazingly, many officers had left the navy to become civil servants, probably the only example of this in the long history of this service. These men were clearly full of confidence in the future of Cochinchina.

It is obviously difficult to classify people's individual motives. However, three groups seem to have played a particularly important role in the establishment of Cochinchina: people emigrating via Bordeaux's commercial networks, people originating from the five trading posts which composed French India and people arriving from La Réunion (the former Ile Bourbon). La Réunion was an important point on the way to the Far East before the opening of the Suez Canal in 1869 and it was a small and overcrowded island. These facts help to explain why people who originated from this 'old colony' were attracted by the opportunities presented by the opening of Saigon harbour. As early as 1860, at a time when French Cochinchina was limited to Saigon and its suburbs, the administration of La Réunion sent a man named Dizac to determine whether La Réunion's rice needs could be met by Cochinchina, rather than by Indian imports. He soon set up in Saigon. He had come from Bordeaux and he invited his fellow-countryman Marcellin Larrieu, who originated from Aire-sur-Adour and was also living in La Réunion, to Cochinchina in 1864.[4] The latter created the Messageries Fluviales de Cochinchine, a transport company which was to play an important role in the economic development of the colony. The cases of Larrieu and Dizac were not isolated and people originating from La Réunion were very influential in the beginnings of Cochinchina. Many noticed that, for administrative matters, political life, and customs, the new colony was organised in the same way as La Réunion. This trend of migration across the Indian Ocean continued up to the end of the colonial period, although after 1900 it was concealed by the larger flood coming from France. The barrister Georges Garros, the journalist Jean Ricquebourg, the Dejean de la Bâtie brothers, Governor Rodier, his son-in-law Chassaing, Governors Drouhet and Douville, all came from La Réunion and all were personalities well known in Indochina, even if they worked mainly in Cochinchina. People originating from La Réunion seemed to specialise as lawyers (Garros, de Cotte[5]) and teachers (Albert Noël, born in 1862, who arrived in Cochinchina in 1891[6]; Rodolphe Pottier, born in 1866, who arrived in 1893[7]; and Raphaël Barquissau, born in 1888, who was head teacher at the Lycée Chasseloup-Laubat in Saigon in the 1920s[8]).

People originating from French India followed a similar pattern. They constituted 12 per cent of the French civilian population of Cochinchina in 1881. Unfortunately, we know less about them. They were not considered 'true Frenchmen' by either the Europeans or the local population, because of the colour of their skin and because their civil and political rights had been contested. They did not therefore mix with other Frenchmen. One of the consequences of this is that eyewitness accounts of French-Indian society are uncommon, apart from those of well-known personalities like the journalists Lucien Héloury (born in Karikal, 1875) or Sombsthay (the pen-name of Pierre Jeantet). French

Indians were to be found particularly in urban transportation, market control and the municipal police. They were very influential in the political life of Saigon because, like many minorities pushed aside by a majority, they lobbied efficiently: at each electoral consultation, candidates had to promise them certain benefits. One of the better-known 'colonial stories' claimed that a Cochinchina *député* paid for hundreds of people to travel from Pondichéry to Saigon so that they could give him their support.

Forty to fifty years after the French landing in Saigon, the proportion of people originating from La Réunion and French India declined but still remained significant: in 1899, 17 per cent of French citizens living in Saigon were born in a French colony, a significant but unknown number of whom came from La Réunion, and 7 per cent in French India. In fact, French migration across the Indian Ocean continued at least until 1914, even if its importance decreased relative to that of French people coming from France and those born in Indochina. For La Réunion and for the five French Indian trading posts, these migration trends are similar to those of people from Senegal emigrating to all of French West Africa (AOF), as has been shown by Henri Brunschwig.[9] Indochina was probably seen as a kind of vital hinterland for La Réunion and French India, two colonies which did not have any such reserves. It offered residents of the latter both economic and employment opportunities and it is thus easy to understand why it was a popular destination for them.

In contrast, migration to Indochina by 'true' Frenchmen (those coming from France) seems to have been uncommon, except for groups originating from south-western France who came mainly through the Bordeaux commercial network, as we have seen with Dizac and Larrieu. But these first settlers did not come directly from Bordeaux. Most had been in the Far East for a long time. Unlike Marseilles or Nantes businessmen, those from Bordeaux had a long tradition of interest in the region,[10] probably because they were regular customers of the Portuguese and Spanish networks to Manilla and Macau and their firms were already active in the Far East before the French navy conquered Saigon. The example of the Roque brothers provides a good example of this. Originally from the Aveyron, a French rural *département* roughly halfway between Marseilles and Bordeaux, they wanted to travel the world. Without their parents' permission, they left for Bordeaux and then went on to Spain, from where they sailed to Manilla.[11] Like people who originated from La Réunion or French India, these men had gained first-hand knowledge of the East and were ready to seize any opportunity when it came. Although the potential of Cochinchina may appear limited to us today, the new colony represented a new opportunity, and an attractive one at the time, for sailors, merchants, traders and other adventurers of the 1860s, not only from Bordeaux, but also from Germany, Britain and the United States.

The first advantage, at least for those coming from Bordeaux, was that the admiral-governors were, like them, French. This could be useful for business. Second, these governors introduced a kind of economic rationality which was beneficial to European traders. Lastly, the army's needs for the war against China created a kind of windfall for business which Bordeaux traders did not want to miss. The example of the Denis family is well known, thanks to the book that one of its members wrote in 1965.[12] The elder brother had been employed for a long time by a Bordeaux shipping house to trade in the Far East. From this base, he bought a ship, *La Mouette*, the main activity of which was the transportation of rice and spices between southern China and the straits of Malacca. As early as 1859, Saigon became the centre of his activities. He built warehouses there, and his brothers came to the Far East to help him. The Roque brothers provide a similar example. They had developed a trading firm in Manilla before 1858 and, when Admiral Rigault de Genouilly landed in Tourane (today's Da-nang), they organised food supplies for the small expeditionary force, via their Philippines warehouses. When Rigault changed his mind and conquered Saigon, the Roque brothers naturally followed.[13] Their activities were so successful that they were able, as early as 1866, to return to France and buy a magnificent manor house, which then became a good advertisement for the new colony. Many other people who originated from south-western France were part of the Bordeaux network to Asia. Originating from Gers, Jean-Baptiste Luro came to Cochinchina in 1864. His brothers Emile and Clément came there with a friend, Labéron. A few years later, his sister came. She married a settler originating from Bordeaux, Louis Andrieu.[14] Germain Lacaze, who came originally from the Rouergue, created one of the first trading firms in Cochinchina, and his brother, a priest, soon joined him.[15] Also from Bordeaux, Paul Blanchy was to become Saigon's mayor in the 1880s and remained in the post until his death at the beginning of the twentieth century.

These life stories may seem anecdotal but, with brothers, wives, cousins, friends and relatives, the Bordeaux connection reveals the main characteristics of French migration trends to early colonial Cochinchina. Those coming directly from France were relatively uncommon: Cochinchina, like Mexico and even Algeria before it, was probably totally unknown to the average Frenchman. The only groups for which Cochinchina was popular were those from the Far East or the Indian Ocean.

The popularisation of Indochina by the conquest of Tonkin

France resumed an expansionist policy at the end of the 1870s, when Gambetta's friends dominated French governments. As far as Asia was concerned, the Upper Burmese and Siamese kingdoms were the first targets of French diplomacy, followed by the remains of Dai-Nam kingdom (the central and northern parts of Vietnam), and finally Tonkin (northern Vietnam). As a result, the need for military personnel increased. 3500 men had been sufficient to ensure French control of Cochinchina in the 1870s, whereas the expeditionary force for Tonkin comprised 30 000 men. Vietnamese resistance was anything but symbolic. Moreover, the conquest of Tonkin had led to war with China, and disease killed many soldiers. Taking account of the turnover of personnel, a total of 100 000 men came to know Tonkin during these years.[16] As the conquest brought about the fall of its main promoter, Jules Ferry, Tonkin seems to have been unpopular, at least among the *députés*. However, soldiers' testimonies paint a different picture, for most of them were enthusiastic. For example, when a warrant officer of a *tirailleurs sénégalais* regiment who was staying in France for a while asked for volunteers for Tonkin, he was inundated with volunteers. In order to extricate himself from this situation, he shouted that he would only register those who 'would buy him a *cassis-cognac*'.[17] The testimony of Poupard, of the Third Régiment de Zouaves, which was stationed in Algeria and abruptly sent to Tonkin in April 1885, shows that troops were happy to experience new horizons, in spite of the difficulties of transportation.[18] Seen through the eyes of a soldier, Tonkin meant adventure.

However, a few years later most of these soldiers were called back to France and they were not replaced.[19] The reason was that the conquest of Tonkin was unpopular in parliament, so that governments had to declare that pacification had ended (which would only be true after 1896), in order to reduce both the number of troops and costs.[20] No new wave of migration replaced the soldiers who had gone home. Indochina's governors did not promote such movements, because they feared competition between *petits blancs*[21] and the local population for agricultural land or junior civil service jobs. For most of these governors,

Indochina needed investment from France and not the development of a white working class. But the presence in Tonkin, albeit for a short period of time, of such a large army had led to an unexpected consequence: thousands of Frenchmen now knew Indochina and they spoke about it to those around them on their return to France.

Many soldiers, former conscripts, chose to return to civilian life in Indochina instead of being discharged in France. Many jobs were available in the early 1890s as junior civil servants, foremen on construction sites, in railway yards or as estate directors. Even Governor de Lanessan, who wanted to build French Indochina through a policy of collaboration with Vietnamese elites and who distrusted the development of a white society, could not avoid such demobilisations in Indochina.

Louis Borel's career is a good example of how Indochina could be popular among ex-soldiers. The eldest brother of four, he came from a small landowning family, which originated from Saint-Julien-en-Beauchêne, a small village in the Hautes-Alpes. This was a mountainous region with poor agricultural potential, apart from some difficult cattle-breeding. Each of the three elder brothers had to leave school early and find seasonal employment in the neighbouring plains. As for Louis, he was a quarryman when he was called up to do his military service in a sappers regiment based in Grenoble. It is therefore easy to understand why he was a volunteer for Tonkin. He arrived there in January 1884 and returned to civilian life during the summer of 1885 in Hanoi, where, he became a foreman in a public builder's yard. He was then employed on a big estate, before returning to work for the administration as a lighthouse builder. The colony obviously needed such men, as Louis Borel invited his three brothers to join him in Tonkin (one of them via the same conscription route). The Borel brothers were also joined by the wives they had married '*au pays*'; and cousins and friends who also originated from Saint-Julien and the neighbouring area soon followed.[22]

Such examples of soldiers from the expeditionary force of 1883–5 abound. Aubert arrived in 1885 as a sub-officer with the Eighth Regiment of Chasseurs à Pied and became an officer in the Garde Indigène (a kind of local police)[23], Eugène Jung became an estate-holder; Louis Bonnafont was employed on the Chinese border railway construction site, Henri Lamagat and Piglowski became journalists and there were many other examples. At the beginning of the twentieth century, those French people who had been established in Tonkin for a long time feared being overwhelmed by this tide of Frenchmen coming from France and in 1904 they decided to found the Association des Anciens Tonkinois. To be a member, one had to have been in Tonkin for at least twenty-five years and the registers of this association show that it comprised almost exclusively people who came originally with the expeditionary force. Whether as volunteers or as conscripts, the colonial infantry had allowed young Frenchmen to get free travel to Indochina: a 'refuge for the poor', the colonial army may be considered to have been a 'springboard' for whose who sought new opportunities and wanted to make a success of their lives.[24]

But the presence of a large army had a second consequence. If many soldiers stayed in Indochina, most of them returned to France and became a living advertisement for Indochina. The colony became more popular among average Frenchmen, especially in those regions to which soldiers returned. The fact that some of them tried to get money in order to return to Indochina and invest in estates or trading firms provided proof to their neighbours that Indochina could be a source of fortune. Others wrote books and articles. Apart from descriptions of wartime violence or the insistence on disease, they were also a source of exoticism and demonstrated a real interest in the civilisations of the Far East. This early familiarisation did not have an immediate effect, however, because Indochina had no need for white men; but it was to have a great influence at the beginning of the twentieth century.

Indochina's call for white workers

Young and dashing, Paul Doumer was appointed Governor-General of Indochina in December 1896. He had big plans to reinforce the French presence in the Far East. His main idea was to build a railway from the Indochinese border into the heart of Yunnan, in the hope that this Chinese province would soon become French. The plan had other aims, such as providing work for the French iron and steel industries and for French banking corporations (since a large public loan was obviously necessary to build the railway). In fact, we still do not know whether the motives for Doumer's conquest of Yunnan province were economic or not, but the consequences for Indochina were in any case the same. Doumer had to organise the Indochinese budget in order to win the support of those Frenchmen who saved money and were looking for safe investment opportunities. Russian or Turkish loans seemed safe; Doumer had to prove that Indochinese loans were just as safe. The main aim of the budget reorganisation was to ensure that the resources of the general budget, against which the 200-million-franc loan was made, came from customs duties, indirect taxes and administrative monopolies. The production and sale of three products – salt, alcohol and opium – were the monopoly of the *régies* (companies run by the administration) or of private firms who paid the colonial state for the privilege.

The reorganisation of taxation and customs and excise duties provided new employment opportunities: for customs officers whose job was to control the borders and keep the Vietnamese villages which tried to produce illegal alcohol under surveillance, for civil servants for the *régies*, for employees for the monopoly private companies, for civil servants whose job was to implement head and land taxes (census and land surveys), for engineers and foremen for railway-building and so on. To give an idea of the scale of this human development, the total number of civil servants was 2860 in 1897, 3778 in 1902, 4390 in 1906 and 5693 in 1911.[25] Furthermore, Doumer strictly forbade civil servants from entering into mixed marriages with Vietnamese women. Unlike in the earlier period, most of these migrants came with their French wives. It can thus be said that French white colonial society was really a product of the Doumer initiative.

But increased employment opportunities cannot on their own explain such migrations: candidates had to be found to fill the posts and the evidence is that this was not a problem. For a young Frenchman, anxious for professional and social success, Indochina seemed full of promise. Officers hoped to obtain glory in daring military campaigns, like their elder brothers of the 1890s, thereby to secure faster promotion. Poor countrymen, like the Borel brothers in a former period, could hope for free land; civil servants who worked in small, grey offices in France could hope to head up important offices in Indochina; and there were opportunities to be had in every profession. The case of women is particularly interesting. At this time, they could not aspire to high-ranking professions in France. They were condemned to marriage or to lower-rank professions. This was not the case in Indochina. The young actress Alexandra David (professional name: Mademoiselle Myrial) could get only small roles in Paris, but she starred in *La Traviata* or *Mireille* in Hanoi.[26] An officer's widow at the beginning of the twentieth century, Louise Alcan became managing director of the newspaper *La France d'Asie*, just like the very young Jeanne Bietry, twenty years later.[27] Even Marguérite Duras's mother's destiny is significant. The novelist insisted on the fact that the life of her mother was sad and poor, and most studies follow this line. But we have to remember that, at home in France, no primary-school teacher could have hoped, as an impoverished widow, to own an estate. In short,

Indochina during this period was a land of promise for people, both women and men, who knew about it.

It is difficult to know who exactly these happy few settling in Indochina were. The evidence suggests that most migrants were young men. The proportion of women to men was one to four in 1907 and one to three in 1922.[28] Many witnesses wrote about French businessmen of questionable honesty who went to ground in Indochina for a while. Others spoke of heirs who had burnt their inheritance or of swindlers who had to escape French justice. It is easy to find such examples: the dishonest lawyer and former *député*, Le Masson, or the colourful adventurer and businessman, Dubois, whose real name is unknown. Other witnesses thought that migrants went from specific French regions. Indochina was described as 'the equivalent of the great India that Dupleix's genius had conquered for France',[29] and many colonial propagandists asserted that the Seven Years War from 1756 to 1763, when France had lost Canada and India, had not been forgotten by French sailors: '[A]mong our valiant populations originating from the coastal regions of Britanny, the Basque country and Provence, these glorious and audacious expeditions have never been forgotten.'[30] Describing new migrants in the year 1883, Paul Bourde had observed that the 'great majority of the civil servants who are to organise the Tonkin administration come from Britanny, sailor country; Cochinchina settlers are merchants originating from Bordeaux or from Marseilles'.[31] If the memory of the Seven Years War had encouraged migration from Britanny or from Provence, we must also add in the memory of the Second Empire's overseas campaigns, as the example of the Cardin family shows. Originating from Brest, the father had fought at Sebastopol in the Crimean War as a ship's boy. The son entered the colonial army and fought in Africa under Mangin, before joining the Garde Indigène in Indochina in 1898.[32]

Besides the numerous migrants coming from Britanny and Provence, there were other networks. Just like people originating from Bordeaux in the 1860s, people originating from Lyons stayed for a long time in the Far East. They were less interested in Cochinchina than in Tonkin. It was closer to China, where their firms had long been established to buy silk. To them, Tonkin represented the same kind of opportunities as Cochinchina had represented to immigrants from Bordeaux. One of the leading figures among these businessmen, Ulysse Pila, described the reasons why he looked to Tonkin from the beginning and why he settled there: 'the headquarters of my firm was in China for twenty years, a country where I had lived, and it has been easier for my firm than for others to keep our commercial network in Tonkin.'[33] Lyons firms were to be less successful in Tonkin than Bordeaux ones had been in Cochinchina, because silk merchants found that Japanese raw material was of a better quality than that from Indochina. But Ulysse Pila became one of the best propagandists for French investment in Indochina, to the point where he was nicknamed the '*vice-roi*' of the colony.

The register of associations of people originating from the same regions reveals other migration trends (see Table 1.1). Even if the custom of setting up such associations was not the same in every region (which explains why there were no associations for those who came from Paris, La Réunion or French India), the evidence is that people from Britanny and Provence were joined by people who did not share the 'Seven Years War tradition': people from Corsica (which was only bought by France in 1768), from Charentes and, as in the earlier period, from the Alps. In 1902, when the newly appointed Governor-General, Paul Beau, who was from Charentes, arrived in Indochina, his fellow countrymen from that region tried to create an association. They claimed that there were 300 of them in Tonkin alone, and three years later the association's festival dinner was attended by 100 people.[35] Apparently less successful, the festival dinner of the Alpine Association, Le Gratin Dauphinois, was attended by only 35 people in Saigon, but it is known that many people who originated from this region lived in Cochinchina.[36] Henri Lamagat wrote about a small village (400 inhabitants) close to Voiron (Isère), Colombe, from which a dozen people went to the province of Cantho (southern Vietnam).[37] Two sons of this French village had settled on a rice estate, and, after making a success of it, they called on others to join them. Their case is not unlike that of the

Table 1.1   The *amicales régionales* at the beginning of the twentieth century[34]

	Saigon	Hanoi	Haiphong
Alsace-Lorraine		Amicale de l'Est	Amicale des Alsaciens-Lorrains
Britanny			Amicale bretonne
Charentes		la Cagouille	
Corsica	Amicale corse	la Corse	Comité d'Initiative des intérêts corses
Côte d'Azur	Amicale de la Côte d'Azur	Côte d'Azur à Hanoi	
Dauphiné	le Gratin dauphinois	le Gratin tonkinois	

Borel brothers, as Saint-Julien-en-Beauchêne was roughly the same size as Colombe.

Up to this point, Corsicans have been absent from this account. This may seem remarkable, since by the 1930s they would represent not less than 6% of all officers and 22% of the sub-officers in the colonial army in Indochina, and in Saigon 12% of those on the electoral register were Corsican.[38] However, they were not so numerous before 1900. They only established themselves in Indochina after this date, when they entered the newly reorganised administration of the Douanes & Régies (Customs and State Enterprises). The first Association of Corsicans was founded in Tonkin and then in Cochinchina in 1905.[39] They developed slowly. However, in 1923 there were 200 people in the La Cyrnéenne Association in Hanoi, which was a significant number, although no higher than the number of those who originated from Charentes.

Thus, apart from the tradition of migration from coastal regions, which has been remarked upon by journalists and novelists, migrations from Charentes, Corsica or the Alps reveal the main motives of migrants to Indochina. There were regional networks driving the 'rural exodus' from poor regions to any place where jobs were available, whether in the colonial Empire or elsewhere: migrants from the Barcelonnette valley went to Mexico and from the Basque country they went to America; migrants from Auvergne or Britanny who went to Paris were motivated by similar reasons to those from Saint-Julien or from Colombe who went to Indochina. The only difference was that Indochina was far away, but the journey was free for most of the migrants and the fact that the country was French must surely have made things easier for them.

Conclusion

In so far as emigration to Indochina may be considered a proof of the popularity of that colony, we may conclude that it was genuinely popular, but perhaps no more so than any colony or any other overseas region. Until the 1880s, Cochinchina was neither popular nor unpopular; it was almost unknown in France, except to those French people who were already established in the Far East or who had interests in overseas enterprises, such as naval officers. There were very few of them. Knowledge of Indochina grew, thanks to the presence of a large number of French soldiers at the time of the Tonkin conquest, but this does not mean that the colony had become popular with French people in general. All the soldiers in Indochina were volunteers, and those who made this choice came from social classes that were aware of the opportunities presented by the colonies. Only specific groups were concerned, such as people from the coastal regions of France or from poor or overcrowded regions, mainly in the mountainous south of France. Britanny and Provence were examples of such regions.

After the First World War, migration trends were very different. Emigration may appear common, as the white colonial population grew from around 20 000 in 1920 to 40 000 in 1930, before levelling out in 1945. But in reality this growth was partly the result of a large difference between births and deaths. This does not mean that emigration had stopped, but it became more and more difficult to obtain employment in Indochina from France. On the one hand, more and more job opportunities were filled by local people, such as Asians, whites and métis, who were now more numerous and better qualified, thanks to the opening of Hanoi University. On the other hand, thanks to its popularisation by returning groups, Indochina became popular after 1918 as the richest, the safest and the most attractive of all the colonies, with the result that more French people wanted to go there.

Notes and references

1. A. Ruscio, 'L'opinion publique et la guerre d'Indochine. Sondages et témoignages', *Vingtième Siècle*, 1991, 1, pp. 35–46, and J. Thobie, G. Meynier, C. Coquery-Vidrovitch and C.-R. Ageron, *Histoire de la France coloniale*, vol. II (Armand Colin, 1992), pp. 364–5.
2. R. Girardet did pioneering work in this field with his *L'Idée Coloniale en France de 1871 à 1962* (La Table Ronde, 1972). Recent books published about Indochina include: A. Ruscio, *Le Credo de l'homme blanc* (Complexe, 1995) and H. Copin, *L'Indochine dans la littérature française des années vingt à 1954. Exotisme et altérité* (L'Harmattan, 1996).
3. Official name of the Vietnamese state to 1945.
4. E. Denis, *Bordeaux et la Cochinchine sous la Restauration et le Second Empire* ([n.p.], 1965), p. 295.
5. AOM GG 49674. (AOM: Archives d'Outre-Mer.) Files issued by the Indochinese administration which were relocated to France after 1954.
6. AOM GG 7539.
7. *L'Indochine Française* (newspaper), 26 May 1893.
8. *Hommes et Destins* [Biographical Dictionary], tome 1, Paris, Académie des Sciences d'Outre-Mer, 1979, pp. 54–6.
9. See H. Brunschwig, *Noirs et Blancs dans l'Afrique noire française* (Presses Universitaires de France, 1983).
10. For example, during the Restoration period (1815–30), Bordeaux *députés* lobbied in order to lower customs duties on Asian trade to France. D. Bouche, *Histoire de la colonisation française. Vol. 2: Flux et reflux (1815–1962)* (Fayard, 1991), p. 41.

11. E. Denis, *Bordeaux et la Cochinchine*, p. 276, and A. Benoist d'Azy, 'L'Expédition française de Cochinchine', *Bulletin de la Société des Etudes Indochinoises (BSEI)*, 1928, 1, p. 29.
12. See note 3.
13. Denis, *Bordeaux et la Cochinchine*, p. 277.
14. L. Malleret, J. Périn et G. Taboulet, 'Jean-Baptiste Eliacin Luro', *BSEI*, 1940, 1 and 2.
15. *La Cochinchine française* (newspaper), 28 March 1908, and *L'Avenir du Tonkin*, 13 May 1911.
16. C. Fourniau, *Annam-Tonkin. Lettrés et paysans vietnamiens face à la conquête coloniale* (L'Harmattan, 1989), p. 254.
17. L. Bonnafont, *Trente Ans de Tonkin* (Figuière, 1924), p. 9.
18. C.-A. Poupard, 'Souvenirs d'un troupier: la prise de Hué, colonnes de police', *Bulletin des Amis du Vieux Hué*, 1939, p. 239.
19. See the example of one company of a sappers regiment that arrived in 1884 with 83 men. 12 had been discharged in Indochina and 22 came back to France; M. Borel, *Souvenirs d'un vieux colonialiste* (Six-Fours: Compte d'Auteur, 1963), p. 49. We do not know if the 49 men missing pursued their military career or if they died.
20. As C.-R. Ageron has shown in *L'Anticolonialisme en France de 1871 à 1914* (PUF 1973), anticolonialism was common before the 1880s and many *députés* wanted France to devote its energies exclusively to the restoration of Alsace-Lorraine to France.
21. *'Petits blancs'* literally means 'small whites' and is the expression used to refer to unqualified or poorly qualified Europeans.
22. For a full account of the history of this family, see Borel, *Souvenirs*.
23. *L'Indépendance Tonkinoise* (newspaper), 9 December 1905.
24. J.-L. Pretini, 'Saigon-Cyrnos', *Autrement*, série Mémoires, 17, p. 99.
25. A. Métin, *L'Indochine et l'opinion* (Paris, 1916), p. 90.
26. J. Chalon, *Le Lumineux Destin d'Alexandra David-Neel* (Perrin, 1985), pp. 102–10.
27. P. Salinger, *De Mémoire* (Denoël, 1995), pp. 16–17.
28. ANSOM Indochine AF c. 111 and *Annuaire statistique de l'Indochine*, 1927.
29. R. Postel, *A travers la Cochinchine* (Challamel, 1887), p. VIII.
30. P. Vial, *Nos Premières Années au Tonkin* (Baratier et Mollaret, 1889), p. 4.
31. P. Bourde, *De Paris au Tonkin* (Calmann-Lévy, 1885), p. 5.
32. Interview with Louis Cardin, 24 February 1992; G. de Gantès, 'Coloniaux, gouverneurs et ministres. L'Influence des Français du Viêt-Nam sur l'evolution du pays à l'epoque coloniale, 1902–1914' (unpublished PhD thesis, Université de Paris, 1994), p. 532.
33. Quoted by J.-F. Klein, *Un Lyonnais en extrême-orient. Ulysse Pila, vice-roi de l'Indochine, 1837–1909* (Editions Lugd, n.d. [1995]), p. 52.
34. De Gantès, *Coloniaux, gouverneurs et ministres*, p. 30.
35. *Le Petit Tonkinois* (newspaper), 14 May 1903; *La France d'Asie* (newspaper), 23 May 1903 ; *Le Courrier d'Haiphong* (newspaper), 20 March 1906.
36. *La France d'Asie*, 9 August 1904.
37. H. Lamagat, *Souvenirs d'un vieux journaliste indochinois*, vol. III, Saigon, IDEO, 1942, p. 138.
38. J.-L. Pretini, 'Saigon-Cyrnos', pp. 97, 100.
39. *La France d'Asie*, 5 September 1905.

2
A Campaign of Colonial Propaganda: Gallieni, Lyautey and the Defence of the Military Regime in Madagascar, May 1899 to July 1900

Pascal Venier

Field Marshals Joseph Gallieni (1849–1916) and Hubert Lyautey (1854–1934), undeniably two of the most outstanding figures in French colonial history, have both left a profound mark on the history of French colonisation. It is due to a great sense of public relations that both men, the master, Governor-General of Madagascar from 1896 to 1905 and his disciple, the general resident commissioner of France in Morocco between 1912 and 1925, have become legendary figures. This chapter sets out to study the case of the campaign of colonial propaganda led by the two officers during their stay in metropolitan France between 1899 and 1900.

On 24 May 1899 the Governor-General of Madagascar, General Gallieni, disembarked at Marseille with his main collaborators: Noguès, Lallier du Coudray, Roques and Lyautey. The 'Pacifier of Madagascar' was welcomed triumphantly. However, he had to share the limelight among public opinion and the press with Major Marchand, who had recently returned from Fashoda with members of the famous Congo-Nile mission.[1] The Minister of the Colonies, Antoine Guillain, paid tribute to Gallieni at the Pavillon de Flore on 26 May, where he was decorated with a gold medal. Four days later, it was the turn of the President of the Republic, Emile Loubet, to welcome him at the Elysée.

Despite the fatigue experienced by the men in Gallieni's team following a prolonged posting overseas – Lieutenant Colonel Lyautey had only just recovered from a tropical disease which nearly cost him his life – they nonetheless were very active during the year they spent in metropolitan France. This involved not only defending the interests of the new colony and, more broadly, the colonial role of the army, but at the same time not losing sight of their own career prospects. Accordingly, Gallieni divided his time between his family and the needs of his mission, concerning himself with the definitive organisation of Madagascar from the office of the Pavillon de Flore which was put at his disposal.[2] The main questions they had to deal with were those concerning the draft bill on the colonial army, the demands for finances for Madagascar, the defence of the naval base of Diego-Suarez and the project for the Malagasy railway.

The approach here adopted to analyse this stay will be at three complementary levels, reflecting the concerns of those in charge of the colony of Madagascar, which centred around three main priorities: convincing the political decision-makers that the measures they were recommending were desirable, on a wider scale, defending the role carried out by the army in the colonies, primarily in Madagascar, and finally encouraging the development of colonisation and its development in Madagascar. For each of these priorities a specific communication strategy was favoured, based respectively on personal contacts, speeches and letters, and on the use of an information bureau and the Paris colonial exhibition of 1900.

This study is based on the analysis of a series of both public and private archive material. At the Centre des Archives d'Outre-Mer in Aix-en-Provence, the papers from the collections of the colony of Madagascar as well as the papers of the Comité de Madagascar and the Union Coloniale Française, kept in the collection of the Comité Français de l'Outre-Mer, have been of special interest, as have the Lyautey papers at the National Archives in Paris. Unfortunately, the major part of the Gallieni papers are still kept by his family and are not generally available for consultation.

Public relations and personal contacts

The study of this stay in France by colonial officials shows the importance of personal contacts, not only with government officials and parliamentarians but also with members of colonial pressure groups. One could perhaps object that this does not, strictly speaking, constitute propaganda activity. Nevertheless, for colonial officers, a visit to Paris was primarily an exercise in public relations.

If Gallieni chose to be accompanied by Lieutenant-Colonel Lyautey, who served as his chief of staff during his stay in France, it was because he knew that he would be invaluable to him, not only because of his talent as a writer and his capacity to work under pressure but also because he was extremely well connected. A very active correspondence had allowed him to keep in touch with his numerous and influential personal relations during his two colonial tours in Indochina and in Madagascar between 1894 and 1899. Lyautey, who had led a very active social life when he was posted to Saint-Germain-en-Laye near Paris in the late 1880s and early 1890s, had a very good introduction into some of the most prestigious Parisian salons, where he was greatly welcomed.[3] Lyautey enjoyed being on the social circuit as much as it profoundly irritated Gallieni, who felt ill at ease in the salons.

Thus did Lyautey prove himself to be particularly valuable owing to the privileged relations he maintained with some key cabinet ministers of Waldeck-Rousseau's government of republican defence formed in June 1899, such as the War Minister, General Galliffet, a fellow Cavalry officer;[4] the Minister of the Colonies, Albert Decrais;[5] and the Naval Minister, Jean-Marie de Lanessan, the former Governor-General of Indochina, with whom he had forged close links in Hanoi.[6] These relations undoubtedly facilitated the advancement of many Malagasy issues with the relevant ministerial departments.

A large part of the work undertaken in public relations aimed to convince the decision-makers as well as the civil servants. The Government-General and its team learned the ropes of lobbying in the corridors of power. They also appeared before a number of parliamentary commissions and participated in meetings organised by the colonial groups of the Senate and of the Chamber of Deputies.

The links Gallieni and his chief of staff had established with the *parti colonial* (colonial lobby) showed themselves to be of particular importance.[7] In this respect Lyautey seems to have played a major role. The analysis of his correspondence and of his diary for 1900 shows how he maintained privileged contacts with most of the main personalities in the *parti colonial*.[8] Here we discover the names of Eugène Etienne, the Prince of Arenberg, Joseph Chailley-Bert, Jules Charles-Roux, Adrien de Montebello, Paul Bourde, Robert de Caix de Saint-Aymour and even Alfred and Guillaume Grandidier, René Millet, Jules Siegfried and Auguste Terrier. The personal contacts he cultivated with Jules Charles-Roux, the Marseilles shipowner, politician, president of the Comité de Madagascar and also commissioner of the colonial section of the 1900 Paris Universal Exhibition, proved to be of special value.[9] The same is also true of the close contacts he had with Joseph Chailley-Bert, head of the Union Coloniale Française.[10]

Just as important were the links both Gallieni and Lyautey had with a number of associations which were campaigning in favour of the colonial empire. Thus Lyautey became a member of the Société de Géographie, the Société de Géographie Commerciale de Paris, the Union Coloniale Française, the Comité de l'Afrique Française and, of course, the Comité de Madagascar.[11]

Writings and propaganda speeches

Writings and propaganda speeches formed a second category of propaganda activity. Gallieni attached great importance to the publication of solidly documented books of propaganda. In a letter to Lyautey, he insisted on the fact that 'serious works, based on sound documentary evidence [had] great influence on informed public opinion ... These documents allow us to not reply to ill-informed attacks against, and criticisms of, our accomplishments in Madagascar.'[12] He had already often resorted to such works during his long and distinguished colonial career.

Anxious to present his achievements in a convincing manner, he attached great care to the preparation of his general report. Lyautey's talents as a writer were put to good use in the drafting of the report.[13] The imposing 'Rapport d'Ensemble du Général Gallieni sur la Situation Générale de Madagascar', which appeared initially in the *Journal Officiel* then later in the form of two large volumes representing more than 900 pages, was exemplary.[14] As a result, it was extremely well received in both the colonial and national press.[15] Journalist Edouard Payen considered the report as 'a true manual of colonial policy [from which] one could extract a whole range of excellent maxims'.[16] In the same vein, Gallieni also published works such as *Trois Colonnes au Tonkin*, relating his role in the pacification of the upper region of Tonkin in 1894–95 and *La Pacification de Madagascar*, a work prepared by one of his officers, Lieutenant Hellot, based on his general report.[17]

In his role as chief of staff for the Governor-General of Madagascar, Lyautey participated in the drafting of the general's report as well as in the drawing up of texts destined to be published in the form of articles to be used as propaganda. His role was also to prepare the documentation, letters and notes of synthesis which provided the raw materials for articles favourable to the work of Gallieni in Madagascar. This was what happened in the case of an article on Gallieni published by Jules

Charles-Roux in the *Bulletin du Comité de Madagascar*,[18] and again with a series of articles, based on notes drafted by Lyautey, published by the historian Ernest Lavisse in *La Revue de Paris*, of which he was the general editor.[19] In 'Une méthode coloniale' he emphasised the exemplary character of the Gallieni method and, in the context of the Dreyfus affair, presented an interesting defence of the role of the army in the colonies.[20]

During their stay in France, Gallieni and Lyautey gave a large number of speeches and lectures. In particular the general gave speeches to the Union Coloniale Française, the Comité de Madagascar, the Chambers of Commerce of Marseilles, Lyons and Rouen, the Sociétés de Géographie of Paris and Marseilles, as well as to the Sorbonne. His chief of staff was not far behind. On 29 November 1899, in the presence of Gallieni, Lyautey gave a speech to the annual meeting of the Parisian group of the Société d'Economie Sociale.[21] On 21 December, at the Terminus hotel, at the monthly dinner of the Union Coloniale Française and the Comité de Madagascar, he gave a lecture on the use of the army in the colonies, on which he based his famous article 'Du Rôle colonial de l'Armée'.[22] On 19 February 1900, at the 38th dinner of the Réunion des Voyageurs Français, chaired by the Prince of Arenberg, he outlined the main ideas from his article.[23]

At a time when the policies undertaken in Madagascar since 1896 were being sharply criticised, the Gallieni team had to defend and justify themselves by presenting positive results. In doing this, they had to tread a careful path between anti-colonialism at one extreme and colonial propaganda at the other.

This politically delicate period was marked on the one hand by the Dreyfus affair, and on the other by the Voulet-Chanoine affair.[24] Colonial antimilitarism, a phenomenon to a certain extent linked to the antimilitarist tendency resulting from the Dreyfus affair, which had been in evidence since 1898, grew greatly in intensity between 1899 and 1900.[25] Articles on the theme of colonial militarism multiplied at the very time when the excesses of the military in the colonies were being denounced. The excesses of the occupation forces in Madagascar were vehemently denounced by Paul Vigné d'Octon in a series of articles, and in his very controversial book *La Gloire du Sabre*.[26] At the same time, two leader-writers on one of the main colonial newspapers, *La Politique Coloniale*, C. Lamy and J. Carol, also denounced the military regime in Madagascar.[27] Behind the scenes, several leading civil servants from the Governor-General of Madagascar led their own campaign against the military administration in Madagascar, hoping to see Gallieni replaced by a civilian.[28]

To offset this wave of criticism, Gallieni and his team launched a propaganda campaign to defend the legitimacy of the army's role in the colonies. The main contribution to this debate was provided by Lyautey's article 'Du Rôle colonial de l'Armée' published in *La Revue des Deux Mondes* and soon re-issued as a pamphlet.[29] This text, which constitutes the manifesto of the new French colonial military school, was to become a classic of French military thought.[30] While it is often considered as an apology for a military regime in the colonies, it must be stressed that this was in no way Lyautey's intention. Far from it: in a speech made on 19 February 1900 at the meeting of French explorers, Lyautey revealingly emphasised what he considered to be the 'main idea' of his article, which was the defence of a 'mixed regime' in the colonies.[31] In the article itself, Lyautey clearly and unambiguously stated that it was not his intention to defend 'an exclusively military regime'.[32] He repeatedly emphasised that 'the actual name of the regime' mattered little and that the question 'of the respective merits of a military regime versus a civil regime' must no longer be presented as alternatives, as it was in fact choosing the right men for the job that mattered most.

The Comité de Madagascar, the colonial exhibition and the promotion of mise en valeur

The last sort of propaganda activity used can be studied by examining the work of the information bureau, which was particularly active during the colonial exhibition of 1900. In this case the main concern was to promote the development of the colonisation of Madagascar and the *mise en valeur* (economic development) of the island.

Gallieni had been able to establish collaborative links with the Comité de Madagascar which, under the driving force of Jules Charles-Roux between 1898 and 1905, began to operate as an unofficial agency of the Government-General of Madagascar.[33] General Gallieni quickly understood all the use he could make of the committee in order to make the public more aware of the colony and to favour the economic development of Madagascar. He endeavoured to establish relations of cooperation with the committee, and from 1898 an annual subsidy was made available to it by the colony, which usefully contributed to the latter's funding.

The statutes of the committee, drawn up in 1900, laid out that

> the Comité de Madagascar aims to raise awareness about our new colony, to help by all available means the colonisation, as well as

the economic and commercial development of Madagascar, by examining questions of general interest relevant to the colony, and by enabling each of its members to defend their own particular interests'.[34]

The publication of periodicals and books destined to raise awareness about Madagascar was one of the main activities of the committee. Indeed, its president, Jules Charles-Roux, announced to the general assembly of 1899 that

> our main concern is to raise awareness about Madagascar in all its different aspects, to follow in the footsteps of our soldiers, so to speak, the various ways in which the *mise en valeur* of the island is being pursued, so as to demonstrate to everyone the resources available to science, industry and commerce, in a word to show what is available to the activity of our compatriots. There is no more effective way of achieving this than to make the most comprehensive and up-to-date publications widely available throughout the country. That is to say, we must spread far and wide new ideas about the colony of Madagascar and give precise and accurate information about its political and economic situation.[35]

A journal, *La Revue de Madagascar*, thus regularly published articles publicising 'the Island and the population of Madagascar, from a historical, ethnographic, economic and scientific point of view.

An important achievement of the committee was the publication in June 1899, to coincide with the return of Gallieni, of a guide for potential settlers in three volumes, the *Guide de l'Immigrant à Madagascar.*[36] In fact this was the second edition, greatly revamped, of a work initially published in 1896, immediately after the Madagascar campaign. The guide was in three large volumes, in octavo, with plans and maps. It was largely based on the work of civil and military collaborators of Gallieni, the main part of which was compiled by Captain Nèples.[37] The leading specialist of Malagasy studies, Alfred Grandidier, compiled the book and was responsible for editing it:

> The material for this great work was supplied to M. Grandidier by the Governor-General and the officers under his command, but it was M. Grandidier who, during an uninterrupted period of six months, did all the hard work necessary to complete the work.

Extracts were taken from this work to produce a small volume in the form of a practical manual aimed at future colonists and immigrants.[38]

Included in these propaganda activities were those carried out by the Bureau de Colonisation (Immigration Bureau). In 1898, during a trip to Antananarivo, Clément Delhorbe had got General Gallieni's agreement to entrust the running of the Bureau de Colonisation to the Comité de Madagascar. Gallieni wanted the bureau established in Paris[39] and granted an annual subsidy of 12 000 francs to the committee for this purpose. As Jules Charles-Roux put it, 'from then on the association became the official intermediary between the government of the island and the metropole for colonial matters.'[40] One of the functions of the bureau was to deal with the placement of employees in the colony. At the same time, the committee also became the official representative of the colony in Paris and official stockist of its publications.

The highpoint of the propaganda campaign organised by the Government-General of Madagascar during Gallieni's visit to France was undoubtedly the participation of the colony in the Paris Universal Exhibition of 1900. As expected, the Comité de Madagascar played a fundamental role here. It is worth noting that the committee was one of the small group of colonial societies which had put forward the idea of organising a colonial section at the universal exhibition.[41] In fact, in April 1898, the presidents of the Union Coloniale Française, the Comité de l'Afrique Française, the Society of Colonial Engineers and the Comité de Madagascar had suggested to the general commissioner of the Universal Exhibition of 1900 the organisation of a colonial congress, which was to lead to the organisation of the colonial exhibition.[42] Moreover, the president of the committee, Jules Charles-Roux, was appointed commissioner of the colonial exhibition, which contributed to the fact that the committee was well represented. The task of organising the participation of the colony of Madagascar in the exhibition was naturally entrusted to two active members of the committee, Anthony Jully and Etienne Grosclaude.

The Comité de Madagascar was represented both at the collective exhibition organised by the Union Coloniale Française and at the Madagascar Pavilion, where it occupied a prominent place. Lyautey and Gallieni did not miss the opportunity to honour this event with their presence. An exhibition of samples of agriculture, forestry, mineralogy and local crafts, as well as 'samples of population' (*sic*) from Madagascar, was organised jointly by the government-general and the committee.

Conclusion

The study of this visit to the mother country, France, between two colonial tours of duty, illustrates an essential aspect of high-ranking colonial officials, which was to represent the colony in question in Paris. The campaign, led by Gallieni and Lyautey, which was both exemplary and remarkably modern in its conception, was the product of a profound talent for public relations.

If it is difficult to analyse the impact Gallieni's team had on general public opinion. The campaign of communication and propaganda which it undertook seems to have been very successful, despite the fact that it left Gallieni and Lyautey with a bitter taste in their mouths because of the political climate of the time. The general kept his position as Governor-General of Madagascar, which was not necessarily a foregone conclusion before the visit. The reorganisation of the local government of Madagascar, which he envisaged, was accepted by the Minister of the Colonies, Albert Decrais, and a Superior Command of the South was created and placed under Lyautey, who had recently been promoted to the rank of full colonel. The Malagasy loan was rescinded (law of 14 April 1900) and the law of 20 July 1900 concerning colonial defence allocated 10.5 million francs for the defensive organisation of the naval base of Diego-Suarez. A law on the organisation of the colonial army, voted in July 1900, transferred the marines from the navy to the War Ministry.[43] If this was not exactly what Gallieni and Lyautey had hoped for, it nevertheless seemed to them to represent a step in the right direction.[44]

Notes and references

1. On the return of the Marchand mission, see M. Michel, *La Mission Marchand* (Mouton et Ecole Pratique des Hautes Etudes, 1972), pp. 239–41.
2. *La Dépêche coloniale* (hereafter D.C.), 25–26 June 1899.
3. A. Le Révérend, *Lyautey* (Fayard, 1983), pp. 125–66.
4. Cf. National Archives, Fonds Lyautey (hereafter F.L.), 475 AP 282, undated manuscripted note by Lyautey regarding his relations with General Galliffet.
5. F.L., 475 AP 262, letter to Blanche d'Aligny, 26 May 1892.
6. P. Venier, *Lyautey avant Lyautey* (L'Harmattan, 1997), p. 66.
7. On the colonial party, see C.-R. Ageron, *France coloniale ou parti colonial* (Presses Universitaires de France, 1978); C. M. Andrew, P. Grupp and A. S. Kanya-Forstner, 'Le Mouvement Colonial Français et ses Principales Personnalités 1890–1914', *Revue Française d'Histoire d'Outre-Mer*, 62, 1975, pp. 640–73, and C. M. Andrew and A. S. Kanya-Forstner, 'The Groupe Colonial in the French Chamber of Deputies, 1892–1932', *Historical Journal*, XVII, 1974, pp. 837–66.

8. F.L., 475 AP 259–314, private correspondence, and 475 AP 227, Lyautey's agenda for the year 1900.
9. F.L., 475 AP 272, correspondence with Jules Charles-Roux. On Charles-Roux, see B. Chevalier, 'Un Essai d'histoire biographique: un grand bourgeois de Marseille, Jules Charles-Roux (1841–1918)' (MA thesis, Faculté des Lettres, Aix-en-Provence, 1969), and S. M. Persell, 'The Colonial Career of Jules Charles-Roux', *Proceedings of the Western Society for French History*, I, 1974, pp. 306–23.
10. F.L., 475 AP 271, correspondence with Joseph Chailley-Bert; and C.A.O.M., Fonds du Comité Français de l'Outre-Mer (hereafter C.F.O.M.), Union coloniale Française 306, Lyautey Dossier. On Joseph Chailley-Bert see S. Persell, 'Joseph Chailley-Bert and the Importance of the Union Coloniale Francaise', *Historical Journal*, XVII, 1974, pp.176–85.
11. Venier, op. cit., p. 144.
12. F.L., 475 AP 42, letter from Gallieni to Lyautey, Saint-Béat, 2 November 1899.
13. F.L., 475 AP 42, letter from Gallieni to Lyautey, 14 April 1899.
14. General Joseph Gallieni, *Rapport d'Ensemble du Général Gallieni sur la situation générale de Madagascar* (Imprimerie Nationale, 1899), 2 volumes.
15. See for instance its analysis in Renseignements coloniaux, supplement to *Bulletin du Comité de l'Afrique Française*, July 1899, pp. 101–12.
16. E. Payen, 'L'oeuvre du général Gallieni', *Bulletin du Comité de l'Afrique Française*, July 1899, pp. 204–6.
17. General Gallieni, *Trois Colonnes au Tonkin (1894–1895)*, (Librairie Militaire R. Chapelot, 1899) and *La Pacification de Madagascar* (Opérations d'octobre 1896 à mars 1899), (Librairie Militaire R. Chapelot, 1900).
18. J. Charles-Roux, 'Le général Gallieni', *Bulletin du Comité de Madagascar*, 1899, pp. 7–23 and F.L., 475 AP 272, letter from Charles-Roux to Lyautey, 8 July 1899.
19. Sending Lyautey a first draft of his 'Rapport d'Ensemble', General Gallieni wrote to Lyautey : 'I am sending you the promised report . . . see what you can extract from it in favour of Lavisse, who asked me for a note which would allow him to publish at the time of my return to France one or two articles on our achievements in Madagascar in the Revue de Paris'. F.L., 475 AP 42, letter from Gallieni to Lyautey, 14 April 1899.
20. E. Lavisse, 'Une méthode coloniale', *Revue de Paris*, May and June 1899.
21. Lieutenant-Colonel H. Lyautey, 'La Colonisation à Madagascar par les Soldats', *La Réforme Sociale*, 1 January 1900, pp.129–39.
22. 'Une Conférence du Lieutenant-Colonel Lyautey', *La Quinzaine Coloniale*, 10 January 1900, pp. 31–2.
23. H. Lyautey, *Paroles d'Action: Madagascar, Sud-Oranais, Oran, Maroc (1900–1926)* (A. Colin, 1928), pp. 3–9.
24. F. Fugelstad, 'A propos de travaux récents sur la mission Voulet-Chanoine', *Revue Française d'Histoire d'Outre-Mer*, LXVII, 1980, pp. 73–87.
25. See for example, J.-L. de Lanessan, *La République démocratique* (Alcan, 1898), pp. 128–9.
26. P. Vigné d'Octon, *La Gloire du Sabre* (Flammarion, 1900).
27. J.-P. Biondi and G. Morin, *Les Anticolonialistes (1881–1962)* (Robert Laffont, 1992), pp. 52–6 and Y.-G. Paillard, *Les Incertitudes du colonialisme. Jean Carol a Madagascar* (L'Harmattan, 1990), pp. 5–34.

28. F.L., 475 AP 42, letter from Gallieni to Lyautey, 10 October 1899.
29. 'Du Rôle colonial de l'Armée', *Revue des Deux Mondes*, 15 January 1900, pp. 308–28 and *Du Rôle colonial de l'Armée* (A. Colin, 1900).
30. D. Porch, 'Bugeaud, Galliéni [sic], Lyautey : The Development of French Colonial Warfare', in P. Paret, ed., *Makers of Modern Strategy from Macchiavelli to the Nuclear Age* (Oxford University Press, 1986), pp. 376–407.
31. Lyautey, *Paroles d'Action*, pp. 3–9.
32. 'Du Rôle Colonial de l'Armée', reprinted in H. Lyautey, *Lettres du Tonkin et de Madagascar* (A. Colin, 1933), p. 629.
33. On the Comité de Madagascar, see P. Venier, 'Le Comité de Madagascar (1894–1911)', *Omaly sy Anio (Revue d'Histoire, Université de Madagascar)*, 28, 1988, pp. 43–56.
34. C.F.O.M. 443, Statutes of the Comité de Madagascar, 1900.
35. C.F.O.M. 443, Charles-Roux's speech at the general assembly of the Comité de Madagascar, 31 May 1899.
36. *Guide de l'immigrant à Madagascar* (A. Colin, 1899).
37. C.F.O.M. 443, Charles-Roux's speech at the general assembly of the Comité de Madagascar, 31 May 1899.
38. Ibid..
39. C.F.O.M. 319, U.C.F., Paris Universal Exhibition of 1900, press dossier.
40. C.F.O.M. 443, Charles-Roux's speech at the council of the Comité de Madagascar, 19 June 1898.
41. C.F.O.M. 443, minutes of the council of the Comité de Madagascar, 29 April 1898.
42. C.F.O.M. 319, U.C.F., Paris Universal Exhibition of 1900, press dossier.
43. J.-C. Jauffret, 'La loi du 7 juillet 1900 sur l'organisation des troupes coloniales : un accroissement de la Puissance?', in P. Milza and R. Poidevin, *La Puissance française à la 'Belle Epoque', mythe ou réalité* (Complexe, 1992), pp. 51–62.
44. Venier, *Lyautey avant Lyautey*, pp. 132–4.

3
Drawing Settlers to New Caledonia: French Colonial Propaganda in the Late Nineteenth Century

Isabelle Merle

New Caledonia, annexed by France in 1853, was the scene of an original experiment in settlement. It had been thought of as a possible territory for the 'white race' and throughout the second half of the nineteenth century it was subjected to a double process of immigration. The first was compulsory and, from 1864 to 1897, brought in thousands of prisoners condemned to hard labour, political deportation and banishment. They were supposed, once they had served their term in the penal settlement, to become honourable settlers on plots of land granted by the penal administration. The second was voluntary, comprising emigrants who, as was the case elsewhere, undertook the colonial venture in the hope of improving their lot and above all to acquire what at the time appeared to be the most valuable possession of all: land.

Over a period of 30 years, France sent about 30 000 convicts of various types to the antipodes. Soon the 'penal' population – convicts and ex-convicts, some of them settled on granted land – made up the majority and was omnipresent on the island. The 'free' population, on the other hand, hardly increased, as the rate of voluntary immigration was low. The French do not emigrate very readily and did not find much to attract them in so remote an island populated by convicts and Kanaks. The latter were said to be fierce and cannibalistic.

The French metropolitan authorities did not share this view and saw New Caledonia as a highly promising country that should not be left, like Guyana, to convicts. Up to the end of the nineteenth century France tried to convince its citizens to go and settle in the archipelago. A particularly strong effort to this end was made during the last years of the century under pressure from the governor who had been appointed in 1894, Paul Feillet. He had arrived on the island with definite plans for the future: to put a stop to the shipping of convicts and to transform New Caledonia into a 'healthy white' colony like the nearby New Zealand. The publicity for New Caledonia in colonial circles thus turned into a veritable propaganda campaign for a policy of voluntary emigration and settlement.

This chapter looks at the details of this operation as a specific, significant example of colonial propaganda. Just how were several thousand French persuaded to leave home for the Pacific? What means were employed? What arguments? What promises were made? What advantages offered? The propaganda developed between 1892 and 1900 to support French emigration to New Caledonia was a distinct change from the earlier 'publicity'. It was more efficiently organised and aimed at different sectors of the public. The settlement idea which had formed the basis of French colonisation of the island since 1853 reached its high point at this time. The results of the experiment, however, entailed its inexorable decline.

Forms and aims of the propaganda

What was generally known about New Caledonia towards the end of the nineteenth century? Next to nothing, complained a member of the Conseil Général of the colony in 1891: 'In France the general public has an erroneous idea of New Caledonia and sees it as uninhabitable, not only because of the climate but also because of the transportees and the natives.'[1]

New Caledonia did in fact have a poor reputation. Up to 1880, '*La Nouvelle*', sung by Bruant, was a destination for convicts of 'white race'. The French government did not do much about voluntary emigration. The Ministry of the Navy and the Colonies published succinct, dry information sheets for prospective candidates.[2] It also financed occasional special operations, such as the transfer of female orphans of the Assistance Publique,[3] the settlement of refugees from Alsace-Lorraine after the defeat of 1871,[4] the shipping out of a few impecunious emigrants[5] or the settlement of soldiers demobilised on the spot.

The situation changed at the beginning of the 1890s, when France became aware of the extent of European emigration to the New World and of the strategic importance of populating the empire it was in the process of building. Emigration to the colonies then became a major preoccupation not only for the colonial lobbies but also for the government itself.[6] The former fiercely denounced the stay-at-home character of the French, which they took to be a sign of the hopeless decline of the nation, and scrutinised the globe in the search for lands to 'populate'. In 1889, the authorities reacted against the setting up on the national soil of recruiting agencies for Argentina or Brazil and appealed to the prefects and chambers of commerce to redirect candidates towards French possessions, including New Caledonia.

Although New Caledonia was in 1889 – except by reputation – still largely unfamiliar to the general public, it was not so in specialist and colonial circles. Since 1853 when it was annexed by France it had been the subject of an impressive literature: officers' reports, travellers' tales, studies by engineers, colonial administrators, doctors or other civil servants, not to mention missionary publications, doctoral theses or essays.[7] Not a year went by without the publication of at least one article, for example in the journals of learned societies, missionary annals or travel journals. There was an accumulation of data about the inhabitants, the fauna, the flora, the nature of the soil, agricultural and mineral resources, and future prospects. Naturally, the aim was not primarily to promote colonisation and people the island, though the topic was frequently raised and discussed. But the gradual building up of a body of scientific knowledge was part of what could be called 'diffuse' propaganda. It provided a variety of information for the interested or knowledgeable reading public among whom there were certainly potential candidates for emigration. This knowledge was widely popularised in the specialised journals created to handle colonial matters and read by emigrants and prospective emigrants, such as *La Revue Coloniale, La Quinzaine Coloniale* and *Le Bulletin de la Société de Géographie de Paris*.

Of course, what could be called active propaganda was more narrowly targeted and aimed at a much wider public than the readers of specialised works or journals. Not only information but also various advantages were offered candidates to encourage them to leave.

As early as 1887 the Under-Secretary of State for the Colonies, Etienne, launched an appeal for emigrants to New Caledonia and Guyana and planned the development of new agricultural centres based on free grants of land previously cleared by penal labour.[8] Three years later the Minister for the Colonies was asked to strengthen his information service and increase the number of brochures and information sheets about French territories, among them New Caledonia.

New Caledonia benefited in fact from special publicity instigated by the Union Coloniale, which made it a priority. This association, founded in 1893 on the initiative of Marseilles and Bordeaux businessmen, was to become a veritable institution in the service of French colonial interests for the first half of the twentieth century. Under its president, Joseph Chailley-Bert, it chose New Caledonia as its first field for experimentation by supporting Paul Feillet. In 1894 it published *Le Guide de l'Emigrant en Nouvelle-Calédonie* by Dr Lavillé which was given publicity in a very optimistic article in the January 22 1895 issue of *Le Petit Journal*, a popular metropolitan paper with a large circulation. Response to the article was highly enthusiastic, as the Committee of the Union Coloniale observed when it subsequently distributed 4000 copies of the guide and received an avalanche of written and oral inquiries.[9] The big Parisian dailies such as *Le Temps* or *Le Figaro* followed suit and regularly informed their readers about colonisation in New Caledonia. This was also taken up by provincial newspapers. In all, 10 000 copies of the guide were printed. It was reprinted in 1897 and again in 1901. The Union Coloniale for its part opened the columns of its fortnightly journal *La Quinzaine Coloniale* to promoters of New Caledonia colonisation and reproduced in full the speeches of Governor Feillet. This information activity, which ranged from general considerations about the colony and colonisation to detailed practical advice for emigrants – the special field of the Union Coloniale – was also supported by other associations such as the Comité Dupleix, by the specialised journals which published numerous articles on the subject and by lectures organised in the large towns in France.

The Union Coloniale did, however, have a special place in this picture, in that it did not just circulate information but rapidly became a veritable agency for advice and guidance. Prospective colonists came to its Parisian headquarters to ask for information and for each case a file was opened.[10] The union aimed to follow the Caledonian project from beginning to end, from the moment the individual entered their office in Paris to his settlement in New Caledonia. In exchange for its help it requested newsletters, which were published in *La Quinzaine Coloniale* when they were favourable. Thus, the emigrants themselves were asked to take part in the propaganda operation by recounting their experience. Some, like François Devillers or Michel Villaz, even had their story published directly by the Comité Dupleix.[11]

The state itself provided special facilities, at both the metropolitan and colonial levels. New Caledonia was the only destination for which the journey was entirely free, covering not just the voyage from Marseilles to Nouméa but also the train fare from the home town to the port of embarkation.[12] On arrival, emigrants were received by the governor in person and a representative of the Union Agricole Calédonienne, who gave them advice and information about their future settlement.[13]

Then came the round-the-island tour and the first visit to the concession under the watchful eye of the local authorities, surveyors and
gendarmes. This careful organisation of the reception of these *'colons
Feillet'*, as they came to be called, was part of the propaganda aimed at
conveying a reassuring image of the colony as a generous country
where life could be good.[14]

Propaganda arguments and the audience targeted

New Caledonia was vaunted above all for its mild climate, often compared
to that of the South of France, where the European in particular could
put all his energy to use:

> The emigrant can work by himself just as easily in New Caledonia as
> in France. The country is even more clement because a good worker
> who conducts himself well is sure rapidly to attain a satisfactory
> degree of prosperity. There is help from the administration, a prom-
> ising future, assurance of good health, no winter to put up with, no
> fear of destitution.[15]

This was not the case in other tropical colonies which were too hot or
humid for whites.[16] The island climate was also presented as exception-
ally healthy compared to other colonies, in particular the nearby New
Hebrides where malaria was rife. Thus, emigrants could go out without
fearing for themselves or their young children, to a country without a
winter and as healthy as any part of France. Finally, New Caledonia
boasted an abundance of fertile land perfectly suited to small- and
medium-scale settlement. Stress was laid on the variety of crops, both
European and tropical, the advantage of the latter being that they
would not be in competition with French produce (unlike Algerian
wine-growing, for example). All sorts of crops had been tested, from
sugar cane to rice, cotton, vegetables of all kinds, fruit trees, rubber and
hemp. But in Feillet's time coffee was seen as *the* crop which could
ensure the colonists' future prosperity.

The colonial guidebooks presented the country as rapidly developing,
with roads under construction, villages springing up, schools opening
and even railways being built. They wanted to convince emigrants they
would benefit from the same services as in metropolitan France, which
was being rapidly transformed at the time. According to an article in
La Quinzaine Coloniale, the penal settlement (*bagne*) 'is confined within
set limits. Free settlement centres were separate from penal centres and

a free settler is in no danger of coming into contact with the convicts'.[17] As for 'the Caledonian native', he was 'no longer the fierce islander of earlier days'.[18] 'Natives', along with Javanese and New Hebrideans under bond, could provide useful labour. The guidebooks enumerated the respective merits of each type of worker, conjuring up in the eyes of prospective emigrants the role of master so often associated with the image of the colonist.[19]

Governor Feillet also vaunted the mineral resources of the country and appealed in 1900 for the immigration of labourers.[20] But the project did not take off, because in the nineteenth century the really basic idea behind settlement colonisation remained that of the ownership and working of the land. This is obvious in the orientation of propaganda, which sought first and foremost to attract small farmers with the qualities of 'the sturdy race of French peasants' described by the Union Coloniale in 1898 as 'sober, thrifty, hard-working, patient and tenacious, who give themselves body and soul to the land and towards whom the land is not ungrateful'.[21] This was the quintessential age-old France, rooted in the land, attached to its fields and meadows. But the call for colonists was not aimed at the poorest, for there was a requirement of a minimum capital of 5000 francs, though this was not in fact enforced in all cases. The problem was to dissuade the really destitute and to attract rather the shrewd French small landowner, who was canny, enterprising and who possessed some modest savings to tide him over the first years and guarantee success. In *La Quinzaine Coloniale* in 1897 Chailley-Bert declared, 'our colonies are at the age of agriculture', but advocated 'colonisation by specialists', using up-to-date techniques.[22] One year later an article about New Caledonia in the same *Quinzaine* warned the reader about those who 'left without preparation, with no knowledge of farming, or the physical and moral capacity for the hard life in the bush, nor the necessary capital', concluding 'they are bound to fail, but whose fault is it if not their own?'[23]

Effects and limitations of a propaganda campaign

In 1899, an article in the journal *Annales des Sciences Politiques* took stock of the results of the Feillet colonisation and emphasised the propaganda efforts it had involved:

> the means of propaganda used, although quite new in this country, have been tried and proved effective elsewhere, in particular in England, where they were wholly successful. There were not only numerous

letters and visits to the Union Coloniale and to the Ministry for the Colonies . . . , but also a good number of colonists of the right type presented themselves straight away.[24]

The means employed over the last five years of the century to promote emigration to New Caledonia were indeed exceptional. They succeeded in replacing the poor image from which the territory had suffered up till then and, in the limited circle of individuals tempted by the colonial adventure, New Caledonia suddenly became a desirable destination. A note circulated by the Ministry for the Colonies shows that in 1895, leaving Algeria aside, New Caledonia came second after Indo-China among the colonies chosen by emigrants. It came first in 1896 and 1897.[25]

The absolute numbers were not high: 115 applications in 1895, 163 in 1897. However, in the history of New Caledonia they were exceptional, for the island had never before attracted such a large influx of emigrants as it did during the last five years of the century. Each year several dozen families arrived. Overall 300 households landed from metropolitan France beween 1895 and 1902, a total of 787 persons.[26]

Some of these 'colons Feillet' did correspond to the type of earlier emigrants of humble origin and it is doubtful whether they began with a capital of 5000 gold francs. Others, however, had obviously been recruited from the better-off classes of French society.[27] The Feillet programme undeniably attracted individuals with financial resources or educational records of a relatively high level for the period. On arrival, the former often bought property that had already been farmed rather than clear the 25 hectares of their free concession. The latter had often had professions before their departure that placed them in the middle class. They were, for example, doctors, engineers, pharmacists and non-commissioned officers. The most extreme case was that of Marc Le Goupils, graduate of the Ecole Normale Supérieure and lecturer at the Sorbonne, who settled as a colonist in New Caledonia with his two brothers, one a teacher and the other a doctor, and was to tell his story in a book entitled *Comment on Cesse d'Etre Colon* ('How One Gives Up Being a Colonist').[28]

Judging from these social profiles, the effectiveness of the propaganda at the end of the century is indisputable. Otherwise it is impossible to see what future a graduate from the Ecole Normale Supérieure, a pharmacist or an engineer could expect in a colony at the other end of the earth in a remote New Caledonian valley. The letters sent to the Union Coloniale, the first ones at any rate, expressed real enthusiasm, pride in being among those who had the courage to leave to begin anew, pride also in their participation in a great endeavour, that of empire-building. These testimonies show a strong feeling for the land, even among those who had not been farmers before they went out and who were in a sense going "back to the land". There was a feeling of joy in working new ground, trying new crops, seeing them thrive and little by little organising the bush round about into a semblance of a familiar landscape, a rather exotic but still very French rural scene. Admittedly the letters available are from the more enthusiastic among them and are written by colonists who had at least made an attempt at agriculture in New Caledonia, for some fled their concession almost immediately after arriving. Still, the initial enthusiasm was undeniable, as was the sense of adventure the land inspired, pioneer adventure that was still possible in New Caledonia at the end of the century. Perhaps this was the reason middle-class colonists dreaming of a return to the land chose the Pacific island rather than the already highly developed Algeria with its solid, close-knit, colonial society.

But the campaign also showed its drastic limitations when it came into collision with reality. New Caledonia turned out to be a trap, both for its promoters and for the settlers whose illusions were soon to collapse.

The colonisation plans for 1896, 1898 and 1899 clearly show the scale of the effort undertaken and the dogged determination of Governor Feillet. The aim was to open New Caledonia to new emigrants while brutally displacing the Melanesian population. Though some agricultural centres on the coast were enlarged, the main effort was directed towards the east coast of the territory and the colonisation of narrow valleys inhabited until then by the Kanaks.[29] But above all Governor Feillet dreamed of taking over the mountainous centre, where he planned to settle large numbers of colonists. For example, in a barely accessible area at over 1000 metres on the high crests of the Tables-Unio he planned to settle more than 300 families. After 1896 the members of the Conseil Général became concerned about the haste with which the governor's subordinates operated and about unkept promises. A colonist spoke of plots divided up 'just any way', while the planned roadworks were never completed. Feillet talked about already populated centres, whereas a *conseiller* reported that in one 'he found an ex-convict, twelve empty huts and not a single settler'.[30] In another, where the governor claimed ten plots had been allotted and 11 000 coffee bushes planted, the same *conseiller* retorted:

There is no arable soil, only red clay covered with niaoulis. There are clumps of forest in the bottom of the valley and with the first rain the soil is washed away. The colonists who had been settled here had so little hope of success that they all left. There is only one still there.[31]

In fact it was by no means rare for newly arrived migrants to leave by the next boat in view of the difficulties awaiting them. The letters received by the Union Coloniale, although still positive, also mentioned the conditions of settlement, the hard toil, the struggle against wild vegetation, the isolation, the lack of roads, the fear of ex-convicts, the scorching sun. One of them said, in reference to prospective emigrants:

These gentlemen should recall that here, more than anywhere, the beginnings are hard, extremely hard, and that if they come they'll find what almost amounts to a village, whereas when I arrived, there was an Indian camp in the midst of bush and reeds, and in the evening there was a piece of damper and a tin of sardines by the fire, creek water and three comfortable logs to sleep on. One broods a lot and curses the well-fed officials who sit in their armchairs and point to a spot on the map 50 kilometres away … Now all that is forgotten.[32]

He concluded with the following recommendation:

I cannot end this long letter without imploring them to think carefully and to give up the idea of coming out if they do not feel they can do without the comfort, housing and food they are used to for a year at least.

The Union Coloniale itself asked questions and sent out a questionnaire in 1897 in order to ascertain the exact situation of the emigrants it had sent to New Caledonia.[33] Was it their intention to defend the work of Feillet or was the union beginning to feel uneasy about the results?

Most Feillet colonists settled on land in the narrow valleys on the east coast that had just been wrested from the Kanaks, who were banished to poor reservations. They were relatively isolated places and sadly lacking in means of transport, with the promised roads amounting to no more than rough tracks. This absence of roads soon became a nightmare for the settlers and the administration, who were unable to solve the problem. The country that had been claimed to be rapidly developing turned out to be one where everything remained to be built: housing, tracks, fields, schools were all lacking. One Union Coloniale correspondent complained about the retrograde step he had made in coming to New Caledonia, especially for the future of his children.[34] Others stressed the peculiar nature of white society with ex-convicts roaming the roads and frightening honest settlers, or the threat of the Kanaks who lived so close and were so different, and probably hostile.[35] Settlers knew they were on their former lands.[36]

As well as loneliness, privation and uncertainty, would-be colonists also had to face the rigours of a climate which was anything but Mediterranean. The years 1895–1900 were particularly bad and there was a succession of cyclones, floods, droughts and other natural disasters such as plagues of grasshoppers. Each time a long, risky job had to be begun all over again, for coffee takes five years to reach maturity and yield a full crop. Moreover, coffee prices collapsed after 1898 under pressure from Brazilian competition, which led to the ruin of colonists who in the end asked to be repatriated to France, leaving a colony in the throes of depression in both agriculture and mining.[37]

Conclusion

Admittedly circumstances were against the Feillet colonists, but it can also be claimed that the propaganda was often over-optimistic. Earlier experiences of settlement could have served as examples and drawn attention to climatic extremes and the fragility of the soil. Former colonists could have told of their loneliness, their communication problems and their fear of others, convict or Kanak. When I did a field investigation in 1990, one colonist told me:

> My grandfather was one of the original Feillet settlers. He had thought there were railway lines and all. He thought it was a country on the move. When they saw all that! Go to Caledonia they'd been told, there's this, there's that, a new country, you'll make money. The poor things! They'd been poor in France too. It was the same privation, here they found even worse. They made a Feillet colonist of him, he built a hut to begin with. Poor devils, water from the *touque* (cut-off tin), working like a navvy. When I think that today they throw money around and we starved.[38]

Among the reminiscences of Feillet descendants I gathered, ones like this are frequent and symptomatic: memories of having been deceived by a highly optimistic propaganda, of going backwards and starting from scratch. The disappointment was in proportion to the promises. The Feillet colonists found it more difficult to accept the hardships of colonial settlement than their predecessors to whom nothing had been promised except sweat and toil. Governor Feillet suffered the consequences of the reaction against his enthusiasm. At the turn of the century he was discredited and in France he appeared as a caricature of the unscrupulous colonial promoter, protected by distance and the slowness of communications. His emigration policy entered the annals of the alluring but dangerous colonial world the French fundamentally never ceased to mistrust. When Feillet left, France changed its strategy and abandoned the policy of encouraging emigration to New Caledonia, and then to the empire as a whole, when, in 1908, it did away with the budget in support of colonial emigration.[39]

The idea of peopling New Caledonia was, however, tenacious. Born again from its ashes in 1925 under Governor Guyon, it was regularly relaunched in the specialised journals between the wars and again in the 1950s and 1960s.[40] In 1972, the prime minister of the time, Pierre Messmer, was still urging emigration to the Pacific island.[41] A tenacious idea therefore, but during the twentieth century it was no more than that and not really supported by any deliberate policy.

Notes and references

1. Conseil Général, session of 1 September, 1891.
2. Cf. Ministère de la Marine et des Colonies, *Note sur la colonisation à la Nouvelle-Calédonie* (Imprimerie Nationale, 1872).
3. Ministerial Dispatch, 3 March, 1873 in *Bulletin Officiel de la Nouvelle-Calédonie*, 1873.
4. Ministerial Dispatch of 19 November 1872 in *Bulletin Officiel de la Nouvelle-Calédonie*, 1873.
5. For example, those settled at Koné, a centre founded in 1880.
6. Cf. H. Bunle, *Mouvements migratoires entre la France et l'Etranger* (Imprimerie Nationale, 1943); C.-R. Ageron, *France coloniale ou parti colonial* (Presses Universitaires de France, 1978); R. Girardet, *L'Idée coloniale en France* (La Table Ronde, 1972); I. Merle, *Expériences coloniales. La Nouvelle-Calédonie, 1853–1920* (Belin, 1995), pp. 45–62. Cf. also P. Leroy-Beaulieu, *De la Colonisation chez les peuples modernes* (Guillaumin, 1891 (1st edn, 1874)); C. Lemire, *La Colonisation et la question sociale en France* (Challamel Aîné, 1885); E. Poiré, *L'Emigration Française aux colonies* (Plon, 1897); J.-B. Piolet, *De l'Emigration* (xerox, n. d.), AOM, Fond Union Coloniale, 553.
7. P. O'Reilly, *Bibliographie méthodique, analytique et critique de la Nouvelle-Calédonie* (Publication de la Société des Océanistes, no. 4, Musée de l'Homme, 1955).
8. The first experiment of this kind was the settlement of Ouaménie; Merle, *Expériences coloniales*, pp. 227–34.

9. The Union Coloniale received more than 500 written and 300 oral inquiries about settlement in New Caledonia after the article was published in *Le Petit Journal*. This over-enthusiasm worried the Union Coloniale, which insisted the paper publish a rectification on 30 January 1895 giving exact conditions for emigration, in particular the necessary capital estimated at 5000 gold francs, AOM, session of 12 February, 1895, Comité de l'Union Coloniale, Fonds Privés, Union Coloniale, Procès-verbaux de séances, register 1.
10. Cf. settlers' files, Fonds Privés, Union Coloniale, AOM.
11. M. Villaz, *Débuts d'un emigrant en Nouvelle-Calédonie* (Challamel Aîné, 1897); F. Devillers, 'Installation d'un colon', in *La Vie du colon en Nouvelle-Calédonie* (Comité Dupleix, 1898; 2nd edn: The Kiwanis Club du Mont Dore, 1975).
12. AOM, note from the Ministère des Colonies, carton 10, Fond géographie, Nouvelle-Calédonie.
13. Cf. emigrants' letters published in *La Quinzaine Coloniale*. For description of a detailed follow-up, cf. *Le Bulletin de l'Union Coloniale Française*, January 1896, 2nd year, 1.
14. *La Vie du colon en Nouvelle-Calédonie*.
15. E. Lavillé, *Le Guide de l'emigrant en Nouvelle-Calédonie* (Union Coloniale, 1894).
16. Emigrants were, however, advised not to land during the hottest season, November-March, which 'is disheartening', *La Quinzaine Coloniale*, 25 February 1897, pp. 120–1.
17. Mgr Fraysse, 'La colonisation en Nouvelle-Calédonie. Réponse de Mgr Fraysse au R. P. Piolet', *La Quinzaine Coloniale*, vol. 3, 28, 25 February 1898, p. 98.
18. Ibid.
19. Cf. Merle, *Expériences coloniales*, pp. 227–71.
20. Conseil Général, session of 28 April, 1895.
21. 'La colonisation agricole en Nouvelle-Calédonie', *La Quinzaine Coloniale*, 10 July 1898, p. 390.
22. J. Chailley-Bert, 'Faites des spécialistes', *La Quinzaine Coloniale*, 10 October 1897, p. 193.
23. 'La colonisation agricole en Nouvelle-Calédonie', p. 391.
24. E. Payen, 'La colonisation libre en Nouvelle-Calédonie', in *Les Annales des Sciences Politiques*, 14, 1899, p. 199.
25. AOM, undated note, Fond géographie, Nouvelle-Calédonie, carton 10.
26. Merle, *Expériences Coloniales*, pp. 319–45.
27. Ibid.
28. M. le Goupils, *Comment on cesse d'être colon* (Grasset, 1910).
29. Merle, *Expériences coloniales*, pp. 319–45.
30. Conseil Général, 1896, examen du projet de budget pour l'exercice 1897, quoted in Merle, *Expériences coloniales*, p. 326.
31. Ibid. Niaoulis (*Melaleuca quinquenervia*) are trees of the eucalyptus family. They are common in New Caledonia and are the country's emblem.
32. Letter from a former civil servant turned settler to the Union Coloniale, published in *La Quinzaine Coloniale*, 25 April 1899, p. 254.
33. Questionnaire sent by the Union Coloniale to 138 settlers in January 1898, of whom only 25 responded. Cf. 'Emigration en Nouvelle-Calédonie', in *La France Australe*, 15 April 1898; 'La vérité vraie sur la colonisation feuilletiste.

Réponse d'un nouveau colon', in ibid, 24 May 1898; 'Un document', in ibid., 2 March 1899; 'Le questionnaire', in *Quinzaine Coloniale*, 10 January 1899.

34.   'I have decided to close down my business and leave. I came to this colony in the belief that I could create a better future for my children than in France . . . but I was mistaken . . . I cannot even give them the education they need as most settlements have no school' – letter from Plesnel to the Union Coloniale, Nakéty, 30 March 1900, AOM, Fonds privé, Union Coloniale.

35.   Ex-convicts, most of them obliged to remain in the colony for life, scoured the bush for means of survival, for example by working in mines or on farms. This contact between ex-convicts and 'honest folk' created a feeling of insecurity among new settlers who, as one of them put it in a letter to *La Quinzaine Coloniale*, saw them as 'degraded creatures with every vice written in their faces'; AOM, Fonds privé, Union Coloniale.

36.   See the account of Ludovic Papin, a settler who went to live in a valley close to Hienghène in 1900 and who was killed by the Kanaks in 1917, in B. Papin, *Vie et mort de Ludovic Papin chez les canaques* (L'Harmattan, 1997).

37.   Merle, *Expériences Coloniales*, pp. 319–45.

38.   Ibid, p. 328.

39.   J. B. Alberti, *Etude sur la colonisation à la Nouvelle-Calédonie, colonisation pénale, colonisation libre* (doctoral thesis, Larose, 1909), p. 219.

40.   Cf. A. Arnette, 'Au sujet de la colonisation en Nouvelle-Calédonie', *L'Océanie Française*, 35th year, 1939, pp. 75–6; H. Bonneaud, 'Nouvelle-Calédonie, terre française du Pacifique', *France Outre-Mer*, 27th year, 1949, pp. 197–8.

41.   Quoted in A. Bensa, *Nouvelle-Calédonie. Vers l'Emancipation* (Gallimard, 1998).

4
The Dissenters: Anti-Colonialism in France, *c.* 1900–40

Jonathan Derrick

In 1931, 8 million people visited the Colonial Exhibition at the Parc de Vincennes in Paris, held from 6 May to 15 November. The elaborately planned and spectacular celebration of empire undoubtedly succeeded in its propagandist aim, besides making a profit of 30 to 35 million francs.[1]

Towards the end of the exhibition, a 'counter-exhibition' was held in Paris by anti-colonialists. They issued a short brochure, *Le Véritable Guide de l'Expo Coloniale*.[2] At the same time 12 leaders of the Surrealist artistic and literary movement issued a leaflet, *Ne Visitez pas l'Exposition Coloniale*. The 'counter-exhibition' gave information about colonial oppression and crimes besides showing some works of art from Africa, Oceania and the Americas. Open from 19 September to 2 December 1931, it had precisely 4226 visitors.[3]

Allowing for the possibility that a few of the 8 million may have left the main exhibition unimpressed by the wonders of the French empire, allowing also for the fact that the 'counter-exhibition' was a communist venture (which would put many people off visiting it), this contrast shows that anti-colonialists were a minority in France, as in Britain, in the 1930s. That is unquestionably true whatever definition one adopts of 'anti-colonialism'.

For the purposes of this chapter, anti-colonialism means opposition on essentially moral grounds to colonial occupation and rule, for two major, related reasons: the ill-treatment and oppression of those who were, at the time under study, commonly called – even by anti-colonialists – 'natives' or *indigènes*, and the role of European militarism and capitalism. Opposition to colonialism for material, France-centred reasons – on the grounds that it was a waste of money or, in the early phase in the 1880s, that it was a harmful distraction from the confrontation with Germany – is thus not considered here.

Protests and campaigns before 1914

The anti-colonialists included some who totally opposed annexations or called unambiguously for withdrawal from the colonies later. But they can reasonably be taken to include also at least some of the more numerous people who, while condemning what was in fact happening in the colonies, called for improved colonial rule and believed that to be possible.

It was natural for left-wing writers and politicians from the Radical Party and from the parties united in 1905 to join the SFIO to have words to say against the colonial expeditions from an early date. One historian of French anti-colonialism has said that the socialists' anti-colonial views from 1880 to 1905 showed more affinity with the liberal and humanitarian tradition than with Marxism.[4] Besides revulsion against capitalism, which did not originate with Marxism, there was revulsion against militarism to which the Dreyfus case had given a great impetus. Referring to colonial abuses, Jean Jaurès said they made the conquests like 'a sort of permanent Dreyfus case'.[5] Anatole France, aroused to political activity by the Dreyfus case, wrote in 1904 that 'a syndicate of financiers and industrialists has made an alliance with the generals' party to drag us into Morocco'.[6]

The long-drawn-out French occupation of Morocco was the major focus of anti-colonial protests for years. At an early stage in the French intervention Gustave Hervé, at the Congress of the Parti Socialiste Français in 1902, applauded the Moroccans and told French troops that he hoped they would be welcomed as the Italians had been in Ethiopia in 1896.[7] Fiercely anti-militarist also, he expressed similar views in the weekly *La Guerre Sociale* which he edited from 1906. But he suddenly abandoned his campaigning against 'colonial banditry' after one of many spells in prison, in 1912.[8] Most of his fellow socialists had never gone as far as Hervé, although many on the left attacked the Morocco campaigns strongly, one extra reason being the danger of European war. However, the Radicals had a quick change of attitude, exemplified by Clemenceau, and soon fully accepted the colonial empire and joined in governing it.

Socialists generally accepted some sort of colonialism from an early stage,[9] even though the SFIO's Nancy Congress in August 1907 passed a strong resolution declaring that

> socialism is necessarily hostile to colonialism, which relies on violent conquest and institutionalises the subjection of Asiatic and African

peoples...Colonialism contributes to the transformation of the world by exacerbating the antagonisms which constitute the very foundation of the capitalist system.[10]

Victor Basch wrote in 1908 that the Malagasys, the black peoples of the Congo and Guinea, and the Moroccans had as much right to defend their 'integrity and honour' as the Boers, who had been widely supported in France a few years before. But he also wrote: 'it is highly desirable that the superior nations should make the inferior nations participate in the benefits of civilisation which they enjoy'.[11] Jaurès eventually came out against imposition of a 'protectorate' by force of arms, but agreed to peaceful extension of French influence and held out hope for improved colonial rule, though he said only socialism could bring it about. A study of French anti-colonialism concludes that socialists generally adopted a paternalist attitude:

The 'master' arrogated to himself, with a good conscience, the right to define the ways to happiness and progress for the 'slave' or the 'pupil'; everyone, left and right, used the same standard or model (that is, France) and the same basic ideas about civilisation and barbarism; the left, then and later, was not immune to ideas, encouraged by the anthropology of the time, about 'inferior' civilisations and one single, inevitable form of human evolution.[12]

The Ligue des Droits de l'Homme (LDH) took up cases of injustice in the colonies, essentially showing the same approach: defence of people against colonial interests on many occasions, while accepting that colonialism should continue and be improved.[13] Some prominent French people called *indigénophiles*, in the early years of the twentieth century, opposed colonial abuses and called for reforms but appealed to a better side of France to install improved colonial rule; they included Catholics and Protestants as well as Freemasons and the LDH.[14] A number of them formed the Alliance Franco-Indigène in 1913, headed by the economist Charles Gide who was also a member of the Comité de Protection et de Défense des Indigènes whose leading figure, at the turn of the century, was Paul Viollet.[15]

Indigénophiles' views parallelled to some extent those of the early Algerian and Tunisian political campaigners who called for greater equality with French citizens under French rule, such as the Jeunes

Algériens and Emir Khaled. Commenting on the Jeunes Algériens' demands, Khaled's biographers argue convincingly that

> in the colonial context, to challenge the status of the 'natives', even in a mild way, was to challenge the Algerians' status in relation to the Europeans of Algeria. It was to contest French domination which was signified in Algeria by those same Europeans who truly represented French power on the spot.[16]

Indeed, critics – people of the colonies and French sympathisers alike – who believed in improved colonialism could still highlight ill-treatment of Indochinese, Maghrebians and black Africans, and make demands on their behalf, in a way that potentially threatened the colonial order. That was all the more so when particular forms of oppression were at the very basis of the local colonial setup: land expropriation in Algeria, or extortionate impositions in the French Congo (later French Equatorial Africa).

The protest campaign over the misrule of the concessionary companies in the French Congo in 1905–6 was one of the high points of anti-colonialism before 1914. The exposure of quite exceptional atrocities and the despatch of Savorgnan de Brazza to head an inquiry were followed by a massive cover-up, but initially the ordinary daily and weekly press played an important part in exposing the crimes. This happened on other occasions also, and the contribution of the press to negative publicity about empire must not be underestimated: it could disturb good feeling about colonialism more than Marxist analyses did. This may have been true also of the novelist Vigné d'Octon, who highlighted colonial crimes while not adopting any consistent anti-colonial position, and was to be quoted in the left-wing *Le Paria* in the 1920s.[17]

One campaigner prominent in the Congo protests was to remain an outstanding leader of French anti-colonialism for decades: Félicien Challaye, chairman of the Ligue Française pour la Défense des Indigènes du Bassin du Congo.[18] Challaye was remarkable because he moved from a position of believing in reformed and improved colonialism before the First World War to rejection of all colonialism later. The more normal trend was in the opposite direction; after the First World War the empire seemed more than ever to be a part of the landscape. But one consequence of the war was the emergence of communism, which became, in France, the first major political movement strongly and consistently opposed to imperialism.

Communism against empire

The majority at the SFIO congress at Tours in 1920 voted to form the Parti Communiste Français (PCF) and adhere to the Third International, accepting the 21 conditions laid down for admission, including the eighth condition which stated that a party must support 'all movements for emancipation in the colonies', demand 'the expulsion from the colonies of the imperialists of the metropolitan country', encourage 'fraternal sentiments' towards the working people of the colonies and the oppressed nationalities among European workers, and keep up constant agitation among European troops against 'oppression of the colonial peoples'.[19] In the succeeding years the PCF was criticised from Moscow for failing to do its anti-colonial duty sufficiently, while the Algerian settlers who joined the party strongly opposed any commitment to emancipation for the Algerian Muslims, concealing basic settler sentiments behind the argument that only the revolution in France itself could bring emancipation to the empire, until they were obliged to submit outwardly, at least, to the party line.[20] But in fact the PCF organised an active campaign among North African troops in the French occupation of the Ruhr in 1923, and a more extensive campaign (again including appeals to troops, following the antimilitarist tradition) against the Rif War in Morocco in 1925–6. In this and other anti-colonial activity, the PCF worked with the communist trade union body, the Confédération Générale du Travail Unifié (CGTU) and with the Secours Rouge International (SRI: International Red Aid). It had its Commission Coloniale from 1924 to 1934, initially run by members of the Jeunesses Communistes among whom there was considerable anti-colonial enthusiasm.[21]

Whatever ambiguities and cross-purposes in its attitudes may be discerned, in the context of the 1920s the Communist Party was seen as the party working against the French Empire. It was seen as such both by governors and defenders of the empire and by early colonial nationalists. From the 1920s there were students from colonial territories in France, very few compared with a later generation, but also attracted to nationalism like that generation. Far more numerous in the inter-war period were the immigrant workers, especially the Algerians; despite efforts to restrict the migration, 82 000 were counted in 1937.[22] It was among them that an early militant nationalist party, calling for independence, grew up in the 1920s: the Etoile Nord Africaine (ENA), organised mainly among Algerians in France.

Some people from the colonies, such as Nguyen Ai Quoc, who became the famous Ho Chi Minh, and the Algerian Abdelkader Hadj Ali, joined the PCF. Others worked closely with it in the Union Interco-lonial and with the newspaper *Le Paria*. The Union was a small but energetic group of people from the colonies, headed by Nguyen Ai Quoc and then by Hadj Ali.[23] *Le Paria*, which published 38 issues from 1922 to 1926, was a militant periodical dealing with colonial crimes and the colonial subjects' sacrifices in the First World War, among other themes.[24] From an early date the communists were ready at least sometimes to work with nationalists whose basic beliefs were unlike theirs, such as Khaled in Algeria; in 1922 the newspaper *Ikdam*, support-ing Khaled, had said the communists 'treat us as equals'.[25] This was a constant asset for the PCF in relations with activists from the colonies.

Later it was claimed that Khaled had been the real founder of the ENA in 1924, but this seems to have been a legend developed after the ENA and the communists parted company.[26] In fact the ENA was founded in 1926 in close cooperation with the PCF, but relations between its general secretary, Messali Hadj, and the PCF were always difficult and eventually, when the ENA was revived by Messali in 1933 after a ban in 1929 and years of difficulty, it was as an independent organisation.[27]

The basic problem between nationalists like Messali and the commun-ists was that the latter wanted to run everything their own way. This problem arose with various organisations founded by black residents in Paris from the West Indies, Africa and Madagascar, such as the Comité de Défense de la Race Nègre (CDRN) in 1926–7, and then the Ligue de Défense de la Race Nègre (LDRN) from 1927 to the 1930s.[28] Much of the initiative for such activist groups came from colonial citizens and subjects living in France. The communists had considerable finan-cial power over allied groups, which usually had no other sources of funding, but this was resisted, and initiative mattered as well as money. However, at the time opponents of communism – politicians, colonial governors and administrators, pro-empire journalists and others – saw the communists as the masters and those Vietnamese, Arabs and Africans who opposed imperialism as mere tools of Bolshevism. An extraordin-ary example was the suggestion by Prime Minister Painlevé that Abd el-Krim had been pushed into attacking France by the Comintern.

The Rif War protests and after

When Abd el-Krim, by then ruler of a *de facto* independent territory in Spanish Morocco, invaded French Morocco in 1925, protests against the French military response were organised by a special Central Committee against the War in Morocco, headed by the young Maurice Thorez.[29] Jacques Doriot emerged to prominence then as a leading communist spokesman on colonial affairs.[30] Communist campaigning emphasised the danger of wider 'imperialist war' and said the war against Abd el-Krim was a bankers' war, a war for plunder of mineral wealth, for which the French workers and peasants would pay, while their sons would die in Morocco.[31] During the campaign a CGTU meeting on 12 June 1925 called for 'an intensive propaganda campaign in order to attract the support of the proletariat and to make peace with a people who have no other desire but to live in the land of their ancestors'.[32] Earlier Hadj Ali spoke at a meeting on the Rif in Paris 30 September 1924 praising Abd el-Krim 'who is fighting, like Abd el Kader before, for the independence of his country'.[33]

The climax of the protest campaign – which also supported the Syrian uprising of 1925 – was a general strike on 12 October 1925. However, this was followed by only about 50 000 to 100 000 people, a clear sign that the mass of French workers and others cared only slightly about colonial issues.[34] Direct communist-organised arms supplies to Abd el-Krim were inevitably suspected, but not proved.[35] But there were appeals (with little success) to troops to refuse to fight the Rifis or fraternise with them, and such direct appeals to insubordination by soldiers, always considered intolerable in Western countries, were for years made consistently by the PCF. As early as 1921–2 it was worried about the possible use of colonial troops against European workers. A new version of this concern was expressed by Moscow after the 1928 Comintern congress, when there was a genuine or contrived fear of new Western military intervention against the USSR and it was considered important to urge colonial troops not to let themselves be used in such a venture.[36] But throughout the 1920s the much-dreaded communist activity in Algeria amounted to very little, and apart from Algeria there was very little communist organisation in the colonies in the inter-war period except for Indochina and (on a very small scale) Tunisia and Madagascar.[37] Generally the colonial red-phobia had a large element of paranoia; vast volumes of police and intelligence reports about subversion in Morocco had little basis in reality, and the idea of communist plotting behind the Gbaya revolt in French Cameroons and Ubangi-Shari in 1928 was fanciful.[38]

An important communist initiative in 1927 was the Brussels conference which led to the foundation of the League Against Imperialism (LAI). Then, in 1928, communist policy all over the world was changed by the sixth Comintern Congress, which imposed a rigorist, sectarian approach, rejecting alliance with non-communist left-wing parties in the West and with non-communist 'bourgeois nationalists' in the colonies. In France this policy meant more determined PCF efforts to control the colonial peoples' own activist groups.[39] But although more isolated, the PCF was as militant in its opposition to colonialism as ever. Both the party and the French section of the LAI, the Ligue Anti-Impérialiste, declined in influence for a few years after 1929, and anti-colonial militancy went through a relatively fallow period; hence the weakness of reactions against the celebrations of the centenary of the occupation of Algiers in 1930, and against the colonial exhibition the following year. However, the Colonial Commission, after several rather inactive years, had a new lease of life for a time under André Ferrat.[40] The PCF declared support for the great revolt in Indochina in 1930. Communist campaigning against imperialism continued until the mid-1930s, in *L'Humanité*, in other publications, in the National Assembly and elsewhere.

Communists and others

However much the PCF was acting under Moscow's orders, it would be wrong to see in all communist anti-colonial and anti-militarist activity mere cynical manipulation from the top. At that time there was no motive for Frenchmen to join the PCF except conviction. The conviction that led people to embrace communism, especially at the time of the Depression, was notoriously followed after a few years by disillusion among a good many, especially intellectuals; and before disillusion there came denial or whitewashing of Stalin's crimes and, where colonial matters were concerned, uncritical enthusiasm for the vaunted progress in the Soviet Asian republics. But a genuine moral, humanitarian conviction was there initially. Among the rank-and-file, the Communist Party can be seen, for about fifteen years, as the main heir to the humanitarian tradition of opposition to imperialism, militarism and capitalism. Its anti-imperialist propaganda appealed to a sense of outrage at oppression and exploitation, as in the *Véritable Guide de l'Exposition Coloniale*.

That sense of outrage obviously extended beyond the ranks of the Communist Party. One cannot make a hard-and-fast distinction between Marxist theorists and instinctive protesters. Many sorts of people were aroused to anger, and aroused others, over specific events in the colonies. Communists responded to concern or outrage over events highlighted by people who might not share their basic views, but who knew about abuses such as the continuing crimes in French Equatorial Africa – notably the conscription of forced labourers (of whom at least 16 000 died) for the Congo-Océan Railway completed in 1934.[41] This was exposed by André Gide in *Voyage au Congo* (1927) and *Le Retour du Tchad* (1928), and by Albert Londres in *Terre d'Ebène* (1929). Gide did not end his grim account with a call for immediate French evacuation of the African colonies, but accounts like his contributed to anti-colonial campaigning.

Other literary people contributed to anti-colonial sentiment in the 1920s. Among intellectuals and artists the widespread post-war disillusion with European 'civilisation' may have encouraged disillusion with empire, which was based so much on a conviction of superior civilisation. The Surrealists took this disillusion to extremes with their peculiar ideology; although that ideology was really far removed from the communists', Louis Aragon, André Breton and Paul Eluard joined the PCF in the late 1920s, and Surrealists produced the pamphlet *Ne Visitez pas l'Exposition Coloniale*.[42] However, it is questionable how much influence the questioning of western civilisation had. The feeling of superiority encouraged by the 1931 Exhibition probably remained fairly general. The inter-war black vogue in Paris (Josephine Baker, the biguine and so on) was quite compatible, in the minds of French people, with belief in the benefits of colonial rule over black people and others.[43]

There was some anti-colonial militancy among minor left-wing and pacifist groups and individuals.[44] Challaye was always active, taking part in the foundation of the LAI in 1927 and leading a minority in the LDH calling for decolonisation. At the LDH's Vichy congress in 1931 he put forward a minority motion (defeated) calling for equal rights, the quickest possible liberation of peoples constituting 'true nations' when they obviously called for independence, and provisional international trusteeship for 'primitive groups who are not conscious of being peoples'.[45] But among socialists the humanitarian impulses regarding 'natives' of the colonies had by the 1920s been turned into a concern to ensure that colonial rule really brought them benefits.[46]

But there was anti-colonial protest from within the SFIO. During the campaign against the Rif War, communists and socialists collaborated to some extent in the protests in the Lyons area.[47] There were stronger anti-colonial sentiments expressed on the left of the SFIO, for example in the newspapers *L'Etincelle* and *La Bataille socialiste*. Socialists protested against certain incidents; on the eve of the colonial exhibition, while *L'Humanité* headlined the case of the Annamite (Vietnamese) student Nguyen Van Tao, under arrest and facing deportation from France,

Léon Blum, head of the SFIO which did not condemn the Expo, wrote in *Le Populaire* (7 May 1931) about the killing of many people by police in Saigon on 1 May.[48] In the early 1930s two young socialist activists, Robert-Jean Longuet and Daniel Guérin, took up the cause of Moroccan protest leaders.

The Moroccans' protests were catalysed by the 'Berber Dahir' of 1930, a decree (*dahir*) nominally issued by the Sultan but in fact drawn up by the French government, aiming to separate Berber-speaking areas of the protectorate from the rest and encourage their development away from Arab and Islamic influence. Anger against this divide-and-rule measure led to publication of the brochure *Tempête sur le Maroc* by leaders of the new Jeunes Marocains movement in collaboration with Guérin in 1931, the launching of the magazine *Maghreb* in Paris (1932–5) through contact made by three Moroccan student leaders with Longuet, and a comprehensive Plan of Reforms for Morocco was presented to the French government on 1 December 1934.[49] A *comité de patronage* for the Plan of Reforms included radical and socialist *député*, Challaye, Magdeleine Paz – an anti-colonial and pacifist SFIO activist, as was her husband Maurice Paz – and a prominent journalist close to the communists, Andrée Viollis.[50]

Obviously several parties, associations and individuals could speak out separately or together about an issue or a country. On Morocco, the PCF denounced the 'reformist' activities involving Guérin and Longuet. On 30 June 1933, there was a debate in the Chamber in which the communist *député* Gabriel Péri denounced the final stage of 'pacification' then going on, saying: 'The mountain people on whom we are waging war want to live as free men'.[51] After a mass trial of communists and Trotskyists in Indochina in 1933, an amnesty committee was formed, largely communist-backed, including Challaye and Henri Barbusse.[52] But the Catholic journal *Esprit* (see below) also drew up a petition in 1934 on Indochina, calling for an inquiry, an amnesty and 'a profound revision of the colonial principle, which accepts a minimum degree of freedom of opinion and equality of rights', while Viollis published *Indochine S.O.S.* in 1935.[53] On the Maghreb, concern was shared at that time by Challaye, the Catholic writer Emile Dermenghem, the Comité de Vigilance des Intellectuels Antifascistes (CVIA) set up on 3 March 1934 with Paul Rivet as chairman (in its bulletin *Vigilance* for example), and the LAI which had a revival in 1933, published the *Journal des Peuples Opprimés*, and issued an appeal on behalf of the Tunisians in 1934.[54] The LAI also issued a major response, signed by many leading intellectuals, to other writers defending the Italian aggression against Ethiopia in 1935.[55] One contributor to the *Journal des Peuples Opprimés* as well as to *L'Humanité* and *Monde* was Léonie Berger, alias Léo Wanner, who was particularly interested in the Arab world where she travelled frequently.[56]

Longuet and Guérin were out of their party's favour with their activity over Morocco, partly because of the French left's phobia (then as now) about Islam.[57] Also, several Catholic intellectuals, centred particularly around the journal *Esprit*, were thinking seriously about the morality of colonialism in the 1930s. Some French Catholic writers, including François Mauriac, Emmanuel Mounier and Jacques Maritain, condemned the Italian invasion of Ethiopia in 1935. But to put this in context one must recall that there was also a 'Manifesto of the 64' in support of Italy, as well as the CVIA's response mentioned above, which was not positively sympathetic to Ethiopia.[58] Intellectuals, it seems, were not generally anti-colonial. Those who were included notably Henri Barbusse and Romain Rolland, editors of the magazines *Monde* and *Europe* respectively. Challaye, Guérin and Charles-André Julien (the activist and scholar specialising in North Africa, active in the PCF for a few years in the 1920s and then in the SFIO from 1934) were among anti-colonial contributors to *Monde* in 1930–1.[59] Barbusse, who helped found the LAI, contributed to a debate in the magazine *Clarté* among intellectuals on the Rif War which showed distinctly limited support for the Rifis.[60]

Anti-colonial minorities in the Popular Front era

There is no space here to recall the sequel to the Popular Front victory in the French empire, to which a recently published volume has been entirely devoted.[61] The important point is that in spite of exaggerated hopes placed in them by opponents of empire, the Popular Front parties did not promise anything for the colonies before the election except for a parliamentary commission of inquiry, which was set up but did not complete its work.[62] The new government in fact did considerably more: amnesties and immediate relaxation of restrictions, changes of governors, introduction of trade union and other social legislation, and formal enactment of the ILO Forced Labour Convention.[63] But all this fitted well into the SFIO's already well-known policy of seeking to improve lives for colonial subjects while not calling French rule into question. As regards political rights for those subjects, the main initiative was the Blum–Viollette bill for extension of full French citizenship rights to a small number (about 20 000) of Muslim Algerians. This was defeated by obstruction from a powerful lobby and opposition from the *colons*, but it was also rejected by the ENA, which Messali was now able to implant in Algeria itself.[64] The ENA was soon banned, on 27 January 1937, while nationalist activities and popular protests led to repression in Morocco later that year and in Tunisia in 1938.

One reason for these developments was that the Communist Party, which supported the Popular Front without joining the government, had by 1936 adopted a new line on the colonies, involving acceptance of continued colonial rule for the time being. This was one consequence of the new communist policy of cooperation on the left against the Nazi–fascist danger since 1934–5. This policy involved putting calls for colonial independence on hold and the PCF thus turned quite sharply against the colonial nationalists. Its general secretary, Thorez, said at the party's ninth congress in December 1937 that it called for 'the right to independence' but added, 'Recalling words used by Lenin, we have already said to the Tunisian comrades, who agreed with us, that the right to divorce does not mean an obligation to divorce.'[65]

The activists from the colonies in France, whose contribution to anti-colonial activity has been stressed in this chapter, were always few in number and easily ignored, especially when the main party supporting them changed its line. The Parti Populaire Algérien (PPA), founded in 1937 to replace the ENA, felt lasting resentment against the communists, while Challaye ceased to be their fellow-traveller. But to many metropolitan French people, preoccupied with the Nazi menace, it must have seemed completely reasonable to put colonial issues on the back burner at that time; and those Arabs, Africans and Asians who knew about Nazism could not (except for a few) doubt that it was far worse than French imperialism had ever been.[66] However, there were some anti-colonial activists who could not accept that the Nazi danger meant leaving the colonial governments to do as they liked.

Local socialists in Morocco condemned the repression in 1937, as did the CVIA.[67] When the nationalist leader Allal el Fassi was deported to Gabon, a petition for him to be moved to a healthier place of banishment was signed by Maritain, Louis Massignon, Gide, Mauriac and others.[68] When Spanish Morocco backed Franco from the start in the civil war many suspected the nationalists of French Morocco of similar sympathies, but others defended them; Wanner called on Maghrebian nationalist leaders to intensify anti-fascist propaganda among the Arabs, and with Robert-Jean Longuet travelled to French Morocco to try to get a stronger anti-Franco commitment from the Moroccan nationalists;[69] Guérin and Ferrat (now out of the PCF and editing the monthly *Que*

Faire?) believed that they were in fact anti-fascist.[70] Guérin was increasingly at odds with the SFIO; after he had harassed the Popular Front Ministers for the Colonies (Marius Moutet) and the Interior (Marx Dormoy) over repression in the colonies, he was disavowed by the SFIO national council. He continued his militant anti-colonial activity in the company of individuals like Magdeleine Paz and Challaye and the Gauche Révolutionnaire, which was founded in October 1935 and committed to 'liberation of the colonial peoples';[71] it split from SFIO in June 1938 and was turned into the Parti Socialiste Ouvrier et Paysan (PSOP). The militant anti-colonial cause was kept alive in several publications such as *Que Faire?*, *La Révolution Prolétarienne*, *Juin 36* and *Les Cahiers rouges*. It was pursued also by the Bureau de Défense des Peuples Colonisés, created in March 1939 by Marc Casati (ex-mayor of Saigon), Longuet and Colette Audry.

But now all this was the work of small groups and marginal individuals not easily able to interest a country preoccupied with the threat of war; and when war broke out anti-colonialism was put aside 'for the duration'.

Conclusion

Jean-Pierre Biondi, in his study quoted frequently in this chapter, sums the anti-colonialists up well as 'the men who clearly and consistently took up the cause of dominated peoples and the reality of their experience'.[72] Theirs was an essentially moral stance opposed to oppression and exploitation of colonial subjects.

For fifteen years the Communist Party voiced, channelled and encouraged those sentiments. Genuine moral motivations, including anti-colonialism, though that may not have been usually dominant, turned people towards communism initially in the inter-war period; while activists from the colonies themselves, in their campaigns against colonial rule, found sympathy – though subject to the party leadership's calculations – in the Communist Party, as they were to do again after 1944.

Anti-colonialism existed among many other metropolitan French people also, including some intellectuals. All those people were swimming against the tide at that time of general acceptance of colonialism. Not all were formally and publicly committed to the ending of colonial rule, but anti-colonialism cannot properly be defined as limited to those with such a commitment. Press articles, books, organisations, meetings, National Assembly debates and questions, pamphlets, demonstrations and rallies by people of varying convictions all contributed to the challenging of empire, by exposing ill-treatment and casting doubts on the belief that colonialism was good for everyone.

Notes and references

1. C. Hodeir and M. Pierre, *L'Exposition coloniale* (Complexe, 1991).
2. Reproduced in C. Liauzu, *Aux Origines des tiers-mondismes: Colonisés et anti-colonialistes en France 1919–1939* (L'Harmattan,1982).
3. Hodeir and Pierre, *L'Exposition*, pp. 125–34; Liauzu, *Aux Origines*, p. 39n.; P. Dewitte, *Les Mouvements nègres en France 1919–1939* (L'Harmattan, 1985), p. 292.
4. C.-R. Ageron, *L'Anticolonialisme en France de 1871 a 1914* (Presses Universitaires de France, 1973), p. 21.
5. J.-P. Biondi, *Les Anticolonialistes (1881–1962)* (Laffont, 1992), pp. 12–13.
6. A. France, quoted in ibid. p. 59.
7. Ageron, *L'Anticolonialisme*, p. 79.
8. Biondi, *Les Anticolonialistes*, pp. 76–80.
9. Ibid. pp. 74–6; R. Thomas, 'La politique socialiste et le problème colonial de 1905 à 1920', *Revue Française d'Histoire d'Outre-Mer*, vol. XLVII, 2nd quarter, 1960, pp. 213–45.
10. 'le socialisme est forcément hostile au colonialisme, qui repose sur la conquête violente et qui organise l'asujetissement des peuples asiatiques et africains ... Le colonialisme contribue à précipiter la transformation mondiale, en exaspérant les antagonismes qui sont au fond du système capitaliste', Biondi, *Les Anticolonialistes*, pp. 81–2.
11. G. Oved, *La Gauche française et le nationalisme marocain 1905–1955* (L'Harmattan, 1984), vol. I, pp. 15–16.
12. Biondi, *Les Anticolonialistes*, pp. 12–13.
13. Liauzu, *Aux origines*, pp. 88–90; Biondi, *Les Anticolonialistes*, p. 97.
14. Liauzu, *Aux origines*, p. 87n.
15. A. Koulakssis and G. Meynier, *L'Emir Khaled premier Za'im? Identité algérienne et colonialisme français* (L'Harmattan, 1987) p. 74; Ageron, *L'Anticolonialisme*, pp. 35–6.
16. Koulakssis and Meynier, *L'Emir Khaled*, p. 53.
17. Biondi, *Les Anticolonialistes*, pp. 53–5, 69–73; R. Jeaugeon, 'Les sociétés d'exploitation au Congo et l'opinion française de 1890 à 1906', *Revue Française d'Histoire d'Outremer*, vol. XLVIII, 1961, pp. 353–437.
18. Liauzu, *Aux origines*, pp. 248–50; Biondi, *Les Anticolonialistes*, pp. 71–2.
19. E. Sivan, *Communisme et nationalisme en Algérie 1920–1962* (Presses de la FNSP, 1976), p. 14.
20. Ibid., ch. 1 *passim*; Biondi, *Les Anticolonialistes*, pp. 121–3
21. Ibid., p. 135; Liauzu, *Aux origines*, pp. 18 ff.
22. On the immigrant communities in France in the inter-war period, see e.g. Liauzu, *Aux origines*: ch. 4, 6 and (on students) ch. 5; B. Stora, 'Les Algériens dans le Paris de l'entre-deux-guerres', ch. IX, and P. Dewitte, 'Le Paris noir de l'entre-deux-guerres', ch. X, in A. Kaspi and A. Marès eds, *Le Paris des étrangers* (Imprimerie Nationale, 1989).

23. Liauzu, *Aux Origines*, pp. 105–13; T. Trang-Gaspard, *Ho Chi Minh à Paris (1917–1923)* (L'Harmattan, 1992), pp. 140–3; Dewitte, *Les Mouvements nègres*, pp. 98–118.

24. Liauzu, *Aux Origines*, pp. 108–10, 113–30; T. Trang-Gaspard, *Ho Chi Minh*, pp. 202–26.

25. Koulakssis and Meynier, *L'Emir Khaled*, pp. 257–63; Sivan, *Communisme*, pp. 34–5.

26. B. Stora, *Messali Hadj (1898–1974), Pionnier du Nationalisme Algérien* (L'Harmattan, 1986), pp. 45–64; Koulakssis and Meynier, *L'Emir Khaled*, pp. 305–17.

27. Stora, *Messali Hadj*, pp. 67–104.

28. The main studies of these organisations and their activists are J. S. Spiegler, 'Aspects of Nationalist Thought among French-Speaking West Africans 1921–1939' (DPhil, Oxford, 1968), and Dewitte, *Les Mouvements nègres*, esp. pp. 153–216.

29. On the Rif War protest campaign see Liauzu, *Aux Origines*, pp. 25–30; Oved, *La Gauche française*, vol. I, pp. 206–35; and some of the contributions to the Paris symposium in 1973 whose proceedings were published as *Abd el-Krim et la République du Rif: actes du Colloque International d'Etudes Historiques et Sociologiques, 18–20 janvier 1973* (Maspero, 1976) (no editor named; Charles-André Julien chaired the symposium); for example P. Isoart, 'La guerre du Rif et le Parlement français', pp. 173 ff., and C.-R. Ageron, 'Les socialistes français et la guerre du Rif', pp. 273 ff.

30. Biondi, *Les Anticolonialistes*, pp. 137–9.

31. Liauzu, *Aux Origines*, pp. 27–8.

32. M. Kharchich, 'Left Wing Politics in Lyons and the Rif War', *Journal of North African Studies*, vol. 2, 3, winter 1997, pp. 34–45.

33. Oved, *La Gauche française*, vol. I, p. 240.

34. Ibid., vol. I, pp. 261–73.

35. Ibid., vol. I, pp. 290–6.

36. E. T. Wilson, *Russia and Black Africa Before World War II* (Holmes & Meier, 1974), pp. 205–8.

37. Sivan, *Communisme et Nationalisme*, pp. 38–70.

38. Oved, *La Gauche Française*, vol. I, pp. 162–85.

39. Stora, *Messali Hadj*, pp. 80–91; Dewitte, *Les Mouvements nègres*, pp. 189–216, 305–8.

40. Biondi, *Les Anticolonialistes*, pp. 197–200.

41. G. Sautter, 'Notes sur la construction du chemin de fer Congo-Océan (1921–1934)', *Cahiers d'Etudes Africaines*, vol. VII, 1967, pp. 219–99.

42. See H. Abdel-Jaouad, 'Le Surréalisme et la question coloniale', *Bulletin of Francophone Africa*, vol. 5, 10, winter 1996–7, pp. 60–73.

43. Dewitte, *Les Mouvements nègres*, pp. 251–75, 349–60.

44. Liauzu, *Aux Origines*, ch. 2, 'Les minorités de gauche et l'anti-colonialisme'.

45. Liauzu, *Aux Origines*, pp. 89–90.

46. See F. Tostain, 'The Popular Front and the Blum-Viollette Plan', in T. Chafer and A. Sackur, eds, *French Colonial Empire and the Popular Front* (Macmillan, 1999), pp. 218–29.

47. Kharchich, 'Left-wing Politics'.

48. Hodeir and Pierre, *L'Exposition*, p. 113.

49. Oved, *La Gauche Française*, vol. II, pp. 31–7, 77–8; Biondi, *Les Anticolonialistes*, pp. 190–2.

50. Oved, *La Gauche Française*, vol. ii, p. 88; Biondi, *Les Anticolonialistes*, pp. 200–1.
51. Ibid., vol. i, p. 324.
52. Liauzu, *Aux origines*, p. 42n.
53. Ibid., p. 84.
54. Biondi, *Les Anticolonialistes*, p. 203.
55. Ibid., p. 160; Liauzu, *Aux origines*, pp. 84n, 257–62.
56. Biondi, *Les Anticolonialistes*, p. 193.
57. Oved, *La Gauche Française*, vol. ii, pp. 59–60, 62.
58. See Liauzu, *Aux Origines*, pp. 84n, 257–62, reproducing the texts with lists of signatories.
59. Biondi, *Les Anticolonialistes*, pp. 116–17; Liauzu, *Aux Origines*, pp. 69–80.
60. Ibid., pp. 80–84.
61. Chafer and Sackur, *French Colonial Empire*.
62. It did produce valuable research findings, for example on women in French West Africa: 'Women, Children and the Popular Front's Missions of Inquiry in French West Africa,' in Chafer and Sackur, *French Colonial Empire*, pp. 170–87.
63. See for example N. Bernard-Duquenet, *Le Sénégal et le Front Populaire* (L'Harmattan 1985) and C. Coquery-Vidrovitch, 'The Popular Front and the Colonial Question. French West Africa: An example of Reformist Colonialism', in Chafer and Sackur, *French Colonial Empire*, pp. 155–69.
64. See F. Tostain, 'The Popular Front and the Blum Viollette Plan', p. 220; F. Gaspard, '"Viollette l'Arabe"', *L'Histoire* special issue 'Le temps de l'Algérie française', 140 (January 1991), pp. 68–72.
65. Sivan, *Communisme et Nationalisme*, p. 97.
66. The few Arab political activists who sought help from Germany and Italy included notably Shakib Arslan, the outstanding pan-Arabist from Lebanon, inspirer of the Moroccan nationalists and now an object of suspicion for the French Left as he had been of the colonial governments for years: see W. Cleveland, *Islam Against the West* (University of Texas Press, 1985), *passim.*
67. Oved, *La Gauche française*, vol. ii, p. 119.
68. Ibid., vol. ii, p. 121.
69. Biondi, *Les Anticolonialistes*, pp. 233–4; Oved, *La Gauche française*, vol. ii, pp. 157–8, 164–79. Oved describes here a fascinating and little-known incident in the Spanish Civil War.
70. Ibid., vol. ii, pp. 176–7; Biondi, *Les Anticolonialistes*, p. 232.
71. Liauzu, *Aux origines*, p. 66.
72. Biondi, *Les Anticolonialistes*, p. 13.

Part II
Representations of Empire

5
Imperial Façades: Muslim Institutions and Propaganda in Inter-War Paris

Neil MacMaster

In recent years there has been a growing interest in the interrelationship between expressions of colonial power, orientalist architecture and town planning.[1] Attention has centred on the syncretic relationship between western and Islamic architecture and design, both overseas in the British and French colonies or spheres of influence (from Istanbul and Cairo to Algiers and Rabat) and in the imperial heartland. Within western Europe a major field of innovation and influence was the great exhibitions and world fairs, from the Crystal Palace exhibition of 1851 onwards. In Paris, for example, elaborate complexes of Arab villages and pavilions, often constructed by North African craftsmen and inhabited by natives in *tableaux vivantes*, were designed for the exhibitions of 1867, 1889, 1900 and 1931.[2]

This chapter centres on an interrelated group of neo-Mauresque or 'Arab' style buildings constructed in Paris during the inter-war period: the Paris Mosque and Institute (completed in 1926), the Franco-Muslim Hospital (opened in 1935), and two associated complexes, a hostel for North African immigrant workers at Gennevilliers (1928) and a Muslim cemetery and religious buildings in Bobigny.[3] Most orientalist buildings in Europe, from the Brighton Pavilion to popular cinemas, were designed for the pleasure of Europeans. The Paris buildings were unique in that they were specifically planned by the colonial power for Muslim subjects.

A comparison of the founding of the two key projects, the Mosque and the Hospital, provides an insight into the contradictions between the officially stated purposes of these buildings, enunciated through an overt imperial discourse, and their concealed segregationist and policing

71

functions. The costly and lavishly ornate Mosque, located in the heart of the imperial metropolis, was a show-case for French propaganda, a symbol of French claims to global leadership of Islam. However, the Franco-Muslim Hospital, which had a cheap and thin veneer of Orientalist styling, was located on the periphery of the city, in a heavily industrialised and polluted suburb. The Mosque was designed for the use of French and Muslim elites, while the many thousands of immigrant workers from French North Africa were relegated to the isolated Hospital, which was directly administered by a colonial police official. The location of the Muslim institutions within the urban space illustrates the extent to which the informal 'apartheid' practices of the colonial system were reproduced within the metropolitan centre.

The best known of the various projects, the Institut Musulman de la Mosquée de Paris, located in the fifth arrondissement, consisted of an imposing and lavish complex which during the inter-war period included not only the Mosque prayer room, but also a library, conference centre, café-restaurant, Turkish baths, curio shop and medical dispensary. This prestigious building had its origins in plans to counter a German threat to French influence in the Arab world. During the First World War a well-organised German propaganda campaign set out to establish an image of imperial Germany as the global champion of Islam: under the leadership of the Emperor 'Haj Guillaume', a holy war or *jihad* would drive the infidel French from the Middle East and North Africa. In October 1916 the Commission Interministérielle des Affaires Musulmanes, which oversaw French propaganda and relationships with the Maghreb and Middle East, established a special committee, under the presidency of Edouard Herriot, to plan the Mosque as a riposte to the German challenge.[4]

The thinking behind this initiative arose from a counter-strategy to demonstrate French identity with Islamic faith and culture by the location of a lavish mosque in the symbolic heart of the *ville-lumière*. Although the Mosque was not built during the war, various colonial interests pressed on with the project after 1918 in response to rising Arab nationalism, the war in the Rif, and a generalised threat to French power in North Africa. During a ceremony to mark the beginning of construction on 19 October 1922, Marshall Lyautey emphasised the function of the mosque as a symbol of the integration of Islam into the heart of Christian French society: 'When the minaret which you are about to build has been erected it will offer up to the beautiful sky of the Ile-de-France yet one more prayer of which the Catholic towers of Notre-Dame need not be jealous'.[5] After 1918 the project also served as a symbol of imperial gratitude towards the North African soldiers, some 25 000 men in all, who had made the ultimate sacrifice for the *patrie* during the First World War, and as an acknowlegement that the Maghreb, and Algeria in particular, had remained loyal.

By the time of its opening in 1926 the Mosque had become a site of conflict between French colonial interests and Maghrebian nationalists. In general the lavish facility was reserved as a centre of prayer and entertainment for the conservative Muslim elites, the francophile aristocracy and political leaders, the *caïds*, *bachagas* and official *imams*, whom the French cultivated as a bulwark against nationalist and anticolonial movements. In order to give the impression that the Mosque was a genuine initiative and expression of Muslims themselves, rather than an imposed tool of colonial propaganda, the fundraising campaigns in the Maghreb and Middle East were coordinated by Si Kaddour ben Gabrit, who also became the rector or head of the Institute from its opening in 1926. Ben Gabrit, born in Algeria in 1873, had a long career as a roving ambassador for French interests, first with a mission to Djedda in 1916 to guarantee the conditions for *hadj* pilgrims and later as adviser and *chef du protocole* to the Sultan of Morocco.[6] Ben Gabrit was to act as the head of the Mosque from its foundation in 1926 until his death in 1954 and during this period he was utilised by the French (as well as by the occupying German authorities) as the quasi-official leader and voice of Islam in France.

The propaganda functions of the Mosque were further highlighted by the great pomp of its inauguration by Sultan Moulay Youssef of Morocco in the company of the President Gaston Doumergue and numerous government ministers. This event, on 15 July 1926, was also well-timed to celebrate the surrender of Abd al-Krim six weeks earlier and the end of the bloody Rif War that had presented the most serious challenge to French power in North Africa. A commemorative brochure welcomed 'the sovereign who, during the unhappy Rif War...did not cease to give evidence of his affection for our country, of confidence in our efforts and in our prestige.'[7] The propaganda also presented the sultan and other Muslim conservative leaders as the true representatives of Islam, thereby implicitly denying the legitimacy of the populist faith that inspired the nationalism of Abd al-Krim and his followers. The imperial manipulation of an official metropolitan Islam, under the supervision of ben Gabrit as the claimed spiritual leader of Muslims in France, was in line with colonial practice in the Maghreb which set out to smash or weaken the Islamic confraternities, the Koranic schools and other traditional institutions that could serve as a base for cultural resistance to the occupiers, and to replace them with *imams* and government mosques.

However, opposition to the official definitions of Islam was very soon to emerge in Paris itself. The Etoile Nord Africaine (ENA), the radical nationalist movement organised by Messali Hadj among the immigrant workers from the Maghreb, was founded in June 1926, only a month before the opening of the Mosque. The Paris Mosque immediately became one of the central campaigning issues of the ENA and on Bastille Day 1926, the eve of the inauguration, it organised a protest meeting which was attended by some 2000 migrant workers. A leaflet proclaimed: 'Brother Muslims! The puppets, the Sultan Moulay Youssef and the Bey of Tunis, Si Mohammed, are going to banquet with the Lyauteys, the Steegs, etc. The first, like the latter, still have their hands red with the blood of our Muslim brothers.'[8] During the next decade a major complaint of the ENA was that the Mosque practised an exclusionary policy towards the 60 000 immigrant workers of the Paris region, an issue that Messali Hadj raised, for example, at the important European-Islamic Conference in Geneva in September 1935.[9] But while workers were turned away because of their shabby clothing, the Mosque became a popular venue for both Muslim elites and the Parisian bourgeoisie who came to enjoy the couscous, mint tea, and Turkish baths in a sumptuous Orientalist décor.[10] *L'Humanité* pointed to the contrasts between this 'place of insolent luxury' and the 'miserable lodgings, the hovels' of the migrants. The communist Arab-language journal *Al Alam Al Ahmar* also commented on the contradiction between French colonial destruction of traditional North African Islamic institutions and the proclamation of 'France, Muslim nation, France protector of Islam, and other idiocies'.[11]

The second large-scale project, also constructed in a neo-Mauresque style by the architect of the Mosque, was the Hôpital Franco-Musulman, which after a decade of planning was finally inaugurated on 22 March 1935. The Hospital was also intended as a showcase of French humanitarian concern for its colonial subjects, but its planning reveals a quite different intent: to segregate and police the immigrant workers. Unlike the extremely elaborate orientalism of the Mosque, a showcase building in the heart of the metropolis, the Hospital – like a Potemkin village – had a mere façade of 'Arab' styling on the gatehouse, while it was spatially isolated far out from the centre in a dreary, industrial suburb. The idea for this well-equipped, modern, 242-bed hospital, which was specifically designed for North African workers, emerged from discussions held during the inauguration of the Paris Mosque and within three months had led to the establishment of a foundation committee (15 October 1926). The leading inspiration behind the project, Pierre Godin, had begun his career as a native administrator and director of security in Algeria. As president of the Paris City Council he was very active in promoting numerous Paris-based projects linked to colonial interests, including the establishment of a special police brigade to gather intelligence on migrant workers and the ENA (the SAINA or Services de Surveillance et Assistance des Indigènes Nord-Africaines), the foundation of immigrant hostels, and the organisation of the Paris celebrations for the centenary of the conquest of Algeria in 1930–1.[12] Godin became the president of the new hospital foundation committee, which also included Si Kaddour Ben Gabrit (vice-president), several doctors from the Algiers faculty of medecine and Adolphe Gérolami, director of the SAINA police in the Rue Lecomte.[13] Like the Mosque, the project was supported by a host of dignitaries, from the Sultan of Morocco and the ministers Sarraut and Herriot to the Governor-General of Algeria, Violette. During 1927–8 this quasi-private initiative was made official and the funding and site location were taken on board by the Paris municipal council and the Department of the Seine.

Some promoters of the project were undoubtedly inspired by genuine humanitarian concern for the North African migrant workers in Paris. Owing to their squalid living conditions, poor diet and long hours of work in dangerous, unskilled work (chemicals, acids, foundries, ceramics, and so on) they suffered from a high incidence of tuberculosis, pulmonary disease, industrial injury and venereal disease. The Hospital had a specially trained staff who spoke Arabic or Berber and who, it was claimed, understood the psychology and special needs of the *indigènes*. Instead of being isolated in the public hospitals of Paris, the migrants could find mutual support, while the dietary and religious needs of Muslims could be catered for. However, this apparently enlightened policy was also driven by considerations of propaganda, segregation and surveillance.

Pierre Godin, in a standard imperial discourse, remarked that a humane treatment of the immigrants, 'the paupers of Islam', would have a profound impact on international Muslim opinion and provide 'a glowing demonstration of our eternal will to action and the subtlety as well as the vigour of our means'. All this made for 'an excellent French policy, which would echo far and wide'.[14] In another speech Godin reminded Paris councillors that

France is no longer simply an old European state, but an Empire, and notably, a great Muslim nation. In the immense and closed world of

Islam everything that is done in Europe, and above all in France, in the religious and social field, carries endless repercussions.[15]

The provision of scientific medical care (such as X-ray equipment, surgery) was emphasised, as a prime symbol of French civilisation and rationality, which would have a profound impact on natives who were still attached to ancient superstitions, magical formulas and the power of the marabouts.[16]

The Hospital, however, just like the Mosque, met strong opposition from the ENA and from the PCF on two principal grounds, first that it represented a segregationist strategy and second that it was part of an apparatus of policing and surveillance.

The Paris Mosque, an elite and highly prestigious building, was deliberately located in the central city as a bold statement of imperial claims to French status as 'a great Muslim nation'. This was not, however, a facility in which immigrant workers were made welcome. In contrast, the Hôpital Franco-Musulman, specifically designed for the migrants, was located far out in the suburbs at Bobigny and the complex planning disputes over this location show that a highly political procedure was at work, rather than a merely technical and administrative one.

The search for a suitable site was initially in the hands of Adolphe Gérolami, head of the Rue Lecomte police. A suburban location was justified on the grounds that central Paris land values were too high, yet several mid-city locations were initially considered in the Rue Gassendi, Rue des Gobelins, Rue Saint-Fargeau, at the Porte d'Orléans and elsewhere but were abandoned because of local political opposition to the presence of North Africans. Likewise several suburban locations were also rejected and, in the case of Bourg-La-Reine, because 'it seems undesirable to construct a hospital for natives in the middle of this residential suburb' since it would have a negative impact on property values.[17] Eventually the Hospital, rejected everywhere else, was forced upon the working-class commune of Bobigny through administrative and legal fiat by the department of the Seine.

The choice of Bobigny was not entirely innocent: the socialist Mayor Clamamus had joined the PCF soon after its foundation in 1920 and by 1925 the Bobigny council was communist and in the public eye the symbol of the 'ultra red Parisian suburb'.[18] Godin and his associates knew that the Hospital project would cause maximum embarrassment for the communists: any local opposition would appear to contradict the anti-racist and anti-colonialist position of the PCF.[19] The council of Bobigny, as well as a citizen petition, did oppose the Hospital on the

grounds that the project had been developed without any consultation, that local people would be excluded from the medical facility, and
that costs (especially of burial) would devolve on the commune. But
ultimately the communists were frustrated in their ability to protest
openly against a project that was, they claimed, planned 'with political
objectives' and which was 'in reality nothing but a systematic and ten-
dacious operation aimed at the commune of Bobigny itself' and a case
of 'bullying'.[20]

A further reason for the high-handed way in which the Paris City
Council and the Prefecture of the Seine pushed through the project at
great speed during 1929–30 arose from Pierre Godin's ambition to see
the foundation stone laid as part of the 1930–1 centenary celebrations of the conquest of Algeria. Godin was particularly active in the
city council to ensure that Paris would celebrate the 1930 centenary
with *éclat* and established an organising commission which noted the
importance 'which is attached to the laying of the foundation stone
of the Franco-Muslim Hospital to coincide with the inauguration of
the festival of the centenary in Algiers'.[21] So keen were Godin and his
associates to press through the project that they even overrode the
recommendations of technical planning experts and of a depart-
mental commission which concluded that the site was unsuitable for
a hospital. The commissioners noted that it was not in the health
interests of hospital patients to be located alongside the Société
Moritz, which daily treated tons of nightsoil brought in by lorry,
while public transport for patients and visitors was totally inadequate.[22]

Not only was the location of the Hospital in Bobigny an indication of
a wish to marginalise the North African immigrants on the periphery of
the city, an urbanist strategy that prefigured the post-war isolationism
of the *grands ensembles* ghettos, but segregationism was even more
apparent in the creation of a facility uniquely intended for Muslim
workers. In a debate in the Paris City Council (9 July 1930) Henri Sellier
supported the Hospital proposal on the grounds that the *indigènes* in
public hospitals 'offended' and 'shocked', 'our fellow hospitalised
citizens for whom the customs and habits of the natives can present
certain problems'.[23] The ENA mounted a strong attack on this form of
apartheid: for Messali Hadj the Hospital was reserved for North Africans, 'as if we were of an inferior, plague-ridden race', and this had
'damaged our self-esteem'.[74] The Confédération Générale du Travail
Unifié (CGTU), in its journal *La Vie Ouvrière*, noted that Muslim workers
were forced to go to Bobigny from every part of the Paris region, even

when there was a nearer hospital, and it demanded the opening of all hospitals to North Africans.[25]

Finally, the political logic underlying the segregation was confirmed for its opponents by the close links between the Hospital management committee and the *Services de Surveillance* of the Rue Lecomte established by Pierre Godin in 1925. The SAINA's public face was that of a welfare agency (provision of worker hostels, health care, location of employment, and so on) and a specialist police brigade for North Africans. Its key function, however, was to gather intelligence on immigrant links to the ENA, the PCF, trade unions and other subversive organisations. One major objective of this surveillance was to control or prevent the transmission by migrant workers returning to North African of radical ideas which could subvert the colonial order.[26] In 1932 André Godin, Pierre Godin's son, replaced Adolphe Gérolami as head of SAINA, while the latter was appointed by the prefect of the Seine as director of the new Hospital. Gérolami was still technically an employee of the Algerian colonial government, a senior administrator of the *communes mixtes* on secondment to the Ministry of the Interior as a specialist adviser on the policing of immigrants.

The placing of a colonial police officer as director of the Hospital was strongly attacked by the ENA and the PCF. Gérolami was well known to the Algerian nationalists as the previous head of the Rue Lecomte. Criticism was also forthcoming in the Paris Council, where Camille Renault commented that the project would be highly beneficial if under the control of doctors and civilians, but the management committee was made up of a majority of police officers, while 'It is intended to put a police commissioner at its head ... What one hopes to achieve through this committee is, above all, to track the North Africans who come to Paris. One wants to know what they are doing and where they are going. This is a social scheme that has been diverted from its aims'.[27] Gérolami had already come under attack from the left for his brutal direction of the SAINA, and the CGTU journal *Le Réveil Colonial* commented on the authoritarianism of this 'former administrator of the *commune mixte*, who receives and speaks to the natives with the customary brutality of the colonial functionary'.[28] Gérolami managed the Hospital in a similar authoritarian way, maintaining, according to the CGTU journal *Le Peuple*, 'a veritable atmosphere of distrust, terror and informing among the personnel and the patients'.[29]

The Hospital was inaugurated with great pomp and ceremony in March 1935 by the prefect of the Seine, the prefect of police, the Governor-General of Algeria, the military governor of Paris, Si Kaddour ben

Gabrit, and a cohort of ministers and officials. Gérolami provided a guided tour of the buildings, which were decorated with the colours of various North African regiments and *anciens coloniaux*. The keynote speech was made by the Minister of the Interior, Marcel Regnier, who had just returned from an official visit to Algeria to take stock of growing political turmoil in the colony. He was then preparing the infamous Regnier decree which introduced highly repressive measures, including up to two years' prison, for Algerians involved in civil disorder.[30] The Hospital, declaimed Regnier, demonstrated

> the true intentions of those who preside over the destiny of France and we ask of the Muslim populations that they see in the opening of this magnificent establishment a further sign of the solicitude of our country and of its government for the future, for the well-being, and for the constant improvement of their situation under the wing and protection of the Motherland.

Godin spoke in similar terms: after a veiled allusion to the disturbances in North Africa among 'those races agitated by so many movements', he declaimed, 'More than ever, Gentlemen, it is towards Paris, initiator of great beneficial projects and social progress, it is towards immortal and generous France, that they direct their attention and their hopes'. The ceremony terminated with the Marseillaise, played by the *garde républicaine*, and the consumption of a giant couscous.[31]

In conclusion it can be noted that the Paris Mosque and Hospital were not only promoted by powerful imperial interests, but that they also reproduced within the metropolitan context, through the segregation of immigrant workers from the French population, the apartheid policies of colonial urban planners in North Africa, particularly the large projects directed by Lyautey in Morocco.[32] Secondly, the flagrant propaganda purposes underlying the Paris Mosque and the SAINA strategy, in its failure to harness the populist but deep religious sentiments of the immigrants, was to have damaging long-term effects for French interests. Their exclusion by the Paris Mosque enabled the ENA and its successor nationalist movements to capitalise on their position as the genuine voice of popular Islamic faith and identity, a source of political mobilisation that prepared the ground for the Algerian War of Independence. France thus failed in its attempt to manipulate official Islam to maintain imperial control over the Maghreb. Lastly, the failure to win acceptance of the Mosque rector as the symbolic head and spokesman of Islam in metropolitan France was a lost opportunity. This has become increasingly apparent during the last two decades as successive French governments, concerned by issues of fundamentalism, youth rebellion and problems of integration, have desperately sought to create a representative Islamic authority within France that could act as an *interlocuteur valable*. The contemporary history of the Mosque has been one of divisive legal and political battles, waged between the Algerian and French governments and other interests, for control of the building, its resources, and symbolic power.[33]

Notes and references

1. See for example M. Crinson, *Empire Building, Orientalism and Victorian Architecture* (Routledge, 1996); J. M. MacKenzie, *Orientalism. History, Theory and the Arts* (Manchester University Press, 1995).
2. Z. Celik, *Displaying the Orient. Architecture of Islam at Nineteenth-Century World's Fairs* (University of California Press, 1992); P. Greenhalgh, *Ephemeral Vistas: the Expositions Universelles, Great Exhibitions and World Fairs, 1851–1939* (Manchester University Press, 1988); H. Lebovics, *True France. The Wars Over Cultural Identity, 1900–1945* (Cornell University Press, 1992); W. H. Schneider, *An Empire for the Masses. The French Popular Image of Africa, 1870–1900* (Greenwood Press, 1982).
3. The Paris Mosque and the Bobigny cemetery buildings still stand. The Gennevilliers hostel has been demolished as has the Franco-Muslim Hospital, apart from the Mauresque gateway, to make way for the modern Avicenna Hospital.
4. On the wartime activities of the Commission see the *Procès-Verbal* in the Archives d'Outre Mer (AOM), Aix-en-Provence, 27 H 20; on German propaganda activities, G. Meynier, *L'Algérie Révélée* (Droz, 1981).
5. G. Kepel, *Les Banlieues de l'Islam: naissance d'une religion en France* (Seuil, 1987), p. 71. Lyautey was renowned for his promotion of architecture and town-planning as a key instrument of 'pacification' in Morocco, summarised in his dictum, 'A construction site is worth a battle.' See J. Abu-Lughod, *Rabat: Urban Apartheid in Morocco* (Princeton University Press, 1980); Crinson, *Empire Building*, p. 7.
6. On Ben Gabrit's background see A. Boyer, *L'Institut Musulman de la Mosquée de Paris* (CHEAM, 1992), pp. 12, 31; Kepel, *Les Banlieues de l'Islam*, pp. 66–8. The French Communist Party regarded him as a traitor to his compatriots, 'sold out to French Imperialism': see C. Ben Fredj, 'Aux Origines de l'émigration nord-africaine en France' (doctoral thesis, University of Paris VII, 1990), p. 373.
7. Kepel, *Les Banlieues de l'Islam*, p. 73.
8. B. Stora, *Ils Venaient d'Algérie. L'immigration algérienne en France 1912–1992* (Fayard, 1992), p. 35.
9. B. Stora, *Messali Hadj (1898–1974). Pionnier du nationalisme algérien* (L'Harmattan, 1986), p. 117.
10. See Ben Fredj, 'Aux Origines', p. 399; also the personal account of visits by Phillipe Decraene in his Preface to Boyer, op. cit., pp. 11–12. The ENA attacked the use of the Mosque as an insult to true religion, an 'Oriental cabaret . . . a veritable den of singing and debauchery'; see B. Stora, 'Histoire

Politique de l'immigration algérienne en France (1922–1962)' (doctoral thesis, University of Paris XII, 1991), pp. 102–3.

11. *L'Humanité*, 21 November 1930, and *Al Alam Al Ahmar*, no. 3 (July 1926), quoted in Ben Fredj, 'Aux Origines', pp. 373, 394.

12. On Pierre Godin and the SAINA, see N. MacMaster, *Colonial Migrants and Racism: Algerians in France, 1900–62* (Macmillan, 1997).

13. A. Boukhelloua, *L'Hôpital franco-musulman de Paris* (Imprimérie Nord-Africain, 1934) pp. 15, 35–6. The hospital archives were destroyed by bombardment during the Second World War: the key sources, in addition to Boukhelloua, are O. Depont, *Les Berbères en France. L'Hôpital franco-musulman de Paris et du département de la Seine* (1937); P. Godin, *Note sur le fonctionnement des services de surveillance, protection et assistance de indigènes nord-africaines* (Imprimerie Municipale, 1933); J. Chevillard-Vabre, *Histoire de l'hôpital franco-Musulman* (thesis for doctorate in medicine, Faculty of Medecine, Saint-Antoine-Paris, 1982).

14. Godin, Note, pp. 43–4.

15. *Bulletin Municipal Officiel* (Paris, 3 April 1931).

16. N. Gomar, *L'Emigration algérienne en France* (Les Presses Modernes, 1931), pp. 133–4.

17. Boukhelloua, *L'Hôpital franco-musulman*, pp. 44–5; Chevillard-Vabre, *Histoire de l'hôpital franco-musulman*, p. 32.

18. Père L'Haude, *Le Christ dans la banlieue de Paris* (1925), quoted in Chevillard-Vabre, *Histoire de l'hôpital franco-musulman*, p. 34.

19. A. Fourcaut, *Bobigny, banlieue rouge* (Editions Ouvrières, 1986), p. 179.

20. Archives Municipales de Bobigny, Cote W 617, *Délibérations du conseil municipal de Bobigny*, 1930–32. Further documents on the Hospital and related cemetery are at W 4433; W 4434; W 2935.

21. Bibliothèque Administrative de la Ville de Paris, Cote 1783, no. 136 – P. Godin, 'Proposition à faire participer la Ville de Paris aux fêtes du centenaire algérien de 1930,' 28 October 1927; also further propositions at Cote 1783, no. 26 (1930) and no. 117 (1932).

22. Chevillard-Vabre, *Histoire de l'hôpital franco-musulman*, pp. 37, 46–8.

23. Paris *Bulletin Municipal Officiel*, 20 July 1930, p. 338.

24. Stora, *Histoire Politique*, p. 121.

25. *La Vie Ouvrière*, 2 December 1937, quoted in Ben Fredj, 'Aux Origines', p. 353.

26. See MacMaster, *Colonial Migrants*.

27. Boukhelloua, *L'Hôpital franco-musulman*, pp. 31–2, 91, 97. Even the francophile young doctor Boukhelloua agreed that 'a constant and humiliating police control' was damaging to the Hospital project.

28. *Le Réveil Colonial* May 1930, quoted in K. Bouguessa, 'Emigration et politique. Essai sur la formation et la politique de la communauté algérienne en France à l'entre-deux-guerres mondiales' (doctoral thesis, University of Paris V, 1979), appendix.

29. *Le Peuple* 15 November 1937, quoted in Ben Fredj, op. cit., p. 354.

30. C.-R. Ageron, *Histoire de l'Algérie contemporaine*, vol. 2 (Presses Universitaires de France, 1979), pp. 430–2.

31. Chevillard-Vabre, *Histoire de l'hôpital franco-musulman*, pp. 73–4.

32. Abu-Lughot, *Rabat*.

33. See Kepel, *Les Banlieues de l'Islam*, and Boyer, *L'Institut musulman*, for the post-war history of the Mosque.

6
The French Provinces and 'Greater France'

Odile Goerg

Over the years, from the conquest of the empire to its exploitation and loss, politicians and colonial societies have complained of the ignorance, coupled with deep disinterest, of the French as regards the colonies, in spite of the efforts made to foster a degree of nationalistic attachment to them. Being the most centralising of countries, France sought to inform public opinion about her vast colonial domain and to instil a certain image of the empire and of its inhabitants. The second most important empire in Europe had in fact been conquered against the will of the French who were little inclined to exploits abroad and unenthusiastic at the prospect of uncontrolled expenditure. The provinces, despite their diversity, were included in this general movement of colonial propaganda. To this end, a variety of different media were used: schools, the national press, lecture tours, exhibition trains.

At the same time, however, each province developed its own specific relationship with the empire and communicated its own image of the colonies according to local particularities. The presence of garrisons, special commercial links with lands overseas, the role of political figures, the establishment of missionary societies, local individuals who in some way left their mark on the history of the Empire, the existence of a geographical society, all of these could be the basis for a link with Empire. This provincial dimension played an important part from the 1880s to the period between the two world wars, a period when technical means were less concentrated and information less standardised. In this chapter, I intend to focus on this local level in order to go beyond the omnipresent image we have of the great international colonial exhibitions. While the colonial exhibition in Paris in 1931 and also the preceding ones in Marseilles (1906 and 1922) do seem to constitute examples of colonial propaganda at its height in France, what do we know of the images or discourse available to those in the provinces and of the way in which they perceived the empire?

This vast subject will be illustrated more specifically using the example of eastern France, and particularly of Alsace, a province marked by the successive tutelage of two colonial powers. Its return to France in 1918 was to be accompanied by active measures designed to integrate the province which had been recently restored to the French nation, a process in which it was fundamental to create some sort of feeling for the colonies. This effort culminated in the organisation of a 'colonial, agricultural and industrial exhibition' in Strasbourg in 1924.

In the course of my investigations into the 1931 exhibition, I was struck by the recurrence in the local press, one of our fundamental sources together with official archives, of advertisements using exotic elements, of publicity for films evoking Africa or Asia and for talks about the Empire.[1] It seemed to me that it would be interesting to go into the question of how the colonies were represented in Alsace, a land characterised by missionary recruits and military vocations in consider-able numbers, but also – because of its history – by departures overseas, essentially to Algeria after 1870.

The agents of colonial propaganda had at their disposal a wide range of means with which to diffuse information about lands overseas and to attract the attention of the nation's population to French possessions abroad. They were assisted in their task by other actors who did not have the explicit vocation of advocating love of the empire, but who nevertheless contributed to the diffusion of certain images or pieces of information among the general public. The latter were communicated as effectively by means of the press (using national dispatches but also local writings), advertising and the cinema as they were by exhibitions and lectures or even military parades.

The precursors of colonial propaganda: the provincial geographical societies

Bearers of an initial form of colonial propaganda, which advocated the constitution of an empire, the geographical societies spread throughout France played a key role in familiarising the French with the colonial idea and with their empire.[2] Their journals, which published reports and accounts of journeys covering the entire planet, contributed actively to this process.

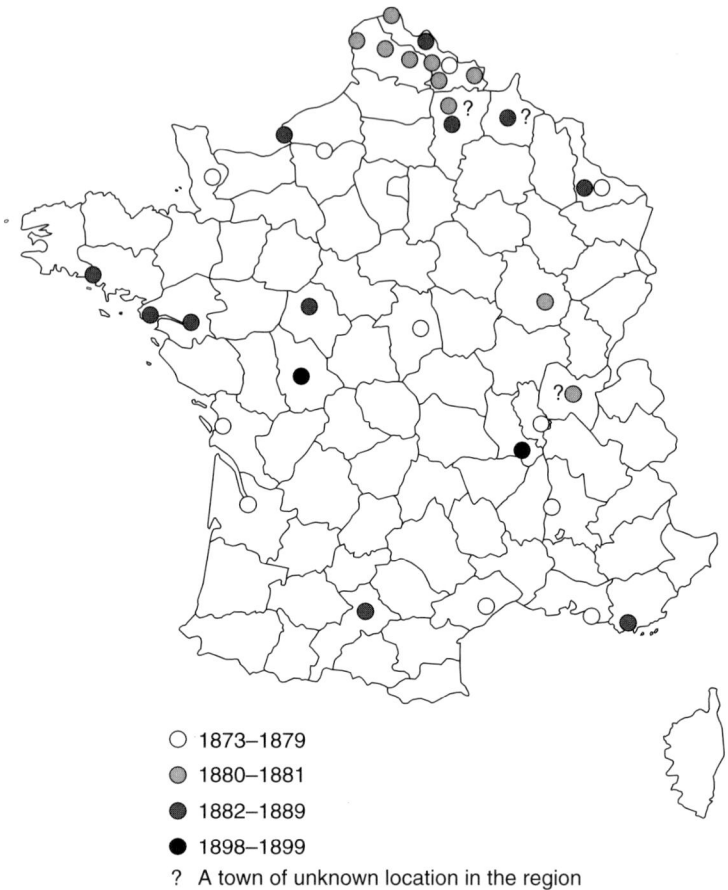

Figure 6.1   Provincial geographical societies, with dates of foundation

Source: Map based on information contained in D. Lejeune, *Les Sociétés de Géographie en France et l'expansion coloniale au XIXe siècle* (Albin Michel, 1993); cartography: Maxime Dondon.

The role of geographical societies in the defence of colonial expansion has often been underlined.[3] Alongside their ancestor, which was born in Paris in 1821, numerous regional societies laboured to the same ends, even if for them the colonial aspect was just one of their areas of interest. Geography was a useful expedient by means of which to arouse curiosity about far-flung lands, to spread information by means of bulletins, to organise lectures or finance journeys, and finally to foster vocations for the colonies. Even if their action as a pressure group was limited, the provincial societies constituted one pole in the diffusion of colonial propaganda, particularly from an economic point of view; by 1890, they had 16 000 or so members (that is, approximately seven times the number in Paris), and 11 700 in 1902. Created principally in the 1870s (10 societies) and 1880s (20 societies), they retained their autonomy from Paris while still functioning according to the same model (see Figure 6.1). The north was well represented (the Union Géographique du Nord de la France had 2662 members shortly after its foundation in 1880, and 2230 members in the town of Lille alone in 1902) and eastern France was also well represented. La Société de Géographie de l'Est, founded in 1879, had its seat in Nancy, complemented by a section for the Vosges (from 1879 onwards) and for the Meuse (1881). With its 950 strong membership in 1884, the heyday of the society, it was one of the largest.[4] Its bulletin enabled the society to advocate colonial expansion from the outset, at a period when the dominant discourse was anti-colonial: its arguments conformed to the usual pattern, though it did emphasise the economic aspect, no doubt owing to the presence of representatives of the business world among its subscribers. When the Association pour l'Afrique Française and the Union Coloniale were created at the beginning of the 1890s, close collaboration was established between the society in Nancy and colonial organisations, even if the two authorities retained their autonomy as regards their ideas and actions: the bulletin published by the Société de Geographie de l'Est gave an account of pro-colonial activities, while the colonial societies provided the lecturers. Appearing four times yearly and totalling one thousand pages in its early stages, the bulletin included various rubrics. 'Colonial geography', an official category, came in second position after 'militant geography:'[5] 40 short notices/ essays per year on average and a total of 56 in-depth articles over 35 years. They treated Equatorial Africa (30 per cent), Indochina (20 per cent), Algeria (13 per cent) and Madagascar (11 per cent). From 1890 onwards, 'colonial intelligence' provided precise information either for candidates for work overseas or for investors. This aspect was the result of a genuine campaign to spread colonial propaganda, 'either to provide the public with the basic information they need to educate the region on colonial questions, or to place the most important information at the disposal of anyone who wants to have, or could have, interests in the colonies'.[6] At the same time as publishing reports, the society organised numerous lectures which allowed it to reach a wider public: of the 238 recorded, 75 were about Africa (of which 55 were concentrated between 1894 and 1905) and 40 were about Asia. Prestigious speakers, such as Savorgnan de Brazza, were invited.

The turn of the century saw the decline of the society, as is evident from the disappearance of active members and the emergence of financial difficulties. This sequence of events is not specific to this particular society. In general, the heyday of the geographical societies coincided with the high point of the conquest of Asia and Africa. Other forms of propaganda developed at the same time, and then other channels took over, the result of both technological innovations and of an evolution in the expectations of the public.

Propaganda by means of 'la leçon des choses':[7] exhibitions and black villages

Among the means used to diffuse a certain kind of image of the empire and its inhabitants, exhibitions with colonial connotations played an important role. The desire to foster in the people of metropolitan France a feeling of legitimate pride, pride that was nourished by concrete information, had found its expression in the numerous colonial sections of the universal exhibitions which had been carefully organised from the middle of the nineteenth century onwards and then in the first colonial exhibitions strictly speaking. The provinces contributed to this general movement.

In order to ensure the diffusion of colonial propaganda, a 'national committee for colonial exhibitions' had been created in 1906 and gained official recognition in 1913. It participated in the constitution of a colonial section at various exhibitions (Nogent, Bordeaux, Roubaix) and then merged in 1924 with the 'French Committee for Exhibitions' so as to improve its efficiency.[8] As heirs to the tradition of medieval fairs, industrial and commercial exhibitions multiplied in the provinces of France in the nineteenth and twentieth centuries. Aimed at promoting local goods, they sometimes included a colonial dimension, which was more or less elaborate, depending on the particular nature of the local economy or on what was at stake politically.[9] If exhibitions of national importance have been the object of detailed studies, provincial events remain unexplored.[10] Limited to a day's consideration here or there, they have rarely been the object of systematic study. It would appear however that the exhibition and fair at Tarbes and at la Bigorre regularly included a colonial pavilion from 1934 to 1948. In 1938 a colonial day, on that occasion a Moroccan day, was organised and marked by the presence of a minister from the protectorate.[11] In the case of national initiatives, notably under the Vichy government, which organised a 'France Overseas Week' in 1941 complete with an exhibition train, and then an 'imperial fortnight' in 1942, colonial propaganda joined the general wave of imperial propaganda without any great degree of originality as compared with local initiatives, where it is possible to detect the influence of local factors. The example of Strasbourg demonstrates this well.

The exhibition organised in Strasbourg in 1924 distinguished itself by its clearly posted colonial dimension and its symbolic significance.[12] Annexed by the Reich in 1870, Alsace had not participated directly in the phase of colonial propaganda, conquest and celebration which affected France from the 1880s and 1890s onwards. Neither was it included in the colonising impetus which marked Germany, albeit more marginally, at this period. Yet, in Strasbourg in 1913, the Reich had organised a presentation of the German colonies for the citizens of the German Empire. It was therefore imperative that the provinces which had been won back be made aware of the existence of this Greater France which they had not known about, that they be offered the necessary information and that there be fostered, in these peoples restored to France, a feeling of national and colonial pride. Thus, the exhibition had to: 'bring to the attention of the people of Alsace-Lorraine the marvels of the French world, which they had not been in a position to appreciate for many years' and 'emphasise the indisputable French flair for colonialism and the indivisibility of France'.[13]

This 'leçon des choses' took on a particular meaning as regards the Alsatians, who theoretically had everything to learn about the French colonies. Different initiatives along these lines had already been undertaken since the war ended: the creation of a colonial institute at the law faculty and the organisation of lectures, notably in the course of a 'colonial week'.[14] In the context of the efforts made to popularise colonial action, Binger himself, born in Strasbourg in 1856, gave a lecture at the university in 1921 on his Sudanese expedition, under the auspices of the Alliance Française. The exhibition of 1924 stands in the same tradition; that is to say, it was organised with an essentially pedagogic purpose. Thus Louis Proust, one of its principal promotors, affirmed that the aim was not 'to amuse the eyes and to arouse banal curiosity ... but to have 'an educative role with practical consequences'.[15] This pedagogy was aimed at a population whose knowledge of the subject was assumed to be zero.

In order symbolically to make up for a break of half a century, the accent was constantly put upon elements of continuity which linked Alsace with the colonies: the reference in Daladier's inaugural speech to 'the eminent role which Alsace played in the formation and exploitation of our possessions',[16] the publication of the biographies of military men or of explorers of Alsatian origin – famous individuals such as Binger or others since forgotten,[17] the recollection of the migrations which led numerous Alsatians to Algeria or Morocco. These themes were dealt with on several occasions in the press and also in lectures.[18]

There was nothing particularly original about the means used: the presentation of products or objects from the colonies, panels and slide shows describing the different territories in the empire, photographs and paintings. In fact, certain individuals, who had little enthusiasm for such exhibitions, pointed to their lack of originality, for the descriptive documents used went around from one town to another.[19] Indeed lack of time and money meant that it was impossible for the organisers to be very original in their presentation of the empire. This was criticised in the local press.[20] The panels and statistics used came from the 1922 Marseilles exhibition. Thus, contrary to the initial intentions of the project, the colonial aspect was itself submerged by other aspects of national life when the exhibition opened.

To judge by the pictures showing in the exhibition halls, one cannot but be struck by their off-putting appearance, both in Strasbourg and at other similar events which were held regularly alongside provincial fairs. Though they were typical of their time, these museographic techniques hardly seem attractive.

Of the approximately 3030 permanent exhibitors in Strasbourg, only 5.5 per cent had made the journey from overseas. Some belonged to private and some to governmental organisations. Because of its economic importance and its geographic proximity, Algeria was preponderant, with 112 out of the 170 overseas exhibitors. At the same time, 184 exhibitors whose headquarters were in metropolitan France also represented the empire. With an approximate total of 354 exhibitors (11.6 per cent) linked to a greater or lesser degree to the colonies, the colonial dimension of the exhibition strictly speaking was marginalised as a result, in spite of its title.[21] However, thanks to the decor and the success of the 'African village', it was nevertheless the colonial dimension which set the overall tone of the exhibition.

The colonised peoples on display: black villages and exotic architecture

Over and above its didactic dimension, the presentation of people and of architecture had to recreate something of the atmosphere of lands overseas: there were stereotypical buildings, exotic plants, but above all a village set up as the principal attraction[22]. Visitors were attracted, not so much by the exhibition's educative approach as by the daily shows drawing on colonial themes and by the 'African village'.

Reutilising the installations used at the Pasteur exhibition in 1923, the Strasbourg exhibition in 1924 did indeed present all the external signs of a colonial exhibition. Even if only a third of the total area of 15 hectares was explicitly devoted to the colonies, the general atmosphere of the event was dominated by the colonial theme: the uniforms of the employees, the architectural style of the new buildings or the dressing up of old ones, the decorations, the advertising posters, as well as the permanent attractions. The following description bears this out:

> Wacken village looks much the same as it did last year. That said, the three entrance arches have had a facelift. In place of their previous grey colour, they are now brick red, or if you prefer 'exaggerated Mara-kesh [sic]', colour and appear vaguely Arabic in style. Also, the ticket collectors in dark tunics and embroidered kepis have been replaced by fine employees dressed in off-the-peg khaki suits and impressive cork helmets. That's local colour for you![23]

To these elements, we might add the touching up of old buildings to give them an oriental look, some of which were crenellated: for example, a brasserie of Indochinese inspiration decorated with dragons, a round 'mosque' which strongly resembled a bandstand, and a 'tata', a sort of defensive tower of West African inspiration. A tower of this type had already been built in Marseilles in 1922, though it was much higher – 63 metres as opposed to 22 in Strasbourg. On the top was a powerful revolving light which swept over the grounds of the exhibiton by night. The commentary accompanying the photo of this edifice, a symbol of technological expertise, bears witness to the prejudices and general incomprehension of those present: 'Here we are, in the middle of barbarous Africa.'

The principal attraction, however, was the African village, made up of a few straw huts and surrounded by a stockade against the prying eyes of those who had not bought their supplementary entrance tickets. As at most of the previous exhibitions, Africa was in the forefront there: it symbolised the most foreign, the most disorienting and, consequently, the most attractive continent. However, the style, which was ill-defined and vaguely Sudano-Sahelian, did not claim to reproduce reality but was an amalgamation of cosmopolitan elements.[24] This is in stark contrast to the care with which villages corresponding specifically to the African regions of Senegal, Soudan or Dahomey were reproduced at the exhibitions in Paris in 1889, in Lyons in 1894 and in Marseilles in 1906 and 1922.[25]

This 'village' was heir to a whole line of spectacles of this type which became extinct after the First World War. Indeed many a town, rather than have its own colonial exhibition, would have a colonial component at a local fair in the form of a so-called 'African' or 'black' village. When the latter arrived in town, it was either at the behest of a municipality or thanks to the initiative of an entrepreneur like Jean-Alfred Vigé, who organised a tour throughout France at the beginning of the twentieth century.[26] This veritable 'tour de France' through its 'villages' (see Figure 6.2), the principal aim of which was certainly recreational, popularised a certain concrete vision of Africa with its 'traditional' chiefs, its artisans, its playful children and its matrons.[27] Series of postcards were sold on these occasions, proving their popularity and spreading their influence beyond these isolated events.

Africans were something of a rarity in Europe at that time and the opportunities to see them were few and far between. The end of the century, however, saw innovations in this respect. On the one hand, African personalities, either hostages or allies, were shown at exhibitions: it was thus that the chief of Rio Nuñez (French Guinea) was invited to the universal exhibition of 1889 in Paris. Moreover, circus tours were organised in which bearded women, giants and living specimens from the African continent were presented on an equal footing. The Germans specialised in these exhibitions of exotic human beings. It was in the context of an 'industrial and craft exhibition', held in the Orangerie park in Strasbourg in 1895, that the Alsatians had the opportunity of seeing an 'exhibition of Schilluk negros from the region of the White Nile' for the first time.[28] These tall pastoralists were taken to be dangerous warriors, which enabled their 'savagery' to be shown off to advantage. One witness, however, remembers that one of the Shilluk spoke to him in basic German. The desired effect was thus countered from the outset.

The First World War had slightly modified French people's actual experience of relationships with colonised peoples by making possible new types of contact, either between soldiers or in the villages where the colonial regiments were stationed. It had helped to reorient the image of those colonised, by relegating their reputation for 'savagery' to the background and praising their good-natured side.[29] Exhibitions which showed 'natives' were progressively replaced by 'folk'-type shows, but the 'African village', which could be visited in Strasbourg, finances permitting, was in the same vein as those which had travelled around

(a) From the 1890s to the First World War

(b) Between the wars

Figure 6.2   The 'Tour de France' of 'black villages' (excepting Paris)
Source: Map drawn up in 1997, based on information available up to that date.

France in the 1890s and 1900s. The visitors became the voyeuristic spectators of a daily life specifically recreated for them and in which 'the daily life and customs of native life are on permanent display'.[30]

The organisation of this African village had been entrusted to an entrepreneur specialised in the field, M. Bouvier. He had brought a group of about 75 people from Senegal, under the leadership of Mamadou and Prosper Seck, natives of Gorée (Senegal) and veterans of colonial exhibitions. The group was made up of Africans from different territories of French West Africa (Guinea, Upper Volta, Soudan and Mauritania[31]). Their task was to reproduce, for an Alsatian public, the activities of daily life in the tropics: culinary preparations, child care, craft activities (weaving, jewellery, shoemaking), prayers and musical interludes. Given the diversity of their origins, the African village could not represent any precise cultural region (the Sahel or forest regions, for example), in contrast to certain earlier exhibitions; in Strasbourg, the village had its origins in a cliché instead and was presented as an archetypal African village, which aimed to meet the expectations of the spectators rather than correct common prejudices. The same was true of the reconstitution of daily life, a sort of summary of life in Africa, simplified to suit a public with preconceived ideas. Thus, several commentators emphasised the easy-going rhythm of the day, the cheerful atmosphere and the laughter. The vocabulary used to describe the activities, attitudes or costumes of the Africans actually corresponded to images and opinions common at the time, bringing out how strange and primitive the Africans appeared. Alternatively there might be an objectivising aesthetic description with an altogether patronising attention paid to certain qualities evident in the Africans present. Aimé Dupuy, signatory to numerous articles, thus speaks of 'gesticulating sorcerers', of a dancer 'who jumps and jigs about' or even of 'three Soussou musicians (Guinea) with their unpolished yet undeniable sense of music'.[32] Elsewhere, he underlines the aesthetic side: 'Our Africans from AOF have today put on their smartest boubous and their brightest *gandourahs*, which further accentuate the oily colour of their black skins.'[33] Together with the lyricism of his style, he reproduces the classic cliché of fascination by Africans, a cliché the flip side of which, fear and rejection, was equally present in public opinion.

Quotations of this type are legion, combining a genuine attempt to understand the peoples under observation with pure and simple disdain. The following extract gives an idea of the tone of numerous articles, which is basically negative but does its best to find a façade that might justify the inferiority of the Africans: 'Although Africans in their own environment do not show clear evidence of intellectual activity, they should not be condemned for this, as they have for many centuries been isolated from the rest of humanity.' And the author concludes logically: 'It is the French who brought them the benefits of civilisation.'[34]

Apart from so-called daily life, various ceremonies were organised in order to give people a reason to return for a second visit, which represented a useful source of income for the organisers. Among the latter, the most common were the baptism of a child born during the crossing and the coronation of Bouppe the First. The former was celebrated in such a way as theoretically to conform to the Muslim ritual (prayer by the imam) while at the same time introducing local practices, notably the presence of a European godmother and the distribution of sugared almonds.[35] Reports describing this celebration are condescending in tone. The enthronement of the 'king' was also set up. This ceremony, presented of course as traditional, cannot but appear incongruous in a colonial context and demonstrates well how little regard was paid to the objective historical situation of the subjects presented.[36] Bouppe the First is said to have come from Dakar with all his retinue, including in particular his 'griot-sorcerers' and a 'marabout', the depository of the crown. His ceremonial dress, the sumptuousness and magnificence of which were underlined, was greatly admired.

Apart from these two outstanding events, we might also mention the feast of Tabaski, organised to mark the end of Ramadan, or the 'black and white dance organised in the negro village'.[37] The numerous postcards published on this occasion and the photographs which appeared in the press attest to the popularity of this attraction.

The exhibition of 1924 was the most outstanding colonial event of the period in Alsace, but we should also mention the colonial and missionary exhibition organised in 1936 by the Société des Missions Evangéliques de Paris or the visit, in the same year, of an exhibition train comprising 18 coaches called the 'France Overseas Exhibition Train' (*'le train-expo de la France d'outre-mer'*).

How far do the impressions gained from these recreated events or from the information diffused support other ways of shedding light on these far-off peoples and countries?

Otherness in daily life: advertising, cinemas and the fine arts as insidious propagandist tools?

In addition to the contribution of exhibitions, which were rare events and carried considerable risk for their organisers, the press diffused a particular vision of non-European peoples through the images used daily in advertising. Who in Alsace did not know the emblematic figure of the African woman on Sati coffee or Banania's famous infantry-man?[38] Local and national images came into contact with each other. How far, however, did the character who was represented in this way still represent someone from the colonies? Did people necessarily make a mental link between the representation of exotic peoples and distant conquered territories? This is difficult to ascertain, all the more so since the presence of images with an exotic theme precedes colonisation. It does, however, seem that the association is present: the increase in the number of references to lands overseas would seem to be proof of this (see Figure 6.3).

An analysis of the advertisements which evoked the African contin-ent as a whole enables us to highlight the clichés and their evolution over the years. If we follow a major regional daily paper, the *Dernières Nouvelles de Strasbourg*,[39] from 1877, the year it was founded, to 1930, it becomes apparent both that there was a rise in the number of references to Africa at the turn of the twentieth century and that they became more diversified. While shows (notably circuses) were important at the beginning of the period, food products (generally more than 50 per cent) predominated, followed by medicines and cosmetic products. Appeal was made to Africa either when the advert was for raw materials

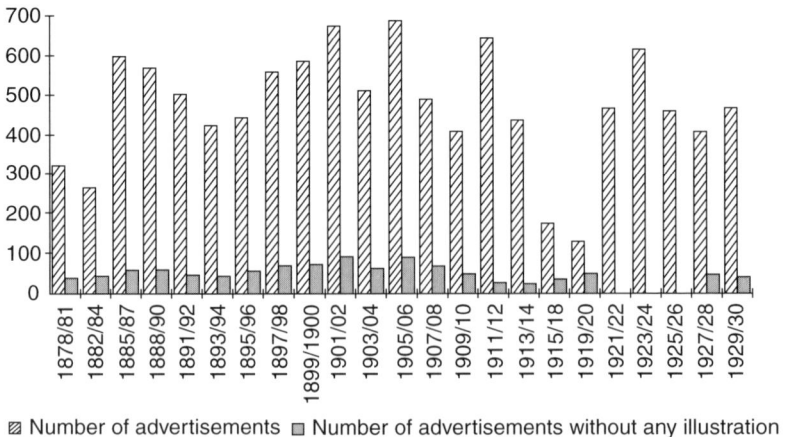

Figure 6.3   Africa in advertising in the *Dernières Nouvelles de Strasbourg*, 1878–1930.
Source: Note that the interval is different for the first years and the war.

from the tropics, and originating principally or even marginally from this continent (coffee, cocoa, vegetable oils), or when they were for products which we associate mentally with this continent. Proceeding by way of antithesis, for example, an advertisement might play on the contrast between black and white, perhaps also drawing on a racist backcloth which links dirt to blackness and hence to Africans, in order to promote cleaning materials (soap powder, soaps, toothpastes). Implicit clichés were also exploited, such as the servility of the blacks, suggested by the famous figure of the groom, their childishness or their capacity for good-natured pranks. A mental link was frequently made with wild animals, leading to images which may be either positive or contemptuous. Thus lions or elephants symbolise strength, monkeys cunning and so on. These advertisements were sometimes the initiative of national campaigns[40] and sometimes inspired locally by Alsatian products or firms. There were restaurants, 'Au Nègre', 'Au Bon Nègre',[41] delivery firms and other types of business. For its advertising in the 1920s, the furniture business Saas & Company repeatedly used the stereotype of a small black with bulging eyes, a flat nose, a smile on his face and a crooked hat. In fact, Africans were most often presented in a manner which either ridiculed or subordinated them. Advertisements for distant voyages, however, should be considered apart as they emphasised the disorienting unfamiliarity of distant paradises and aimed at attracting a limited public to the colonies in the period between the wars.

These representations went beyond the world colonised by France: the frontiers of the continent were vague and spilled over into a mythical Orient, passing imperceptibly from Egypt to the Arabia of the thousand and one nights. Indeed we might ask ourselves if all this was in the realm of colonial propaganda or, more generally, that of exoticism as a commercial medium. Moreover, how far does advertising create the image, or how far does it confirm stereotypes forged by other means? One cannot, however, but be struck by the similarity between the images used in literature and colonial propaganda and those used in advertising, the significance of which in society was growing markedly. As in literature and propaganda, advertising tended to abandon the image Africans had after the First World War of being 'barbarous' or simply 'savage' in favour of a more sympathetic attitude, which was nevertheless somewhat patronising and deprecatory. Some differences, however, do exist between the messages conveyed by advertisments and those conveyed by propaganda. Thus, the 'civilising' dimension of the relationship with Africa is generally masked, although whites were more often put in the position of instructor than one would have expected. They were also set up as models, and technology was located on the European side. Likewise, the way in which women were perceived differed, in so far as the sensual aspect, which was magnified in painting and photography, was minimised. Rather than help to inform the general public, which after all was not its role, advertising tended to perpetuate superficial clichés, an obvious mark of the failure of any real attempt to make the Greater France better known.

The impact of images and words

Advertising is not the only means by which to communicate a certain image of the distant colonies, notably in these days of technological diversification, where there is such a great reliance on the visual dimension. Numerous were the lectures presenting one or other aspect of the colonial realm, as part of fund-raising efforts carried out by missionaries, for example. Over the years, they called upon new techniques, including the sale of objects or the projection of slides. In Strasbourg, too, the cinemas regularly carried documentaries or films in which the Empire formed the backcloth.[42]

From 1921 to 1939 numerous events dealt with the colonies, whether they were films or lectures.[43] A minimum of 122 lectures were organised in Strasbourg during this period. They were set up by societies whose sole function was colonial propaganda, such as the Ligue Maritime et Coloniale, but also by those with a wider vocation: economic actors, such as the chamber of commerce, missions (the Société des Missions Evangéliques de Paris, in particular) or even cultural agents (such as extra-mural classes, Friends of the University). The subjects included the field of religion, which was fundamental in Alsace, the accounts of travellers or colonisers, and also economic and political talks. These lectures had a varied impact, ranging from direct colonial propaganda to the evocation of an exotic dream. In order to attract the public and make their testimony concrete, films or slide shows often accompanied the lectures, though they were also projected independently: approximately 280 colonial films (of which 163 were hitherto unseen) were shown on Strasbourg screens between 1921 and 1939. They were mostly fictional films, for documentaries were in the minority. They concentrated on the exotic nature of the countryside or the strangeness of customs, exploiting, for example, the image of the harem.

As in the lectures, North Africa played the major role: its geographical proximity seemed to induce less of a cultural and psychological distance, allowing spectators to identify with the heroes, some of whom originated in metropolitan France and were cast in the role of the adventurer.

People in the provinces thus had numerous opportunities for familiarising themselves with lands overseas, in a didactic or simply entertaining way. Even if all these events did not strictly constitute colonial propaganda, they did instil a feeling of national pride, glorifying the presence of France overseas and communicating images which converged to form a certain vision of the empire.

These abstract images were relayed thanks to the concrete participation of people originating from the colonies in certain national events. Apart from their walk-on parts in the 'African villages', the empire's subjects could make their presence felt at military parades. This was particularly obvious in eastern France where various regiments were stationed: a batallion of machine-gun *chasseurs* composed of indigenous colonial troops, such as a regiment of the colonial infantry or a regiment of Algerian, Moroccan or colonial *tirailleurs*.[44] There were seven Algerian regiments, one Moroccan regiment and three Indochinese and Madagascan battalions posted in France's twentieth military region (North-East France) between the wars. The theatrical or musical abilities of the Indochinese and Madagascan battalions were moreover put to use at the 1924 exhibition in Strasbourg as the town could not afford to bring in musical groups from abroad. Without any additional cost, the Strasbourg public was offered the opportunity to see Asiatic theatre and hear Madagascan songs. 'Native' soldiers were also present at national celebrations, such as 14 July and 11 November, but also when there were official visits, such as the ones by the minister Albert Sarraut and Maréchal Lyautey to the 1924 exhibition, by President Albert Lebrun in 1936, or by the Sultan of Morocco to Strasbourg in 1939. On both occasions, the Third Regiment of Moroccan infantrymen sent its *nouba*, an orchestra composed of percussion, a flute and bugles. Their success was guaranteed by their shimmering uniforms or their exotic tones, but genuine contact with the population remained extremely limited. The Second World War would arouse renewed interest in these soldiers, especially in regions liberated by troops partly raised in the empire. The numerous tombs of soldiers from the overseas territories who fell on the soil of metropolitan France, which are to be found throughout these regions, are evidence of this, as are the marriages and other links between colonial soldiers and French people that were forged at this time.

In time, although we must wait until the 1950s, another figure from the colonies would appear, that of the student. Thus in 1960–1 half of the African grant-holders (about 2200 students) were dispersed among various provincial towns.

Conclusion

The French had access, therefore, in the provinces and in the capital alike, to a variety of different types of information concerning the colonies. This also came from a variety of sources: lectures, advertising, films, exhibitions but also literature and even stamp-collecting. What impact did this information have? What did the French really know about the empire? And about what empire? We should in fact make a distinction between those parts of Africa which were little known but rich in clichés, Asia which was attractive but far off, and North Africa which was preponderant by reason of its geographic and mental proximity. In order to do this, we come up against the general problem of how to measure public opinion and the effectiveness of propaganda. Thus, in the case of the Strasbourg exhibition, what was the role of the colonial component in its attractiveness to visitors: just an exotic touch, cultivated in order to arouse their curiosity? Or a novel context for what was basically a banal agricultural and industrial exhibition? Our sources are not complete enough to allow us to evaluate with any accuracy exactly how the Alsatians perceived the message which the organisers sought to communicate concerning the colonies. It was nonetheless as a 'colonial exhibition' that this event went down in history. The 'African village' and the shows presented by the colonial troops in the evenings were apparently very successful. But can we go further than this? An administrator named Paira, a student at the time, spoke, for example, of a contradictory reaction; on the one hand, he stated that 'the discovery of the colonial world aroused real interest in the population', and on the other, that 'it was perhaps not very clever to present France to Alsatians in a totally unfamiliar way.'[45] This ambiguity, which in itself is not very surprising, would seem to suggest that some Alsatians were baffled by the choice of the colonial theme, which on this occasion projected only its attractive features.

The distance between the French and their empire does indeed seem to be a constant in the history of colonisation, a distance only overcome by certain recognised figures which barely evolved over time: the pink spots on the map, gallant conquerors, potential wealth, and strangeness and savagery, to name a few.

This chapter constitutes an invitation to do more research at a local level, to deepen study into the specific links between certain provinces and the colonies (for example, by studying those who originated there, such as the armed forces, or commercial links) and, more generally, to gain a greater knowledge of the links between the population of France in all its diversity and the colonies. From this point of view, the local press is a particularly fertile source.

Notes and References

The author and editors are indebted to Jill Husser for the translation of this chapter.

1. In addition to my own research, I am indebted here to master's degree dissertations written under my supervision at the Université des Sciences Humaines, Strasbourg, over the last few years; indeed this contribution gives me the opportunity to pay them tribute and to recognise the worth of research which is often not well enough known.
2. See the panorama presented by R. Girardet, *L'Idée coloniale en France de 1871 à 1962* (La Table Ronde, 1972).
3. D. Lejeune, 'Les Sociétés de géographie en France, dans le mouvement social et intellectuel du XIX° siècle' (thèse d'état, University of Paris X – Nanterre, 1987), published in condensed form as *Les Sociétés de géographie en France et l'expansion coloniale au XIX° siècle* (Albin Michel, 1993).
4. C. Poinsignon, 'La Colonisation française dans le bulletin de la Société de Géographie de l'Est de 1879 à 1914' (master's dissertation, 1990).
5. Over the years 'colonial geography' became usual, a term which reflects the definition adopted: the two types of geography both concern journeys, only the places are different: those dominated by France and the others. This explains how the progressive shift from one category to another took place.
6. *Bulletin de la Société de Géographie de l'Est*, 1894, p. 240.
7. 'La leçon des choses' was the expression used by the Minister for the Colonies, Albert Sarraut, in 1920. It may be translated as 'learning through observation'.
8. *Cinquantenaire 1885–1935. Comité Français des Expositions*, published by the committee, undated, but contemporary with the commemoration, gives only partial information about the provincial exhibitions.
9. This is the case in Marseilles, whose privileged economic links with the southern shore of the Mediterranean explain how two major colonial exhibitions came to be organised in 1906 and 1922.
10. For an analysis of national colonial exhibitions, see C.-R. Ageron, 'L'exposition coloniale de 1931', in P. Nora, ed., *Les Lieux de mémoire* (N.R.F., 1984), pp. 561–91; C. Hodeir and M. Pierre, *L'Exposition coloniale* (Complexe, 1991).
11. Information given to me by M. Auguy, who is completing a master's dissertation under the direction of S. Dulucq (Université de Toulouse – Le Mirail).
12. O. Goerg, 'Exotisme tricolore et imaginaire alsacien. L'exposition coloniale, agricole et industrielle de Strasbourg en 1924', *Revue d'Alsace*, 120 (1994), pp. 239–68. A master's dissertation has clarified this initial approach: S. Gartner, 'L'Exposition coloniale, agricole et industrielle de Strasbourg, 1924' (1994).

13. *Guide spécial*, edited by the regional daily newspaper *Dernières Nouvelles de Strasbourg* (*D.N.S.*), p. 38.
14. *D.N.S.*, no. 109 on 18 April 1924, A. Dupuy, 'Avant l'exposition de Strasbourg', and no. 291 on 20 October 1924, a closing speech by M. Quentin (president of the Paris city council, who mentions the lectures he was responsible for organising). Moreover, on the occasion of the Pasteur exhibition in 1923, the different institutes had been presented, including those located outside France. The Alsatians had certainly been able to have a look at the installations in the Congo (convention with Pasteur Institute in 1909), in Guinea at Kindia (1922) and in Senegal (the Saint-Louis laboratory, created in 1896 and transferred to Dakar, was to affiliate in 1924).
15. *D.N.S.*, no. 33, 2 February 1924.
16. Reproduced in the *D.N.S.* on 6 July 1924. He thus mentions the campaigns of Colonel Moll in Tonkin, then against the Tuaregs by Captain Fiegensihuh and Lieutenant Wirth.
17. 'Un grand colonial alsacien, Binger', *La Vie en Alsace*, no. 7, 1924, pp. 108–13. Binger returned to Strasbourg at the end of the war and left Alsace in 1922. In *D.N.S.* on 23 July 1924, 'Nos colonies et les fils d'Alsace'; A. Dupuy speaks of Admiral M. J. Dupré, who was in Senegal and in Tonkin, as well as of Fuchs and Zeys, who were on active service in Algeria.
18. 'L'Alsace et les colonies' emphasises that many Alsatians died as heroes in the colonies (*Guide*, p. 36).
19. The Ministry for the Colonies specifies that the collections belonging to colonial economic agencies and which figured at the Brussels exhibition (could it be that of 1910?) were to be available in Strasbourg (Archives municipales de Strasbourg/AMS., d. 48–379, Proust's letter to the mayor on 11 January 1924).
20. 'Trop d'expositions', *Journal d'Alsace et de Lorraine*, no. 34, 3 February 1924.
21. Gartner, L'Exposition coloniale, pp. 64 ff.
22. On the architecture of colonial exhibitions and notably that of African villages, see S. Leprun, *Le Théâtre des Colonies* (L'Harmattan, 1986).
23. G. Bergner, 'Choses d'Alsace. L'exposition coloniale à Strasbourg', *L'Alsace Française*, 12 July 1924, p. 658. This analysis is confirmed by the metamorphosis of different stands, such as that of Ricqlès, decked out with crenellations in an oriental style (*A travers l'Exposition coloniale*, weekly supplement of the *D.N.S.*, no. 4, 15 August 1924).
24. A sketch of the doorway, where the straw huts are visible in the distance, figures in the *Guide*, p. 60.
25. S. Leprun, *Le Théâtre des Colonies*, makes a detailed analysis of their scenography, paying attention not only to the architectural choices (pp. 160–80, 'Le village, scénario africain') but also to the participation of colonised peoples (pp. 181–203, 'Les travailleurs indigènes: présence en acte du "non civilisé" à l'exposition').
26. See his biography in P. David and J.-M. Andrault, 'Le village noir à l'exposition de Nantes de 1904 en histoire et en images', *Annales de Bretagne et des pays de l'Ouest*, 4, 1995, pp. 109–25.
27. See the research in progress under the aegis of the association 'Images et Mémoires' and other recent publications such as *L'Autre et nous: 'Scènes et Types'*, notably the articles on 'L'exhibition de l'autre', pp. 144–77 (ACHAC/

Syros, 1995). On this phenomenon in Germany, see R. Debusmann and J. Riesz, eds, *Kolonialausstellungen – Begegnungen mit Afrika?* IKO-Verlag für Interkulturelle Kommunikation, 1995, notably S. Arnold, 'Propaganda mit Menschen aus Übersee', and H. Sippel, 'Rassismus, Protektionismus oder Humanität'.

28. H. Gachot, 'La grande exposition industrielle et artisanale de Strasbourg (mai-octobre 1895)', pp. 71–82, in *Annuaire de la Société des Amis du Vieux Strasbourg*, IX, 1979.

29. Recent studies on the subject of the infantryman attest to this transformation, cf. J. Riesz and J. Schultz, eds, 'Tirailleurs sénégalais' (Verlag Peter Lang, 1989).

30. *Guide*, p. 42.

31. *Chronique officielle*, no. 10 'Types du village africain' (sketch by M. Hubrecht). *A travers l'Exposition coloniale*, no. 8, 12 September 1924, 'Le village africain', written under the pseudonym Tityre. It is difficult to identify the author of this article, which contains certain phrases published in the *Guide*: are these borrowings or is the author the same?

32. *A travers l'Exposition coloniale*, no. 2, 1 August 1924, 'Au village noir'.

33. Ibid., no. 4, 15 August 1924. A *gandourah* is an Arab-style sleeveless tunic.

34. Ibid, no. 8, 12 September 1924, 'Le village africain', Tityre. Note also the following type of assertion, which is ambiguous to say the least: 'Blacks are people like us, less brilliant but perhaps with more common sense', L.P., *La Vie en Alsace*, no. 8, p. 148.

35. *Chronique officielle*, no. 6, 9 August 1924, p. 64, 'Le baptême d'un bébé selon le rite musulman' and *D.N.S.* on 8 August 1924.

36. *Chronique officielle*, no. 9, 30 August 1924, p. 101 and *D.N.S.*, 21 August 1924.

37. *D.N.S.*, 9 August 1924. The entrance fee was 1 F. Also, A. Dupuy, 'La fête du Tabaski au village Africain', in *A travers l'Exposition coloniale*, 4, 15 August 1924.

38. For a discussion of blacks in advertising, see J. Nederveen Pieterse, *White on Black: Images of Africa and Blacks in Western Popular Culture* (Yale University Press, 1995).

39. C. Dreyfus, 'L'Afrique et les Africains vus à travers les Publicités d'un Journal Strasbourgeois, les Dernières Nouvelles de Strasbourg: les Coulisses d'un Mythe' (master's dissertation, Université de Strasbourg II, 1996).

40. See in particular Bacholet, ed., *Négripub, l'image des noirs dans la publicité* (Somogy, 1992).

41. A tea room of this name still exists in Colmar (Alsace).

42. S. Gontier Ackermann, 'La Propagande coloniale à Strasbourg pendant l'entre-deux-guerres à travers les Dernières Nouvelles de Strasbourg' (master's dissertation, Université de Strasbourg II, 1996).

43. Those which the *D.N.S.* publicise and review.

44. G. Reymond, 'Rôle et Place des Troupes Indigènes dans l'Est de la France, 1919–1939' (master's dissertation, Université de Strasbourg II, 1995).

45. Personal letter, dated 28 March 1992. The analysis comes a posteriori because he does not mention the 1924 exhibition in his memoires *Affaires d'Alsace. Souvenirs d'un Préfet* (La Nuée bleue, 1990).

7
Alienation or Political Strategy? The Colonised Defend the Empire

Catherine Atlan and Jean-Hervé Jézéquel

At the end of the nineteenth century, the 'colonial idea' was far from widely accepted by French public opinion.[1] One of the tasks of the *parti colonial* therefore was to convince a reluctant public of the value of empire. Thus, during the first half of the twentieth century, placing members of the indigenous population of colonial countries in the public arena for propaganda purposes was one of the strategies used in an attempt to achieve this.[2] However, although much is known about the passive role attributed to some of those who were put forward to be seen, admired or feared (for example, in colonial exhibitions), little study has been made of the conditions in which certain prominent African individuals were induced to play a more active part in spreading French imperial propaganda.

One of the distinguishing features of French colonial ideology is the fact that, in Africa especially, it was adopted and promulgated by elite members of the indigenous population who, furthermore, also took part in African proto-nationalist movements. How is this paradox to be explained? Was it simply that these people were alienated? To what extent were they being manipulated by the colonial power, which treated them favourably in return for their services? Were they mainly concerned with furthering their own careers? Or should their actions be seen as part of a socio-political strategy which sought to turn the colonial rules to their own advantage, rather than as simply reflecting a willingness to promote French colonialism?

The phenomenon will be analysed with reference to certain specific instances which occurred in French West Africa over the period from 1930 to 1950. These involved men who belonged to the new political elite to which colonisation gave rise: Blaise Diagne, Fily Dabo Sissoko and Léopold

Sédar Senghor. These men were the precursors of modern African nationalism, yet they were persuaded, on certain occasions, to speak in defence of colonial positions adopted by the French, especially at international conferences. Blaise Diagne supported the case for forced labour at the conference of the International Labour Organization in 1931; Fily Dabo Sissoko, speaking in 1937 at the International Conference for the Cultural Development of Colonial Populations, proposed a model for cultural development of a distinctly African nature, but which would remain under French supervision; and lastly, at the United Nations in 1950 Léopold Senghor supported the French administration in Togo and Cameroon.

These speeches were far more than mere propaganda; they constituted a high point in the careers of the African elites and reflected the particular socio-political positions they managed to adopt within a multifaceted colonial context. The focus of attention here will be these positions as manifested in the three instances mentioned above. Seen in the context of the inter-war years in the cases of Blaise Diagne and Fily Dabo Sissoko, they are examined with a view to piecing together the biographical development – both social and political – of the two men. Senghor's speech, however, coming as it did after the Second World War, will be analysed as illustrative of a pivotal moment in his political career and in his philosophical development.

Blaise Diagne: the first black African to win an election[3]

Blaise Diagne came from the island of Gorée, one of the Four Communes of Senegal legally entitled in 1848 and subsequently from 1871 onwards to elect their own deputy to the French National Assembly. A civil servant in the customs service, Diagne stood in the elections of 1914 and, to widespread surprise, was elected, beating the candidate from the *métis* (mixed-race) families which had hitherto monopolised the seat. Although elected on a somewhat moderate platform, he was a source of irritation to the colonial authorities until the outbreak of the First World War brought an unexpected rapprochement.

In exchange for Diagne's support in the recruitment of *tirailleurs sénégalais*, a law was passed in the National Assembly granting French citizenship to *originaires* of the Four Communes. Rapidly achieving prominence as one who was not to be ignored in matters concerning African troops, in 1917 Diagne was appointed High Commissioner for French West Africa to spearhead an ambitious troop recruitment drive. He obtained a number of pledges advantageous to demobilised infantrymen and, more generally, was instrumental in bringing about improvements in the living conditions of the indigenous population. Placed in charge of the Commission for Black Troops after the armistice, he took an active part in improving the status and welfare of ex-soldiers, seeing them as the agents of progress in Africa.

Following a change of government, however, Diagne resigned his post in 1922 and, although remaining a deputy for Senegal, he withdrew to the sidelines with regard to governmental responsibilities. At the same time he was beset by political problems since he was confronted by competition from the 'pan-*nègre*' movements which, being more radical and inclined towards communism, condemned his policy of cooperation with the colonial authorities. Denigrated to an increasing extent by these anticolonialist groups, Diagne turned to his former enemies in the *parti colonial*. Thus, in 1931, a government of the right chose him to represent France at the Geneva conference on the subject of forced labour held by the International Labour Organization (ILO).

Blaise Diagne at the 1931 ILO conference: the problems of citizenship and African nationality

At the conference a number of colonial powers came together to discuss the question of compulsory labour in the different empires. France came under attack from a group of countries led by Great Britain which accused it of resorting, through forced labour, to virtual slavery for the benefit of public and private interests. In order to strengthen its defence of legislation making the exploitation of local African populations easier, the French government chose a black African to be its representative. In the event, Blaise Diagne had no hesitation in defending the position adopted by the French with regard to forced labour:

> We are in favour of putting a stop, as soon as possible, to this social scourge that afflicts the races, to one of which I belong. However, we entreat you not to provide a two-edged sword which would serve, on the one hand, to sever the bonds of subjugation and, on the other, to leave us in a state of inferiority which is the very condition we want to bring to an end.[4]

Although he still spoke out in support of the interests of Africans, he remained true to the political stance of his early years only in appearance. When, in 1915, he had spoken in support of granting French citizenship to *originaires* or the rights of African ex-soldiers, on the one hand he had acted in the spirit of the colonial situation, and on the other had established himself as the leader of the new African social groups described as being 'assimilated'. Citizenship, both French and African, were to him closely interconnected; he had no difficulty in reconciling the two principal components of his political philosophy. However, the state of urgency caused by the First World War probably made this position easier since France was prepared to grant temporary concessions. After the war, the period of withdrawal to the sidelines through which Diagne went shows the new difficulties he encountered in acting in the political arena. In order to return to the forefront of politics, Diagne had to reaffirm his attachment to France by legitimising its colonial policy.

In 1931 Blaise Diagne still made much of his attachment to the French colonial system, but his defence of African interests in his speech was only apparent. The fact was that at the 1931 conference his arguments were not based on any concrete plan promoting the welfare of Africans. Indeed, in the name of the government, Diagne refused to countenance any proposal to regularise, oversee or reduce forced labour.[5] Thus he betrayed the very essence of his political stance hitherto, which had been based on the defence of the French imperial structure as the route to advocating a programme of reform which would benefit Africans. On his return to France from Geneva, confronted by those who accused him of collaborating with the *parti colonial*, Diagne made no secret of the primacy he attached – and would continue to attach – to the defence of French interests:

> Closely caught up in the cut and thrust of those verbal exchanges in my capacity as representative of the French government, I was better able than anyone to detect the intrigues against our country engaged in, under the mask of humanitarian control, by a coalition of politico-economic interests more intent on hampering than on guaranteeing the happiness of the peoples they purport to protect.[6]

Attacking the approach of the defenders of indigenous populations as 'humanitarian control', Diagne extolled the virtues of the defence of 'our country' against the other imperial powers and postponed until some more favourable future the economic development of Africa.

Blaise Diagne: the political career of an *originaire* in retrospect

Diagne never claimed to be an opponent of the colonial regime, but considered himself, from the outset, to be a responsible politician. This prompted him to ally himself more and more closely as time went by to a *parti colonial* which took little interest in improving the welfare of the indigenous population. In 1931, he was no longer the spokesman for the interests of the *originaires*, for the *assimilés* or for the indigenous peoples; he was simply the spokesman of a colonial state that had mandated him to represent its own interests and which turned to its own advantage his status as a French black African *député*. Furthermore, following the conference he was appointed Under-Secretary of State for the Colonies, a post never before occupied by an African.

From 1914 to 1931 Diagne's political career reflected the failure of a delicate balancing act allying, on the one hand, patriotism and faith in assimilation, and on the other, the wish to represent the interests of the new 'assimilated' African elites. The success of the early years, in the particular context of a state of war, was short-lived. After that interlude, Blaise Diagne was no longer able to urge the adoption of a reformist, middle-way approach by a colonial state which was once more in a position of power. On the contrary, it was precisely the colonial system that eventually brought him into line by recruiting him into its service.

Over the years, Diagne's loss of his sense of direction was much like that of Fily Dabo Sissoko, another African leader who had also chosen to support French imperial propaganda.

Fily Dabo Sissoko: between francophilia and cultural nationalism

The maverick young schoolteacher

Fily Dabo Sissoko was born in about 1900 in Horo Koto, not far from Bafoulabé (in the west of present-day Mali), into a powerful family of chiefs. He was educated first at the School for the Sons of Chiefs (Ecole des Fils de Chefs) in the town of Kayes, and subsequently in the Ecole Normale on the island of Gorée, where he qualified as a primary school-teacher. In 1927 he published an article anonymously in the review *Europe* in which he was severely critical of the French administration and commercial companies, and defended African cultures against reactionary prejudices. It was an article of intense youthful grievance, showing Sissoko to be a teacher of unconventional views who soon came to be viewed with misgiving by the authorities.

The International Conference for the Cultural Development of Colonial Populations, September 1937

Ten years later, in 1937, on the occasion of the Universal Exhibition, Paul Rivet, the director of the Musée de l'Homme in Paris, organised an international conference on the cultural development of colonial populations. It constituted in part a propaganda exercise serving to publicise the changes brought about by the colonial policy of the new Popular Front. There were only two Africans present – Amadou Mapaté Diagne (a Senegalese schoolteacher) and Fily Dabo Sissoko, who delivered a speech which he entitled 'Culture and the Blacks'.

In this speech, he listed eminent intellectual black African figures of the past, pointing out that the contribution of Africans to world culture was far from negligible, despite the existence of a 'dividing-line some seven hundred years old' between blacks and whites. By way of contrast, Sissoko drew up a series of portraits of 'assimilated' Africans whom he pilloried mercilessly: 'the Bourgeois Gentilhomme, the Faux-Semblant (humbug) or White Negro, the *parvenu*, the reprobate, the strutting peacock... Pretentions, idle chatter. But a genuine elite? Certainly not!'[7] Sissoko felt that intellectual and cultural development in black Africa within the framework of colonisation was desirable, but that it should take place in such a way as to remain truly African and in accordance with African tradition.[8] Motivated by associationism, Sissoko summed up these ideas in one key sentence: 'The Black must remain Black, in both life and development.'[9]

This political slogan appeared to echo the defiant tone of the article of 1927. Here, however, it occurred in an altogether different context, since it formed part of a set of papers promoting pro-imperial propaganda. It is true that ostensibly it was critical of the harmful cultural effects of French colonialism on '*évolués*', as they were called, but the speech was in no way anti-colonial. On the contrary, it was in line with the new approach incorporated during the 1930s into colonial policy, which sought to avoid the creation of a class of '*déclassés*' in African societies. To the colonial mind the creation of a dangerous and more or less westernised African 'semi-elite' no longer at ease in its own country was to be discouraged. Thus, Sissoko's comments accorded well with the policy of mistrust with regard to westernised African elites.

Sissoko's political career: an assessment

Thus, while maintaining a certain continuity in his thinking with what he had written in his youth, Sissoko gave up direct criticism of French colonialism and came to support French pro-colonial propaganda. How is this to be explained? First, Sissoko came to realise that it would be to his personal advantage to cooperate with the colonial administration. In 1933, thanks to the backing of the administration which was seeking to promote the appointment of those who were 'scholarly' and compliant to positions of responsibility, he took up the post of senior administrator in the *canton* of Niafunké which had been under the leadership of his family until a few years before.

In a more general sense, though, Sissoko saw himself as the representative of those African elites who, refusing to be over-westernised, favoured a more African option. He maintained that a reformed colonial framework would enable the Africans to develop in a manner more in keeping with their history, under the combined leadership of the colonial administration and the African elites, who would have their former rights and privileges restored. It was consistent with this line of thought that, in 1944, Sissoko formed the Parti Soudanais du Progrès (PSP), composed of both chiefs and the new elites of aristocratic origin who had received a French education – men such as Hammadoun Dicko and Almamy Koreissi, both of whom were former schoolteachers, sons of canton chiefs and future parliamentarians in France. The main aim of the party was to negotiate the more active and meaningful participation of the Soudanese aristocracy in the administration of the colony of French West Africa.

The PSP was, however, used by the colonial power as a weapon in its battle against the much more radical Rassemblement Démocratique Africain (RDA). The blatantly obvious and enthusiastic support given by the administration, however, brought about the collapse of the PSP and, with it, the growing political isolation of Fily Dabo Sissoko. Rejecting to the end all thought of severing ties with France, Sissoko met a tragic death in a prison cell in the newly independent Mali.

The cases of Diagne and Sissoko show how two African political figures became implicated in an imperial propaganda machine which took advantage of the fact they were African. There is no denying that personal advantage and ambition played a part in these rapprochements. It is also true that, each in his own way, the two men sought to speak for African social groups which were anxious to carve out a niche for themselves in the management of the existing colonial regime. Their readiness to cooperate with the colonial authorities was rooted, then, in a genuine socio-political perspective which took into account the emergence of new social groups from which they themselves had sprung. However, apart from periods of crisis, the colonial state played the game by the rules only in so far as to do so was to its own advantage and involved no real departure from its policy. This led to the defeat of the two men, who henceforth switched from a stance of willing *cooperation* to one of grudging *collaboration*, which was more unilateral and which lacked its initial political vision.

However, in the years after 1945, the context had changed, as is evident in the case of Léopold Sédar Senghor, another politician from Senegal, who also faced an occasion when he had to defend a colonial policy of which he did not wholly approve.

Léopold Sédar Senghor at the United Nations (1950): colonial rhetoric and the idea of emancipation

In 1950 Léopold Sédar Senghor had been active in politics for almost five years: he represented Senegal in the French National Assembly where he was part of the ruling parliamentary majority.[10] It was owing to this that in 1950 he was appointed as a member of the French delegation to the United Nations. In this capacity he took part in the work of the Fourth Commission which was concerned with the UN Trust Territories, among which were two territories administered by France: Togo and Cameroon. He was, then, in a somewhat anomalous position: here was an African politician, one always ready to criticise the colonial administration in his own country, having to speak in defence of French policy in so far as it affected neighbouring territories. How did Senghor handle this ambivalent situation? His first speech to the UN, delivered in New York on 3 October 1950, goes some way towards answering the question;[11] in order to assess its significance, we will analyse the arguments adduced by Senghor in the context of his semantic and ideological universe.

Senghor reiterates French arguments in favour of colonialism

At a first reading of the speech, Senghor seems to have trotted out key elements of French colonial propaganda. For instance, he began by stressing the economic effort made by France to promote the the development of its colonies, referring in particular to the FIDES programme (Fonds d'Investissement pour le Développement Economique et Social) which, he said, was of immense benefit to the French territories of Togo and Cameroon. Here Senghor was echoing one of the stock themes of French colonial ideology, namely the '*mise en valeur*' of the colonies, and presenting it as both the reason and justification for colonialism. At that time this was a constantly recurring theme in all speeches on the subject of colonialism, including those delivered by nationals from the colonies. A case in point is that of Douala Manga Bell who, addressing the UN shortly after the war, spoke highly of French achievements in Cameroon – compared with those of Germany – in order to justify the need to maintain French rule.[12]

When addressing the UN, Senghor also echoed another classic line of argument put forward by the colonial powers: whenever he broached the sensitive issue of the French administration in Togo and Cameroon, he would sidestep it by referring to French law and institutions. Hence, on the subject of racial discrimination, he simply reminded his hearers that 'discrimination is declared to be a punishable offence in the preamble to the French Constitution'. In the same way, he supported the official line in playing down the problem of African women's failure to vote in elections: 'French law allows no discrimination in the matter of the emancipation of women.' Finally, on the thorny question of local assemblies in Togo and Cameroon – and their accession to a form of self-government – what Senghor said was deliberately vague. He pointed out that provision had been made for such a possibility in the constitution of the French Union, but produced no timetable for its implementation. This kind of prevarication was typical of colonialist circles in the 1950s. Time and again in those years there was a rush to hide behind every letter of the law as set out in the constitution whenever colonialism came under adverse scrutiny. Instances of this are the ritual formula of a 'single, indivisible Republic' (a formula which, incidentally, Senghor was later prompted to attack), and François Mitterrand's celebrated assertion, made in 1954 when he was minister for overseas France: 'From Flanders to Congo there is the law, one single nation and one single parliament. That is the constitution and that is our will.'[13]

Finally, in his speech, Senghor put forward one other argument which was typical of colonial discourse at the time when he declared, 'France has always paid careful attention to the aspirations of the indigenous people, and more especially to those of their freely elected representatives.' He was implying here that some of the demands made by people in the colonies – those that were made through an official representative – were more legitimate than others. The notion of the '*interlocuteur valable*' ('valid spokesman') that he exemplified was one by which the colonial authorities in France set great store. Indeed, during the period of decolonisation, the claim that it was seeking '*interlocuteurs valables*' enabled the French government to ward off radical opponents in favour of officials who were said to be 'traditional', or those elected representatives who 'played the game by the rules', that is to say, in most cases, the moderates.

Senghor's use of this ploy was particularly noticeable in the case of Cameroon where, in the early 1950s, political activity took two conflicting forms. One, which was within the legal political framework of the

French Union, had all the standard features – parties, elections, locally elected assembly, deputies – and pressed for greater flexibility on the part of the colonial regime. The other shunned official channels, looked to the people and the unions for its support, and demanded an end to French rule; this was the policy of the Union des Populations Camerounaises (UPC), a movement which, ostracised by the French authorities, nonetheless found a platform in the UN by means of the well-known petitions addressed to the Trust Territories Council. France and its representatives saw it as their task to discredit this practice and discreetly cast doubt on the legitimacy of those who engaged in it.

What Senghor was defending, then, was the official French standpoint; indeed he was himself one of the '*interlocuteurs valables*' of the colonial authorities in the tradition of Blaise Diagne and Fily Dabo Sissoko. In pursuing this line, Senghor was also asserting his own legitimacy and at the same time proclaiming his own political position.

A political message

In his address Senghor kept stressing the parliamentary responses made by African representatives in the French National Assembly to the problems concerning Togo and Cameroon: bills relating to the granting of autonomy to territorial assemblies, economic development, the question of racial discrimination, education, working conditions. He cited them one after the other and, so as better to show how effective they were, he ended by saying with something of a flourish: 'More than eighty representatives of overseas territories occupy seats in the French parliament, and on no occasion when their case was made forcefully enough have they failed to achieve what they wanted.' This, of course, was sheer wishful thinking, as he himself well knew, since in another context he lamented the lack of power of the African representatives in French assemblies.[14] What, then, explains his exaggeration before the UN? It would seem that he was not merely resorting once again to French colonial propaganda. By drawing attention to the existence and activities of the overseas representatives in this way, Senghor was sending a message to politicians in both Africa and France.

To the Africans he was implicitly affirming the relevance of the policy of his movement, the Indépendants d'Outre-Mer (IOM), which he always portrayed as being a third way between the 'collaborating' socialists and the 'revolutionary' RDA. This was why, in his UN speech, he so often cited the bills introduced by his parliamentary colleagues, bills which, on examination, prove always to have been submitted by the IOM deputies in his group.[15]

To his 'French' opponents, that is to say the ultra-colonial caucus in Paris, he pointed out that the constitution of 1946 contained political pledges relating to overseas territories, pledges which had not yet been fulfilled and which the Africans were demanding should be honoured. As Senghor said a few years later, in what was an openly combative speech: 'We demand the Constitution, the whole of the Constitution.'[16]

It was, then, alongside official colonial arguments, a highly political message that Senghor intended to convey in his speech to the United Nations. However, he went further than that: he also explored certain cultural ideas to which his philosophical reflections had given rise.

The need for cultural emancipation

The text of Senghor's address shows the major importance he attached to culture. A number of passages underline that for him, in 1950, the emancipation of those living in the colonies should come about initially through education, through a process which should be cultural and only later economic or political. His references to the development of teacher-training colleges, then, fit into this perspective. More clearly, as far as the emancipation of women was concerned, Senghor expressed his belief in intellectual development rather than institutional reform: 'The fact is that the emancipation of women will come about by means of education.' Finally, with regard to the achievement of mature political awareness among Africans, he seems to have favoured progressive training in democracy for, on the subject of the territorial assemblies in Togo and Cameroon, he declared: 'Legislators are not made overnight; that is why the experience of those who represent the overseas territories in the French parliament is of such value.'

This statement sets in high relief an élitist conception of both education and political emancipation which, Senghor seems to have been suggesting, can result only from a prolonged period of training, and which, moreover, must be conducted by colonial elites who have already achieved intellectual and political distinction in their careers. This explains why, in the same speech, Senghor went on to insist on the founding of a university in Dakar and on the appointment of Africans to executive posts in Togo and Cameroon: 'Over half the magistrates in Togo, Cameroon and West Africa are native-born,' he said with a touch of pride. After all, Senghor was himself a striking example of the type of educational and cultural emancipation he was advocating: from humble beginnings in the colonial empire he had gone on to achieve outstanding academic distinction in the French university system. His intellectual development led him to the rediscovery of his own culture and prompted him to fight for the emancipation of Africa. Whenever and wherever he delivered a speech, he never missed the opportunity to draw attention to his exemplary career, not – or not simply – out of self-satisfaction, but because of his firm belief in the cultural values he embodied, values which alone in his view could restore Africa to its rightful place in history. It was for this reason that he ended his address to the United Nations on 3 October 1950 by referring to his own situation: he pointed out that he was 'a native of an overseas territory ... and that the populations in lands under foreign rule were peasant populations with firmly held, concrete values.' It was not for nothing that, after having stressed his position as a diplomat and deputy to such an extent, Senghor should recall his peasant roots. It was his discreet and pithily symbolic way of drawing attention to the cultural diversity and potential of Africa, the accomplished representative of which he held himself to be. The intellectual and peasant, defender of both 'concrete values' and noble principles, Senghor revealed in his speech those ideas and qualities that were close to his heart: the pursuit of excellence, cultural *métissage* (cross-fertilisation), *négritude* and humanism.

Senghor's United Nations speech, then, far from merely echoing French colonial propaganda or even being a means whereby he could defend the part he had played in Franco-African politics, provides a clear insight into his philosophical and cultural ideas concerning the emancipation of Africa. This illustrates, it could be claimed, both the multifaceted nature of the man and more generally the way in which, as late as 1950, the elites of the French empire could position themselves within the limited room for manoeuvre which they were permitted.

Conclusion

All in all, the three cases of African politicians addressing international conferences enable us to comprehend the original way in which French imperial propaganda was received and disseminated by nationals of the colonies concerned. Their activities and speeches were then used by the colonial power to convince French public opinion of the 'humanitarian' benefits that French colonialism brought to the 'natives'. Indeed, this was one of the most convincing arguments in favour of France's 'civilising mission', since it demonstrated how successfully these members of the African elite had been assimilated to French culture and values through their French education, to the point where they were prepared to defend French colonial rule in international fora.

However, what these three men did should by no means be construed in terms of 'collaboration'; rather it would appear that, while defending a certain vision of the Empire, they were operating within the framework of a broader socio-political project. This prompted each of them to assume the role of spokesman, either for emerging social groups or for a new African 'national' conscience, or both. Blaise Diagne, Fily Dabo Sissoko and Léopold Sédar Senghor, then, had aspirations that transcended colonial rhetoric; they wished to defend their own position as members of African elites by acting within the limited scope allowed to them for ideological autonomy by the colonial power.

The fact remains that their speeches – like their actions – were strikingly ambiguous, in that they were continually based on colonial concepts such as the 'citizenship' of the Four Communes (Blaise Diagne), the policy of 'association' (Sissoko) and concern for a strict interpretation of the law of the French Union (Senghor). How, then, are the positions implied by these speeches to be assessed from a historical and political standpoint? Whereas, in 1950, Senghor was on the threshold of a political career in the run-up to independence, Blaise Diagne and Sissoko, in the inter-war period, seemed to be trapped in a political impasse. In order to pursue their own strategy, each decided to turn the machinery of colonial power to his advantage, but this failed to provide the opportunity for either of them to pursue to the very end the political logic which had led them to adopt such a cooperative attitude.

Notes and references

1. See R. Girardet, *L'Idée coloniale en France* (Seuil, 1972).
2. This came to form an integral part of the 'competition' between the colonial powers, notably Great Britain and France, to prove to the outside world that they were 'better' colonial powers than their rivals: see also Chapter 12 by Véronique Dimier in the present volume.
3. The information in this section is based on J. H. Jézéquel, 'L'action politique de Blaise Diagne, premier élu noir-africain à l'Assemblée Nationale' (DEA dissertation, Institut d'Etudes Politiques de Paris, 1993).
4. Quoted in A. Dieng, *Blaise Diagne, premier député Africain* (Chaka, 1990), p. 99.
5. Ibid.
6. Preface by Blaise Diagne to C. J. Fayet, *Travail et colonisation. Esclavage et travail obligatoire* (Chantenay, 1931).
7. F. D. Sissoko, 'Les noirs et la culture', in *Congrès International de l'Evolution des Peuples Coloniaux* (Paris, n.p., 1938), p. 119 ff.
8. Sissoko can here be seen as adopting a stance analogous to that referred to by Anthony Smith as 'reformist-revivalist'; see A. Smith, *Theories of Nationalism* (Duckworth, 1971), pp. 243–51.
9. Sissoko, 'Les noirs et la culture', p. 122.

10. For a general biography of Senghor, see: J.-L. Hymans, *Senghor, an Intellectual Biography*, (Edinburgh University Press, 1971); J. Sorel, *Léopold Sédar Senghor: l'emotion et la raison*, (Sepia, 1977); J. Vaillant, *Black, French and African: a Life of Léopold Sedar Senghor* (Harvard University Press, 1991). On his activities as a politician in the Palais-Bourbon, see C. Atlan, 'Les Indépendants d'outre-mer: députés africains à l'Assemblée Nationale sous la Quatrième République (1948–1958)' (MA dissertation, EHESS/Université de Paris I, 1991); and J. Vaillant, 'African Deputies in Paris: the Political Role of Léopold Senghor in the Fourth Republic', in G. W. Johnson, ed., *Double Impact: France and Africa in the Age of Imperialism* (Greenwood Press, 1985), pp. 141–54.
11. This speech is recorded in the following document: UNO, A/C4/SR.145.
12. E. Mortimer, *France and the Africans* (Faber, 1969), p. 115.
13. Quoted in Girardet, *L'Idée coloniale*, p. 339.
14. Vaillant, *Black, French and African*, p. 279.
15. Assemblée Nationale, *Documents Parlementaires (Législature 1946–1951)*, projets de loi nos. 759, 2167, 3501 and 7072.
16. Assemblée Nationale, *Journal Officiel, Débats Parlementaires*, 16 April 1951.

8
'Propagender': Marianne, Joan of Arc and the Export of French Gender Ideology to Colonial Cambodia (1863–1954)

Penny Edwards

In 1873, ten years after the establishment of the French protectorate of Cambodia, the naval officer and explorer Louis Delaporte petitioned the French Ministry of Public Education for state gifts of European art. Female nudes such as Venus de Milo would be the best bet, Delaporte argued, to 'vanquish the few religious scruples' of Cambodia's cultural guardians, the king and the chief monks.[1] Weeks later, armed with copies of Jean Thierry's *Leda with Swan* and a host of other depictions of women by Raphael, Rembrandt and Rubens, Delaporte set sail on the first of many missions to cull Khmer monuments for Parisian museums. Delaporte's calculated export of female imagery foreshadowed a rich traffic in French ideas of femininity and gender ideology.

This was not a propaganda blitz, but a subtle saturation. Postage stamps and poster art, costumes and currency, maternity wards and monuments, statues and schoolbooks all served to project French ideals of femininity onto Cambodia during the 91 years of the protectorate. Two images in particular stand out: Marianne, the sobriquet of the Republic and Joan of Arc, the darling of royalists and clergy. These symbols of intellectual and political cleavage were twinned by an identical ideal: that the modern nation has a female incarnation.

By the late nineteenth century, the adoption of the female form as a national sign was a mainstay of nationalist movements and state governments in Europe and America. Cambodia, however, had no such history. The very idea of the nation-state as the sacrosanct unit of moral and political belonging was new. Equally novel was the bourgeois binary opposition of femininity and masculinity, and the embodiment of this European gender cleavage in costumes, coiffures and the cult of domesticity.

In pre-colonial Cambodia, gender-specific behaviour was prescribed through didactic verse, oral history, and religious injunction, central to which was the paradigm of the *srey-krup-leakh* (perfectly virtuous woman). Married women enjoyed considerable clout as the keepers of household finances and heads of house (*mee-pteah*).[2] Matrilineal practice reinforced their socio-economic status. Gender equity was subtly reinforced by strong similarities in the traditional clothes and coiffures of men and women.

The colonial encounter attenuated these indigenous ways of seeing and being a woman, crystallising new gender identities around the previously fluid domains of home, hair and clothing. By independence in 1954, the *srey-krup-leakh* had been refashioned into a new symbol of national dimensions which conflated woman and nation. Cultural differences rendered the initial fusion of these abstractions problematic. Cambodia was routinely exoticised, eroticised and iconised as a woman in colonial paraphernalia, literature and propaganda. In their bid to market Cambodia to political constituencies and tourist markets in the metropole, French artists and administrators routinely represented the protectorate as a sensuous, nubile woman seeking protection from an older, wiser nation. Sumptuously dressed royal dancers and bare-breasted girls were standard personifications of Cambodia in monuments, novels, postcards and exhibitions. But in their daily incarnation, Cambodian women struck most European visitors as anything but feminine.

In nineteenth-century Cambodia, women and men both wore short hair and long pantaloons. Unstitched lengths of cloth (*sampot*) were draped, tucked and folded to form baggy-hipped trousers which tapered at the calves, known as *sampot chong-k'ben*. 'It is hard to distinguish men and women from a distance, because of their heavy features and robust limbs: they smoke and usually wear a [*sampot chong k'ben*]', wrote one French visitor to Cambodia in the 1910s.[3] His remarks typified the protectorate's near-century-long chorus of contempt for the androgynous appearance of Cambodian women.

The perceived gender ambiguity of Cambodia jarred with the cultural norms and national imagery of nineteenth-century Europe, where political authorities were actively promoting feminine icons of nation. In France from 1870–1914, the bipolar crucibles of 'male' and 'female' identities were encoded in popular culture and suspended in a 'complementary equilibrium'.[4] Gender relations remained a 'primary way of conceiving identity and power in . . . French politics, culture and society' between Europe's two 'world wars,' when cultural anxieties saw new negotiations and contestations of these constructions.[5] National allegory and popular culture in Vichy France sustained this male–female binary opposition in exaggerated form.[6] Through the prism of gender, and focusing on the iconology of Marianne and Joan of Arc, this chapter will explore the cultural, social and sartorial ramifications of France's attempts to emboss its own image on the Protectorate of Cambodia.

Exporting Marianne: 1884–1918

After France's defeat in 1870, statues and sculptures of Joan of Arc reared on horseback or lifted their hands in prayer in numerous villages and town centres, guarding the frontiers of French national pride and regional culture along the newly hewn Franco-Prussian border. The following decade, the clerical right embraced Joan as the symbolic antithesis of the republican icon of Marianne. When the church launched sacred Joan Days in the 1890s, and began to lobby for their national recognition as a royalist alternative to Bastille Day, alarmed anti-clericals blocked the legislative effort. But they could not prevent the rise of Joan as a symbol of a growing nationalist consciousness.[7]

Despite such competition, Marianne's monopoly of state insignia and republican paraphernalia ensured her mass circulation in the metropole and colonies as the face of France. Her bust presided over the newly created republican holiday of Bastille Day, first celebrated in Phnom Penh in 1885.[8] The 1880s also saw Marianne's debut on Banque d'Indochine banknotes, printed in Saigon, and on the newly minted Indochinese *piastre* coins. Her serene features oversaw colonial attempts to homogenise Cambodia's means of exchange, which ranged from Mexican piastres to thin silver coins minted in the precolonial era, silver bars and Siamese currency.[9] Until the launch of a new series of stamps featuring Cambodian and Cochinchinese women in 1908, Marianne was the dominant philatelic motif in Indochina.[10] She appeared in miniature on official colonial seals and loomed larger than life in imperial monuments such as Théodore Rivière's *La France* (Hanoi, 1908). In the poster art of David Dellepiane (1866–1932) and its amateur equivalents, Marianne invariably appeared as a protective, matronly figure warding grateful, childish natives.[11]

Although lampooned by her French royalist detractors as a harlot, Marianne must have cut a frumpish figure to *fin-de-siècle* Cambodian women of fashion. Her Phrygian bonnet must have seemed a particularly bizarre encumbrance. Cambodian court dancers wore coronets, and peasant women wore broad-brimmed sun hats in the fields, but hats were never seen as a fashion item by Cambodian women. Marianne's long hair, like that of European women in turn-of-the-century Indochina, must have appeared both unkempt and unclean, not least because Cambodians observed a panoply of hair-related rituals. Shorn at birth, cropped on marriage, and shaved in mourning, short hair was a marker of civilisation, matrimony and maturity in Khmer tradition. Long hair was associated with evil spirits and *yeak*.

A Khmer term for giant or monster, *yeak* became street slang for Europeans in the colonial era. Only her plump shoulders – considered one of the five signs of true womanly beauty in Cambodia – would have saved Marianne from outright derision as a *yeak* of truly monstrous proportion and calamitous dress sense.

During the first decades of colonial rule, the circulation of these effigies of Marianne would have been restricted to the corridors of colonial power in the Cambodian capital of Phnom Penh. The means and scope of broadcasting such images expanded in the early 1900s with the establishment of Cambodia's first secular schools for girls and an increase in French female emigration to Cambodia.

The first French women active in social work in Cambodia were the Sisters of Providence, who staffed Phnom Penh's first hospital in the 1880s, and subsequently opened an orphanage for abandoned girls. But the near-complete failure of Catholicism to win Khmer converts in Cambodia greatly curbed the cultural reach of French nuns.[12] Although billed as housewives, at least some French women exerted influence outside the private sphere. One such woman was Madame Russier, who joined her new husband in Phnom Penh shortly after his appointment as head of the Department of Cambodian Education in 1914. Here she worked on the school manual *Histoire Sommaire du Cambodge* (A Brief History of Cambodia), which was subsequently adopted on the history syllabus of colonial schools.[13]

Cambodia's first secular school for girls, the Ecole du Protectorat, opened in 1904. Principally for European or 'assimilated girls', the school had 22 students in its first year. While Indochina's slowly expanding pool of French-native schools dispensed the rudiments of arithmetic, French language, history and geography to native male pupils, the syllabus of Cambodia's first state schools for females centred on hygiene, mothercraft and needlework. In this they mirrored *fin-de-siècle* France's newly established, secular primary schools for girls, which aimed to instil distinct gender roles through lessons in domestic science and childcare.[14]

The destination of most French women in the metropole during the nineteenth century was marriage and the founding of a new *intérieur* (home). Exhibits such as the Hall of Women at the 1900 universal exhibition in Paris validated the distinction between the 'exterior' world of the male and the more 'intimate,' 'interior' women's world of foyer and family.[15] Mindful of these social roles, in 1905 a French architect in Cambodia designed a blueprint for the perfect colonial house. The 'heart' of his ideal home was the corridor where 'the mistress of the house (let us not speak of the man, who is busy elsewhere) will while away the day's long hours in delicious pursuit of little projects of embroidery or fashion'.[16] Although a number of French women journeyed beyond the *intérieur* to work in colonial schools and charities, their pedagogical mandate and philanthropic pursuits generally had a strong domestic orientation.

Like their counterparts in the Dutch East Indies and British Burma, Cambodia's new girls' schools aimed to produce well-dressed and nicely spoken native women who would take France's *mission civilisatrice* into Cambodian homes as the spouses of native civil servants.[17] By teaching young native girls 'housework and mothercraft', homeliness and hygiene, as one prominent colonial lobbyist argued in 1906, French schoolmistresses would cultivate 'good housekeepers' and 'good wives and mothers'.[18] Catholic convents shared this mission to train their few Khmer charges in 'the most delicate points of western etiquette'.[19]

French women in Cambodia also found an outlet for their energies in philanthropic activities. However, the outbreak of the First World War encouraged a European focus, a prime example being the Cambodian chapter of the Croix-Rose. This was founded by a group of French girls in Phnom Penh in 1918 to help 'young Belgian and French girls in the occupied territories'.[20]

While the Croix-Rose staged charity benefits to syphon donations from European pockets, Indochinese women were the target of fund-raising campaigns for the National War Bond. 'Knowing that her feminine arms are too weak to beat the enemy, [she] is arming other, more virile limbs by participating in the Bond,' read one fund-raising poster which depicted a generic 'Indochinese' woman dressed in a Khmer scarf and Vietnamese pants pulling the family savings out of a chest.[21] Such crude characterisations of native women as shrewd money-managers formed the perfect foil for romantic iconisations of *la Française* as a tender-hearted and nimble-fingered 'mother, wife and sister' whose needlework warmed many a fighter's chest.[22]

Cocooned in Phnom Penh's European district, French women rarely came into contact with female residents of the Cambodian quarter. This lack of contact exacerbated the importance and impact of imagery in shaping perceptions and reinforcing prejudices. The end of the First World War saw a shift in the focus of European philanthropic endeavours in Cambodia from battlefields to childbirth. As projects to educate Cambodian women in maternity and modernity moved beyond the classroom, so, too, did the cult of Joan of Arc. Once largely restricted to convent schools, imagery of Joan of Arc began to circulate in the secular domain and to encapsulate notions of national rebirth and feminine virtue.[23]

So long, Marianne: the inter-war years

To a bewildered French public seeking stability in the aftermath of the First World War, Joan of Arc provided a traditional symbol of gender offering an antidote to cultural trauma and social dislocation. In 1920, Joan was canonised with lavish ceremony in Rome. The establishment of an official 'Joan Day' consolidated *la pucelle's* incorporation in France's national pantheon.[24] Joan's trajectory to sainthood and national heroine status coincided roughly with the passage of a new anti-abortion bill by a sweeping majority in France's parliament.

In the aftermath of war, French authorities and media promoted the figure of the mother as a symbol of rebirth, healing, and redemption who promised at once a strong birth-rate and the rebirth of moral virtue. This movement of morals and motherhood had reverberations in the colonies.[25] The Society for Protection of Mothers and Infants of Cambodia (SPMIC) was founded in Phnom Penh by French women in 1926 for the 'protection of pregnant and nursing mothers and new-borns and the care of abandoned children'.[26] Mirroring the motives and organisational apparatus of similar societies in France, SPMIC provided neo-natal and post-natal consultations to Khmer women through a gradually expanding network of provincial branches and the opening of milk banks.

The economic exigencies and social change of wartime irrevocably expanded the parameters of acceptable behaviour and labour opportunity for women. Juxtaposed with the traditional mother-figure in inter-war France was the progressive female parodied as *la garçonne* and associated with rising hemlines, short hair and promiscuity. One offshoot of the war was the rise in unattached women.[27] Some were widowed or had lost their partners; others, like Suzanne Karpelès, chose to live and travel alone.

Karpelès was an outstanding scholar of Sanskrit and Pali attached to the Ecole Française d'Extrême-Orient. A formidable organiser, she arrived in Cambodia in 1922 and carved out her own brilliant career there. Within three years she had established the Royal Library and pioneered Cambodia's first Khmer language journals: *Srok Khmer* (Khmer Country; 1926) and its highbrow twin, *Kampuchea Surya* (Cambodian Sun, a Buddhist journal; 1927).

Kampuchea Surya printed the first known Khmer literary treatment of Joan of Arc. *Katilok: Chbap dunman kluen* (*L'Art de bien se conduire dans la vie*), a normative poem by the highly erudite and acclaimed writer Suttan Prija In (1859–1924), compared Joan to a legendary local hero-ine, Yiyiey (Granny) Taep.[28] Like Taep, In explained, Joan had saved her king and wrested her country back from enemies. This act of national salvation had led to her iconisation. A statue was made in her image, and all of her fellow nationals joined to honour her.[29] Alongside contemporary Vietnamese and Chinese writings on Joan of Arc, In's verse helped to constitute a globalising category of womanhood by uniting indigenous and European heroines in a single, gender-based pantheon.[30]

While indigenous writers constructed cosmological realms of equality between native and western heroines, a strict social and racial hierarchy continued to prevail in the real world. For all her independence and intellectual achievements, Karpelès subscribed to, and actively promoted, the view that French women in the colonies could best serve as civilising agents in the colonies through the moral, social, hygienic and cultural uplift of native women in such fields as education.[31] In 1923 Humbert-Hesse, director of primary education in Cambodia, asserted that it would be 'good politics' to expand education for girls in Cambodia. Praising the industry, dexterity and enthusiasm of girl students in Phnom Penh, Hesse blamed the slow development of girls' schools in Cambodia on the lack of qualified women teachers, and noted a parental preference for female French teachers.[32] In 1927, school inspector Henri Gourdon recommended that the school curriculum for girls in Cambodia be amended to reflect parental preferences for training in practical domestic crafts.[33] The following year, the resident of Kompong Cham reported 'dressmaking' as the chief interest of the 35 girl students at the Ecole de Filles in his province.[34]

By 1931, there were 290 girls enrolled at the protectorate's 3 girls' schools in Phnom Penh, and a further 377 spread among 10 schools in the provinces.[35] 1932 saw the appointment of the School of Young Princesses' first Cambodian headmistress. Under her guidance, the school aimed 'not to form intellects,' but to foster proper social deportment through lessons in French, etiquette and embroidery.[36]

In 1938, *Nagaravatta* summarised the educational gains of the past 20 years of schooling for Khmer girls as 'writing and needlework.' As sartorial indices of national progress, the author suggested, Cambodian women had a special role to play. Most importantly, they should strive for the 'civilised' look of a western blouse, a *sampot* and shoes.[37]

Editorials and articles in both *Srok khmer* and *Kampuchea bodemien* encouraged readers to send their daughters to school. By the late 1930s, the number of eligible girl entrants far exceeded the places at the Ecole Norodom. Female literacy was on the rise. However, in 1938, the sight of Khmer girls reading *Nagaravatta* still made front-page news.[38]

But who provided the role-models for Cambodia's tiny, educated female elite? While the elderly bard In may have compared Joan of Arc to Granny Taep, the teenage graduates of colonial girls' schools are more likely to have identified with Joan's youth and beauty, as portrayed in 1930s iconography. When out of their exotic costumes and jewelled tiaras, the Cambodian ballet corps, sent to Paris in 1931, had begun to emulate the bobbed hair known in France as the Joan cut (*coupe à la jeanne*). By the late 1930s, the bob had spread from the Cambodian capital to the provinces.[39] Hair-cutting ceremonies fell into disuse. Once a field of ritual meaning, hair was increasingly seen as both a gauge of gender and a barometer of civilisation.

The 1930s were tumultuous times for Cambodia's intellectual, cultural and social development. Forums for the circulation of ideas in print and seminars expanded with Karpelès' establishment of the Buddhist Institute in 1930. A think-tank and cultural research centre for Cambodians, the institute provided the impetus for the launch of *Nagaravatta*, the first independent Khmer newspaper, in 1936.

Like its officially sponsored predecessors, *Nagaravatta* was dominated by male writers and initially concerned with such matters as the salary and perks of [male] native administrators. However, as national fields of meaning were drawn around dress, hairstyles, education and etiquette, gendered identities were inevitably constructed. Increasingly, Cambodian nationalists began to map the moral fibre and social dilemmas of the Khmer nation on the body of Khmer women.

Meanwhile in France, caught in a semiotic tug of war between the extreme right and the progressives who adopted her as their bob-cut mascot, Joan's popularity was on the rise. In 1931, Marshal Pétain publicly invoked Joan as a symbol of national unity against 'the external invader and internal disorder'. Three years later, *La Victoire* compared

Pétain to Joan of Arc.[40] When Pétain took power as head of the Vichy Government in 1940, Joan displaced Marianne as the official national allegory.

Joan of Vichy

Like their forebears who had blamed Prussia's victory in 1870 on an 'over-feminised' metropole, many Pétainists blamed France's defeat by Germany in 1940 on the nation's 'effeminate youth'.[41] To reverse this Republican emasculation, Pétain's new government launched a character-firming, body-building youth movement. To feed the flame of youthful patriotism and purchase political loyalty, Vichy encouraged the vigorous promotion of 'national' heroes throughout the French empire. A new cult of Joan, which served the twin goals of inculcating gendered norms and resuscitating past glory, was promoted throughout the Vichy empire.

Vichy ideology was interpreted for native consumption in Indochina by the autocratic workaholic Vice-Admiral Jean Decoux. Decoux's achievements in Cambodia included the abolition of all elected bodies, the violent dispersal of peaceful protests, the internment of Cambodian activists and a crackdown on press freedom which culminated in the closure of *Nagaravatta* in 1942 and the launch of a pro-government Khmer newspaper, *Kampuchea*.

The regimentation of youth was a central plank of Vichy social policy. By January 1941, the Vichy youth movement had spread to Tunisia, where a vast rally of French and Muslim youth swore loyalty to the empire.[42] In February 1941, the Vichy government passed a law enforcing a three-month participation in summer camps for all twenty-year-olds in France, Algeria, the colonies and protectorates.[43] The following month, *La jeunesse franco-indochinoise* launched its monthly revue *Ralliement*. The pilot issue promised its readers that 'we will become real Men, French and Indochinese worthy of the name.'[44] But the construction of 'real Men' entailed the invention of 'real Women'.

Who better to broadcast Vichy virtues to the entire female population of Greater France than Joan, already known and admired? To capture the imaginations of Cambodian youth, Decoux and his skilled team of propagandists manipulated the pomp and pageantry of Joan of Arc.

Schoolbooks reinvented the rebel of Orleans as a role-model of uniformity, submission, and ultimately subjugation for French girls. From Indochina to Madagascar and Senegal, colonised populations incorporated this Joan of Vichy in their national pantheons, and paid homage to her through a pastiche of national ceremony and local ritual.[45] The cult of Joan was also given air-play from Saigon to North Africa through such Vichy radio favourites as Children's Hour.[46]

On 10 May 1941, Vichy Indochina celebrated its first Joan of Arc Day. The recently crowned King Norodom Sihanouk and Khmer ministers accompanied the French resident and French administrators to the Catholic cathedral in Phnom Penh to honour the memory of St Joan. Thousands of soldiers and school youth groups gathered for the minister of education's exhortations to 'sacrifice your life, like Joan of Arc, to save the nation'.[47] In Hanoi, Joan fever had some twelve thousand school children and college students marching through the streets.[48] These commemorative ceremonies sparked a spate of hagiographies. Mirroring Vichy gender ideology, leading Khmer newspapers applauded Joan as both a national martyr and a master housekeeper.[49]

A plethora of articles remade legendary female figures of Cambodian history in Joan's image.[50] These Vichy remakes of old lore cast (British) India and (pro-British) Siam as the eternal enemy. One writer likened Joan's valiant conduct and national devotion to the self-sacrifice of the folk hero Klang Moeung, a sixteenth-century Khmer general whose legendary suicide and subsequent haunting had saved Cambodia from Siamese invasion.[51] Others compared Princess Livi – the mythical creator of Cambodia – to Joan of Arc, praising both as famous female defenders of nation against enemy invasion.[52] Traditional stories of a harmonious marriage between Princess Livi, guardian of the embryonic Khmer state of Funan, and the Indian King Kaundinya gave way to new legends casting Kaundinya as an enemy who emprisoned Livi 'like the English took Joan prisoner'.[53]

The 'Jeanettes', named after St Joan, were one of the many youth groups coordinated by Maurice Ducoroy, appointed as head of the General Commissariat for Physical Education, Sports and Youth for Indochina in May 1941.[54] In 1942, Cambodian women joined French, Lao and Vietnamese women at a training camp for female youth leaders at Dalat in Vietnam.[55] The active participation of Cambodian women in such gender-specific youth groups, and the widespread promotion by French and Khmer writers of such Vichy mantras as 'Travail! Famille! Et puis, pardessus tout, Patrie!'[56] ('Work! Family! And above all, Father-land!') appears to have strengthened the conflation of woman and nation in Cambodian intellectual circles, while reinforcing notions of gender cleavage. School syllabuses also played their part.

An article in May 1940 stressed the need for more education for women so that Cambodian girls could fuse traditional codes of conduct with western notions to help build a better nation. '[Khmer] women ...are still very base in terms of character, knowledge, and livelihood' railed the writer.[57] The following week, another writer announced an initiative by the Ministry of Education to introduce domestic science into the school curriculum in Indochina.[58] In February 1941 the Vichy minister of education announced his intention to make 'girls into wives and mothers'.[59] In 1942, the Vichy government made domestic science mandatory at girls' schools.[60]

The same year, in Cambodia, Khieu Ponnary (founder of Cambodia's first women's journal in the early 1950s, and future wife and mentor of Pol Pot) made front-page news with her success in stage two of her baccalaureate.[61] This feat inspired a lengthy article which cited Marshal Pétain's exhortation to national rebirth through hard work, and stressed the importance of women in making Cambodia grand and glorious.[62]

The SPMIC expanded under Vichy. Under the patronage of King Norodom and Princess Sutharot, it ran an orphanage and a milk bank, held numerous consultations with women, and issued a Khmer manual on motherhood. By 1943, it had expanded its 'fight against infant mortality' across Cambodia and established maternity clinics in every provincial town. Replicating patterns in the metropole, the SPMIC organised nationwide baby contests. In 1944, Prime Minister Pierre Laval recognised the 'public usefulness' of the SPMIC.[63]

By 1944, over 86 000 youth in Indochina had joined sports societies, the Boy Scouts, and the Girl Guides.[64] An enormous statue of Joan was erected in Saigon, forming an impressive stage-prop for Ducoroy's 1944 St Joan Day address to over 20 000 Indochinese youth.[65] This was Vichy Indochina's last Festival of Joan, held simultaneously in Phnom Penh, Dalat and Hanoi. In honour of the occasion, *Kampuchea* applauded Joan as a 'model' whose love of country, king and people was a wonderful virtue.[66] One Khmer writer invited Khmer youth to emulate Joan's selfless devotion to king and country and to commemorate her as a 'proper woman' (*sdray drimdriw*).[67] The following month, *Kampuchea* stressed the importance of decorating, cooking, needlework, childcare and dressmaking, without which no woman could call herself a household head (*mee-pteah*).[68]

The confluence of these gender-specific messages in Vichy media, propaganda and imagery steered Cambodian nationalist discourse towards a conflation of woman, home and nation. It was women's duty to keep a tidy house and dress in a civilised manner to impress the state of the nation on foreigners. Vichy notions of gender cleavage were inscribed onto the female body through a campaign to get men into

European-style trousers or shorts and encouraging women to wear their *sampots* not as culottes (*sampot chongk'ben*) but as wrap-around skirts (*sampot samloy*). Numerous articles on Khmer fashion stressed the historic difference of male and female attire.[69] This process catalysed the abandonment of the once unisex *sampot chongk'ben* by men and women alike, and encouraged the adoption of the *sampot samloy* as the national dress of Khmer woman – at once fusing woman, nation and notions of tradition.

The mass diffusion of gender symbols, reiterated on stages and schools in France and Cambodia, inscribed French notions of gender cleavage on Cambodian society. There emerged a reinvented *srey-krup-leaq*, who outwardly mirrored the European feminine traits of hair and wear, while inwardly adhering to Khmer cultural canons and most particularly the 'Code for Women,' or *chbap-srey*.

In their hair and dress, these daughters of the colonial encounter came to adapt, reproduce and enact French national allegory. Chiefly urban products of the French Protectorate's few schools for girls, they represented a tiny minority of women under colonial rule. Yet they came to represent a powerful force in the nationalist imagination.

Like Delaporte – whose 1873 mission of acquisition to Cambodia saw him perusing one ancient temple after another, and contemplating 'what to take, and what to leave', Cambodian women were the final arbiters of change in deciding which aspects of European gender imagery to emulate and which to reject. Modelled on urban Cambodian schoolgirls, the national figure of Cambodian womanhood promoted by nationalists on the eve of colonial collapse owed as much to Joan of Arc as to Khmer tradition. She had sleek, shoulder-length hair and wore her 'national' identity in a 'Khmer' costume woven from local tradition and French fashion.

Notes and references

1. Centre d'Accueil et de Recherche des Archives Nationales, Fiche 21 4489 3a Delaporte to minister of public education, 16 May 1873.
2. J. Ledgerwood, 'Changing Khmer Conceptions of Gender: Women, Stories and the Social Order' (PhD thesis, Cornell University, 1990).
3. F. Gas-Faucher, *En Sampan sur les lacs du Cambodge et à Angkor* (Typographie et Lithographie Barlatier, 1922), p. 17.
4. R. Nye, *Masculinity and Male Codes of Honour in Modern France* (Oxford University Press, 1993), pp. 7, 10, 217–9, 226.
5. M. L. Roberts, *Civilization without Sexes: Reconstructing Gender in Post-war France, 1917–1927* (Chicago University Press, 1994), p. 8.
6. F. Muel-Dreyfus, *Vichy et l'eternel féminin: contribution à une sociologie poli-tique de l'ordre des corps* (Seuil, 1996); E. Jennings, 'Reinventing Jeanne: The

Iconology of Joan of Arc in Vichy Schoolbooks, 1940–44', *Journal of Contemporary History*, 29 (1994), pp. 711–34.

7. Patrick H. Hutton, ed., *Historical Dictionary of the Third French Republic, 1870–1940* (Aldwych Press, 1986), pp. 377–9, 381.

8. Archives d'Outre Mer (henceforth AOM) INDO GGI 10044 Representative of Cambodia to Governor of Cochinchina, 15 July 1885.

9. L. Henrique, ed., *Les Colonies françaises: notices illustrées: III – colonies et protectorats d'Indo-Chine* (Maison Quantin, 1889), pp. 177–9; AOM INDO GGI 7678 Arrêté autorisant la Banque de l'Indo-Chine à émettre des billets au porteur de la valeur d'un piastre 3 August 1891.

10. R. Despierres, 'Le timbre-poste en Indochine', *Indochine Hebdomadaire Illustrée* (henceforth *IHI*), (11 November 1943), pp. 7–10.

11. R. Bertrand, 'David Dellepiane', in *L'Orient des Provençaux*, November 1982 – February 1983 (Vieille Charité, 1982), p. 31; *L'Exposition de Hanoi en 1902* (Les Actualités Diplomatiques et Coloniales, 1902).

12. AOM INDO GGI 23762 Mme de Villebon to GGI, July 1896.

13. A. le Fol, 'Souvenirs et notes sur la vie et l'œuvre d'Henri Russier', *Revue Indochinoise*, 12 (December 1918), pp. 481–97.

14. K. Alaimo, 'Adolescence, Gender and Class in Education Reform in France: The Development of Enseignement Primaire Supérieur, 1880–1910', *French Historical Studies*, 18, 4 (Autumn 1994), p. 1050.

15. S. Zeyons, *La Femme en 1900: les années 1900 par la carte postale* (Larousse, 1994), pp. 12–13.

16. P. Bergue, 'L'habitation européenne au Cambodge', *Revue Indochinoise*, 1905, 1, April 1905, p. 494.

17. F. Gouda, *Dutch Culture Overseas: Colonial Practice in the Netherlands Indies, 1900–1942* (Amsterdam University Press, 1995), pp. 75–117.

18. E. Heckel and C. Mandine, *L'Enseignement colonial en France et à l'étranger* (Balatier, 1907), pp. 50–1.

19. M. Phal, *The Young Concubine* (Random House, 1942), p. 142.

20. AOM INDO RSC 251 Association de Jeunes Filles de France Croix-Rose, Section du Cambodge (AJFFCRSC) to RSC 9 fevrier 1918; president of AJFFCRSC to M. Maurice Bloch, Paris, 22 October 1918.

21. 'L'emprunt national de 1917 en Indochine', *Revue Indochinoise*, 6, February 1918, p. 229.

22. M. Olivient, 'Femmes de France', ibid., 7, July 1918, pp. 62–3.

23. For convent schools, see Phal, *Young Concubine*, p. 142.

24. Hutton, *Historical Dictionary*, pp. 377–81.

25. See also Chapter 10 by A. Conklin in the present volume.

26. AOM INDO HCC 13 Minutes of Société de Protection Maternelle Infantile du Cambodge (henceforth SPMIC), 6 March 1941, 23 July 1943.

27. Roberts, *Civilisation without Sexes*, p. 20.

28. A. Hansen, 'Religious Identity in turn-of-the-century Cambodia' (paper presented at the Annual Meeting of the American Association of Asian Studies, Washington, 27–30 March 1998).

29. S. P. In, *Gatilok ou l'Art de bien se conduire*, vol. 3 (Editions de l'Institut Bouddhique, 1972), pp. 39–43.

30. See T. E. Barlow, 'Theorising Women: Funu, Guojia, Jiating (Chinese Women, Chinese State, Chinese Family)', in A. Zito and T. E. Barlow, eds.,

Body, Subject and Power in China (University of Chicago Press, 1994), pp. 254, 265; S. McHale, 'Printing and Power: Vietnamese Debates over Women's Place in Society, 1918–1934', in K. W. Taylor and J. K. Whitmore, eds., *Essays into Vietnamese Pasts* (Cornell University Press, 1993) p. 192.
31. M.-P. Ha, 'Engendering French Colonial History: The Case of Indochina', in *Historical Reflections*, 25, 1, 1999, p. 96 fn. 4, p. 114.
32. AOM INDO RSC 304, Rapport Général sur l'Enseignement au Cambodge, 10 January 1923, p. 39.
33. AOM INDO NF 259 Dossier 2226, Rapport sur l'Enseignement en Indochine, p. 9.
34. AOM INDO RSC 648, Extrait du Rapport Politique, Resident of Kompong Cham, 27 August 1928, p. 2.
35. Morizon, R. *Monographie du Cambodge* (Imprimerie d'Extrême-Orient, 1931), p. 185.
36. 'L'Ecole des Princesses', *Le Khmer*, 30 November 1936, p. 6.
37. K. Sotra, 'The Progress of Khmer Girls', *Nagaravatta*, 5 March 1938, pp. 1–2.
38. 'Rongwoen samrap krubangrien' ('Prizes for Teachers'), ibid., 3 December 1938, p. 1.
39. A. Kong, 'Boriyaka tngai siw' ('Saturday Report'), ibid., 15 May 1937, pp. 1, 3.
40. R. Griffiths, *Marshal Pétain* (Constable, 1970), p. 170.
41. *Le Temps*, 17 August 1940.
42. 'Le loyalisme de l'empire', *L'Avenir du Tonkin*, 19 January 1941, p. 1.
43. 'Camps de jeunesse', ibid., 14 February 1941.
44. 'Ralliement', ibid., 18 March 1941, p. 1.
45. Jennings, 'Reinventing Jeanne', pp. 728–30.
46. P. J. Kingston, 'Gerontocracy, Propaganda and Youth: Youth Propaganda in France 1940–1942', *French Cultural Studies*, 1, 3, October 1990, p. 206.
47. *Nagaravatta*, 14 May 1941, p. 1.
48. M. Ducoroy, *Ma Trahison en Indochine* (Les Editions Inter-Nationales, 1947), pp. 24–5.
49. *Nagaravatta*, 14 May 1941, p. 1.
50. A. Gallego *Jeanne d'Arc, la Sainte* (Haiphong, 1942); Christianus, 'Style propre du patriotisme chez une Fille de Dieu', *IHI*, 15 May 1941.
51. P. Andelle, 'Folklore et légendes du Cambodge: le génie Khléang-Muoeung', *IHI*, 21 November 1940, pp. 5–7.
52. 'Ompi virnieri barangmneak' ('About a French Woman'), *Kampuchea*, 4 December 1943, p. 1.
53. 'Karwiphiep champueh nieng san dark' ('The Power of St. Joan'), *Kampuchea*, May 1943.
54. 'Camp de Jeunesse Notre-Dame du Ba-Vi', *L'Avenir du Tonkin*, 6 June 1941.
55. Ducoroy, *Ma Trahison*, pp. 88–9; D. Marr, *Viet-Nam 1945: The Quest for Power* (University of California Press, 1995), p. 78.
56. Penh-Kunh-Ning, 'Muse Cambodgienne: Travail-famille-patrie', *IHI*, 22 May 1941.
57. 'Ompi sdrey jiet barangseh' ('About French Women'), *Nagaravatta*, 4 May 1940, p. 1.
58. 'Srey two mee pteah' ('Women as Heads of Home'), *Nagaravatta*, 11 May 1940, p. 1.
59. Muel-Dreyfus, *Vichy*, p. 271.

60. 'L'enseignement ménager va devenir obligatoire', *La Revue de la Famille*, 27 April 1942.

61. K. Frieson, 'Women, Power and the State' (unpublished paper presented at 'Cambodia: Power, Myth and Memory', Monash University Conference, 1996), p. 7.

62. 'Mien srey kmae prolong joap diet haey' ('Khmer girls have passed the exams again'), *Kampuchea*, 6 June 1942.

63. AOM INDO HCC 13, Minutes of SPMIC, 6 March 1941 and 23 July 1943; President SPMIC to RSC 11 and 21 May 1943; AOM INDO HCC 13: SPMIC *Toromien Mieda* (Imprimerie Henry, u.d.); President of the SPMIC to RSC, 23 July 1914, Decree no. 1338, 2 June 1944.

64. Marr, *Viet-Nam 1945*, p. 76.

65. Ducuroy, *Ma Trahison*, pp. 88–9.

66. 'Ompi Nieng Sandark' ('About St Joan'), *Kampuchea*, 13 May 1944, p. 1.

67. Baan Teng, 'Koorop campueh nieng san dark' ('In praise of Joan of Arc'), ibid., 13 May 1944.

68. 'Vicie mee pteah' ('Household science'), ibid., 30 June 1944.

69. 'Somleak bompeak kmae' ('Khmer Clothing'), ibid., 26 May 1944.

Part III
The Empire and Science

9
Miscegenation and the Popular Imagination

Owen White

French imaginations in the first half of the twentieth century were easily stirred by the subject of miscegenation – the interbreeding of people classified as belonging to different races. Miscegenation is an ugly word, which itself seems almost to imply that somebody has done something wrong. In fact, this was a commonly held view in early twentieth-century France, but, as I will be suggesting later, it does not tell the whole story. Much has been written on the subject of academic and scientific theories of race and miscegenation.[1] Here we are more interested in popular attitudes to miscegenation, in an attempt to elucidate parallels or differences between visions of empire in the minds of those who helped orchestrate and legitimise it, and of those who represented a quite different place in French life.

How are we to measure popular attitudes on this subject? Certainly, there were many novels in which miscegenation was a major theme. Pierre Loti's *Le Roman d'un Spahi*, published in 1881, was a best-seller. The book went through many editions, was turned into a musical in 1897 – surely a rather bleak evening's entertainment – and was still being reworked by other authors into the 1920s, for example in Louis-Charles Royer's *La Maîtresse Noire*. Such novels, though often receiving more attention than their literary qualities deserve, are interesting enough in themselves, and clearly their exotic settings and invariably prurient storylines provided appealing ready-made fantasies for a popular audience.[2]

Even so, the popularity of these literary sources does not seem to me to provide an especially reliable indicator of popular opinion about miscegenation. This is because such works tend to conform to a tragic trope with a long history behind it. From *Othello* through works by

Balzac such as *Le Nègre* and *Le Vicaire des Ardennes*, and indeed, right up to recent films like *Jungle Fever* by Spike Lee, convention dictates that sex across the racial divide invariably comes to no good, and very often ends in the violent death of one or both of the protagonists. In fact, tragic endings to racially mixed romances continue to resonate, perhaps offering a clue to why many people prefer the MI6-conspiracy theory explanation of the death of Princess Diana and Dodi al-Fayed over the banal drunken-driver explanation. Surely this was a tragedy which could hardly have been better designed to conform to the literary trope of inevitable death that foredooms miscegenists. Certainly a French author writing that particular fairy tale in the late nineteenth or early twentieth century would have emphasised the point that their relationship crossed racial boundaries.

A further problem is presented by the fact that whether we are talking about fiction or the parallel fiction of biological speculation about the pros or more usually the cons of miscegenation, opinions expressed on the subject in the late nineteenth and early twentieth centuries are almost always expressed by men.[3] Women, of course, were expected to remain silent on the subject of their sexuality. [4] However, there are at least two compelling sources from the period in question in which women do express opinions on the subject of miscegenation – in articles in French women's magazines, and in an odd cache of letters written by French women to West African soldiers in the Second World War. These somewhat interstitial sources offer an opportunity to understand French women's own theories on miscegenation, sexuality and race, and to judge the potency of racial propaganda and images of blacks which were generated by the architects and theorists of empire.

'Would you marry a man of colour?'

In 1920 a women's illustrated daily magazine called *Eve* – the forerunner of *Elle* magazine – invited its readers to write an essay on the subject 'Would you marry a man of colour?'[5] Before putting this question to its readers, the magazine canvassed the opinions of 35 representatives of the Parisian literati, all but 2 of them men. Several referred to the recent use by France of black troops in the First World War. The novelist Charles-Henry Hirsch claimed that 'thousands' of white women had had relationships with black men as a result of this.[6] The poet Hugues Delorme replied in verse that having defended the homes of the French people, blacks should in return be free to build their own homes in France. Besides, he added, it was better for a French woman to marry a black man than a *boche* (German).[7] The feminist playwright Madame Rachilde wrote that if the events of the past few years had been the product of so-called culture and civilisation, and that if black people were closer to man's animal ancestry than whites, then she would prefer a black man, or, failing that, a monkey. In any case, she argued, the 'natural savage' would be better for reproductive purposes.[8]

The theme of breeding interested other respondents too. Charles-Henry Hirsch noted that cattle-breeders knew the advantages of cross-breeding. There is a suspicion here that people are toying with an answer to the problem of France's low birth-rate and of replacing the losses experienced during the war. Others, however, expressed concern about French civilisation being bastardised. The novelist J-H. Rosny *aîné* contended that there had never been a black civilisation, that blacks were prolific and as a result he could understand their poor treatment in the United States.[9] Others invoked the 'purity' of the blood. Professor Charles Richet of the faculty of medicine at the Sorbonne asked how much cheap wine could be poured into a bottle of Château Lafite 1873. Richet, a former winner of the Nobel prize for physiology, was here restating his unequivocal opposition to miscegenation as set down in his book *La Sélection Humaine*, published in 1919.[10]

Contact between white women and black men was in fact quite a live issue in 1920 when the *Eve* survey was carried out. The debate centred on the posting of French colonial troops to the left bank of the Rhine after the war. This aroused fierce opposition in Germany. Hitler wrote in *Mein Kampf* that 'the main artery of the German people flows through the playground of black African hordes' – once again calling up the image of the purity of the nation's blood, with the word 'hordes' likewise evoking the supposed prolificity of blacks. An American campaign against the so-called 'Horror on the Rhine' was founded, while British opposition was led by the radical politician E. D. Morel, who criticised those who 'thrust barbarians...with tremendous sexual instincts...into the heart of Europe.'[11] In Britain itself, one of the reasons given for the race riots which broke out in Liverpool and Cardiff in 1919 was that black seamen had been forming relationships with white women.[12] In Germany, too, despite the opposition to the black presence along the Rhine, German women engaged in relations with black troops. The children born of these unions were among the first groups to be sterilised after the Nazis came to power in 1933.[13]

To return to the survey in *Eve* magazine, when the presumably largely middle-class readership was asked whether it would marry a 'man of colour' – a phrase which seems to have been generally interpreted to mean a black man – out of 2040 replies, 1060 readers answered 'no', while 980 said yes, they would marry a black man.[14] The results were compiled by the writer Paul Reboux, whose recently published novel *Romulus Coucou* centred on a very light-skinned, mixed-race man in the United States who has a relationship with a white woman, and who, somewhat predictably, is eventually put to death by a lynch mob.[15] Reboux's sympathies lay with the 'yes' camp, although as will be seen the difference in attitude between those who answered 'yes' and those who answered 'no' could be quite minimal.

One of the main reasons for answering 'no' concerned the children that would be born of such a union. Many feared that mixed-race children would risk being rejected by society in later life, which seems a reasonable enough viewpoint given the prevailing racist ethos of the day. It is perhaps not coincidental that only one of the male minor celebrities who offered their opinions to *Eve* magazine stopped to consider what would become of the children.[16] Other women were unsure that their maternal instincts would be the same with a mixed-race child. 'I like *café au lait*, but not in a cradle,' wrote one. Some spoke of blacks' 'natural savagery'. This idea could actually have been fed by the experience of the First World War. As early as 1915, the Germans were making official complaints about France's use of black troops, whom they accused of taking heads, fingers and ears as trophies, and of killing wounded soldiers.[17] Far from seeking to contradict these accusations, the French used them as a way of spreading fear among German troops.[18]

Other respondents claimed that the addition of white blood did nothing to improve the 'brutal and perfidious' black race, because mixed-race people were unstable, whimsical and incapable of decisive action and achievement. These characteristically degenerate traits had long been ascribed to people of mixed race by social scientists and physiologists. For example, Louis Vignon, a lecturer at the Ecole Coloniale, wrote typically in 1919 that people of mixed race were infertile hybrids made unstable by the 'conflict of heredities'.[19] Such ideas were reiterated by those opposing coloured immigration into France in the inter-war period, and these stereotypes also bedeviled the lives of mixed-race people in France's colonies.[20]

Some women cited physical repugnance as a reason for not marrying a black man. They spoke of their horror of light palms, flat noses, big lips – all features so often caricatured when images of blacks were used in contemporary advertising. *Eve* magazine itself was regularly carrying an advertisement for shoe-heels at this time depicting blacks in just such a caricatured fashion. In the absence of direct contact with black people to contradict these caricatures, such responses are not surprising. One reply came from an eleven-year-old girl, whose entry earned her 100 francs for the fourth best essay. She wrote that she would agree to marry a black man later in life, but added:

> I don't think I'd find it very nice to have dinner opposite a black man. In any event I wouldn't want him to eat without putting on white gloves, because he'd always give me the impression that he hadn't washed his hands, and perhaps even that he'd make his napkin or the tablecloth dirty. Apart from that, if I loved him, I don't see what would stop me being happy with him, and I would simply wipe my cheeks after he'd kissed me.[21]

This seems to betray primarily a middle-class obsession with cleanliness, but the girl's impression of black people could have been reinforced by any number of soap advertisements from the time showing blacks scrubbing their skins in an effort to turn themselves white.[22]

What of the 980 women who said they would marry a black man? Some asserted simply that love is blind. Many others gave reasons which offered a more benign view of black people than those who answered 'no', yet which followed a racist logic nonetheless. Some, for example, wrote that blacks were naturally athletic and that they therefore only produced strong and robust children. This at least made a change from the more usual accusation of degenerate physical debility levelled at mixed-race children. Others stated that their physical repugnance at black people would soon wear off once they became used to them, and anyway, what was described as the 'special odour' of blacks was less disgusting than the breath of an alcoholic. Moreover, some observed, the potential for savagery existed in all men. In the majority of these responses, a perhaps well-meaning and broadly liberal outlook was nonetheless accompanied by an axiomatic belief in white superiority. For some, to marry a black man and attempt to improve him would be an act of charity, a personal mission to civilise. Others had less lofty ambitions. In the wake of the war, some women felt that their options were few. 'Quick, a husband, yellow, black, brown or red,' wrote one: 'Faute de grives, on mange des merles' ('beggars can't be choosers').

Most of these women, it seems clear, had had little or no direct contact with black people. One confessed that she had never known a black person, and that the only case of marriage between a coloured man and a white woman of which she knew was between Othello and Desdemona, which, as she noted, had not been a great success. So some perhaps did look to literary works as offering some kind of practical wisdom, which may contradict my earlier caveat about the value of literary evidence. But a few respondents did have personal experience upon which to draw. The woman who won second prize for her essay was married to a black man. She wrote that on meeting her future husband she developed a peculiar obsession to find out whether his feet were as light as the palms of his hands. Her curiosity satisfied, she professed herself very happy with her husband and their child. The winner of the prize for best essay was married to a mixed-race man. She confessed that she had been worried at first about having a coloured baby, but now that her son was four she felt able to say 'I love him despite all the worries he has caused me. Je ne regrette rien.'

Love in the time of war

France's use of African troops during both world wars brought many French women into contact with black men for the first time. In the First World War, according to the testimony of one Guinean *tirailleur*, the French authorities were anxious to prevent this contact.[23] But despite their best efforts it seems to some extent to have happened anyway. A report on the barracks at Fréjus, where many West African troops were posted, claimed in 1916 that the *tirailleurs'* sense of well-being had been improved by contact with local women, who 'take delight in spoiling them. Some of them go even further...'[24] A less direct but perhaps more common link was made by the institution of so-called *'marraines de guerre'* during the Second World War, where French women would sign up to look after individual soldiers. They would act as pen-pals, send gifts and sometimes arrange to meet up with their adopted 'godchildren'.[25] For one woman from Melun, this led in 1945 to an awkward exchange with her 'godson' once he had returned to his home in Niamey in Niger:

> My dear friend, I was surprised and saddened to read your letter. I didn't think your affection for your second godmother had become what seems to be a deeper and more serious feeling. I am distressed to reply that my affection for you is that of a *soeur-marraine*, if you grasp the shade of meaning, and that, if I surrounded you with kind thoughts in letters, if I wanted to meet you in Paris, it was only that you should feel understood and comforted by a young French woman who loves her colonial Empire and who wants to pay homage to those who, like you, have abandoned everything in good faith for

France. I am deeply sorry if my attitude may have seemed provocative to you ... as you know I hate 'messing around' with young people and our friendship seemed to me wholesome and safe, as I knew you to be respectful and sincere. I am sorry that you should have wished for a more personal union of the heart, and I beg your pardon.

Though some women wanted their involvement with black men to remain 'wholesome and safe' (*'saine et sans danger'*), there were others who did form serious relationships. As with the letter just quoted, we are able to gain an insight into some of these because in 1945 and 1946 the French authorities were intercepting correspondence between French women and former *tirailleurs* who had returned to West Africa. These letters survive in the Senegalese national archives in Dakar.[26]

French officialdom was less than enthusiastic when confronted with requests from women to go to West Africa to rejoin men who in some cases they had married during the war.[27] Governor-General Cournarie of French West Africa wrote to the colonial minister in July 1945 that he was not in favour of French women going to live in villages in the bush (*'en brousse'*), adding that for them to live with the natives could only have 'deplorable effects', though he did not specify what these might be. One such relationship involved a 30-year-old Dahomean who served in the resistance, was arrested by the Gestapo and later received the *croix de guerre*. He married a 52-year-old war widow from Dijon and returned to await her in Dahomey. Governor Legendre of Dahomey wrote to the Governor-General that she would not be able to live comfortably in the colony with her considerably younger husband, but as it happened she ignored this official disapproval and went anyway. Unfortunately the sources do not reveal whether the relationship was a success.[28]

On the other hand, the authorities were less concerned about *tirailleurs* who had married French women and who wished to remain in France. In one such case a Senegalese man, Joseph N'Diaye, met a Mademoiselle Renaud from Tarascon. They continued to see each other regularly throughout his posting in the south of France, and N'Diaye stated that he was also welcomed by her employers, and regularly ate at their table. Nine months after their first meeting she had a son, whom N'Diaye formally recognised as his own. Late in 1945 he was repatriated to Dakar, from where he sent her coffee, cocoa, rice and soap. He also planned to send half his salary from his new job in the customs office. The police commissioner in Dakar gave favourable information on N'Diaye, and the colonial minister wrote to Governor-General

Cournarie that he approved his request to return to France to regularise his union with Mademoiselle Renaud and to provide for their son. They also discussed the possibility of helping N'Diaye to find work when he got there.

Other relationships did not end in reunion. One woman from Fréjus wrote to Governor-General Cournarie trying to track down her Senegalese husband. He was traced to Foundiougne, where he was discovered to earn very little. In any case, he claimed that they were not even married, that his alleged wife was resident in a brothel in Draguignan and that he never wanted to see her again. Another woman from Vittel wished to be reunited with her Dahomean fiancé, by whom she had had a child. The Governor-General and the governor of Dahomey agreed that there was nothing to stop him rejoining her in France, beyond the fact that he showed little inclination to do so. She remained convinced as late as October 1948 that only a lack of room on the boat was preventing his return to France, where she and her child were living on the breadline.

Finally, in March 1945 a Breton woman had some important news for her 'godson' in Côte d'Ivoire concerning her friend, Madame Lambert:

> My dear godson, Madame Lambert has just had a little girl, but alas it's the work of Jean Traoré, she's not very black but she'll have the same frizzy hair, she didn't deserve that, she was so good for him, it'll be a broken home now, she's asked me to be the godmother, you know me, I'm too good, I didn't refuse, the baptism's on Saturday. I'll keep you a box of sugared almonds and one for Gaston, and if possible I'll send some things later, because though you're far away you'll always have a part in our celebrations here. Don't talk about this to anyone because Monsieur Lambert is very pleased with his little girl and doesn't know what's happened.

Beyond the obvious, one of the most striking things about this letter is its tone of easy familiarity and the phrase 'you'll always have a part in our celebrations here.'

Between the wars and under the Vichy regime, a man named René Martial wrote books which condemned miscegenation in language little altered from that used by the so-called 'father of racist ideology', Arthur de Gobineau, almost a century earlier. Among other things, Martial claimed that whites felt a natural repugnance which would prevent them from ever having relations with black or 'oriental' people.[29] As the examples given above make clear, this was not a view shared by all white women; and yet Martial held influential views in the fields of public health and immigration, views which, particularly if the Vichy regime had survived longer, might well have led to the kinds of sterilisations seen under the Nazi regime.[30]

It is not possible for us to know whether the women described here having relationships with West African soldiers were untouched by racism; it is not my intention to reclaim or identify populist heroines from the past. What we can say, however, is that these women almost certainly did not care about the views of the likes of René Martial, writing from his Institute of Anthroposociology in Paris, and, more importantly, that they certainly had views of their own. As historians we can deconstruct the published writings of racists as much as we like. Life as it is lived, on the other hand, is far less easily uncovered; and on the occasions when it is uncovered it does not always match our expectations. The racist theories and ideologies so clearly visible in a broad range of printed sources may not necessarily have manifested themselves in the imaginations of magazine-reading women who could consider the question of love across the racial divide, or in the day-to-day interaction between whites and blacks in a nation markedly changed by the experience of empire.

Notes and references

1. On this question see my own analysis, *Children of the French Empire. Miscegenation and Colonial Society in French West Africa, 1895–1960* (Oxford University Press, 1999), esp. ch. 4; also P.-A. Taguieff, 'Doctrines de la race et hantise du métissage. Fragments d'une histoire de la mixophobie savante', *Nouvelle Revue de l'Ethnopsychiatrie*, 17, 1991, pp. 53–100.
2. On the nineteenth century see W. B. Cohen, 'Literature and Race: Nineteenth-Century French Fiction, Blacks and Africa, 1800–1880', *Race and Class*, 16, (1974), pp. 181–205.
3. There are exceptions to this, of course; Clotilde Chivas-Baron is a notable example, although her novel *Confidences de Métisse* (Fasquelle, 1926) conforms to the 'doomed relationship' pattern described earlier.
4. For a good example of how men elaborate on subjects concerning women that are considered indecent for women themselves to speak about, see N. Etherington, 'Natal's Black Rape Scare of the 1870s', *Journal of Southern African Studies*, 15, (1988), pp. 36–53.
5. *Eve* ('Le premier quotidien illustré de la femme'), 5 March 1920.
6. *Eve*, 26 February 1920.
7. *Eve*, 27 February 1920.
8. *Eve*, 26 February 1920.
9. *Eve*, 28 February 1920.
10. The Château Lafite reference appears in *Eve*, 26 February 1920. See also C. Richet, *La Sélection humaine* (F. Alcan, 1919). For more on Richet, see

W. H. Schneider, *Quality and Quantity. The Quest for Biological Regeneration in Twentieth-Century France* (Cambridge University Press, 1990), pp. 109–13.

11. K. L. Nelson, 'The "Black Horror on the Rhine": Race as a Factor in Post-World War I Diplomacy', *Journal of Modern History*, 42, 1970, pp. 606–27; S. Marks, 'Black Watch on the Rhine: A Study in Propaganda, Prejudice and Prurience', *European Studies Review*, 13, 1983, pp. 297–334.

12. P. B. Rich, *Race and Empire in British Politics*, 2nd edn (Cambridge University Press, 1990), pp. 120–1.

13. See P. Weindling, *Health, Race and German Politics between National Unification and Nazism, 1870–1945* (Cambridge University Press, 1989), pp. 385–8, 530, 533.

14. *Eve*, 28 March 1920.

15. P. Reboux, *Romulus Coucou* (Flammarion, 1920). Liberal French writers seem often to have reassured themselves that colour prejudice was someone else's problem; the American setting for Reboux's novel is typical in this regard.

16. This apparent insouciance is evident in the sexual relations of French men with West African women in the colonial period; see White, *Children of the French Empire*, ch. 2.

17. Institut de France, Paris, Fonds Terrier, 5920: 'Emploi contraire au droit des gens par l'Angleterre et la France de troupes de couleur sur le théâtre de guerre', Berlin, July 1915.

18. M. Echenberg, *Colonial Conscripts. The Tirailleurs Sénégalais in French West Africa, 1857–1960* (Heinemann, 1991), p. 37.

19. L. Vignon, *Un Programme de politique coloniale. Les Questions indigènes* (Plon-Nourrit, 1919), p. 369.

20. White, *Children of the French Empire*, esp. ch. 4; on opposition to immigration, see Schneider, *Quality and Quantity*.

21. *Eve*, 19 March 1920.

22. For examples see *Négripub. L'Image des noirs dans la publicité depuis un siècle* (Somogy, 1992), p. 59.

23. J. H. Lunn, 'Kande Kamara Speaks: An Oral History of the West African Experience in France 1914–18', in M. E. Page, ed., *Africa and the First World War* (Macmillan, 1987), pp. 36–8.

24. Archives Nationales du Sénégal, Dakar (ANS), 4D 70, report on the Camp de Fréjus-Saint-Raphaël, 25 November 1916.

25. N. E. Lawler, *Soldiers of Misfortune. Ivoirien Tirailleurs of World War II* (Ohio University Press, 1992), pp. 69, 72–4.

26. ANS, Fonds Moderne (FM), 4D 61.

27. For similar concerns after the First World War, see R. Schor, *L'Opinion Française et les Etrangers 1919–1939* (Publications de la Sorbonne, 1985), p. 130.

28. This and all following examples from ANS, FM, 4D 61. All names of private individuals changed.

29. R. Martial, *Les Métis* (Flammarion, 1942), p. 46. Gobineau claimed that miscegenation was the fundamental cause of the irreversible decline of civilisation. See M. D. Biddiss, *Father of Racist Ideology. The Social and Political Thought of Count Gobineau* (Weidenfeld & Nicolson, 1970).

30. On Martial's influence see Schneider, *Quality and Quantity*, pp. 230–55.

10
Faire Naître *v.* Faire du Noir: Race Regeneration in France and French West Africa, 1895–1940

Alice L. Conklin

This chapter seeks to raise questions for further research about the relationship between certain policies adopted in the metropole and their colonial counterparts under the Third Republic. I contrast a variety of public hygiene, health care and maternalist initiatives taken by the French at home between 1895 and 1940 to combat depopulation with similar policies adopted by the French in West Africa to develop, or '*mettre en valeur*' their inadequate colonial labour force. Through this comparison I hope to establish three points. The first is that the overseas measures in question did echo similar trends in France, where a scientifically based social hygiene and pro-natalist movement, aimed at improving both the quantity and the quality of the French population, began to emerge during the Belle Epoque and reached its fullest expression in the inter-war years. Despite this superficial similarity – and this will be my second point – hygiene and race betterment discourse and policies in West Africa revealed a different underlying logic from that in France. At home, the approach to health care remained, with one important exception, 'individualised', while overseas the French thought primarily in terms of bettering the 'race' as a whole. The important exception to individualised health care in France was the treatment of women. My final point will be that, especially in the inter-war years, women in France were increasingly objectified as mothers at the service of the state in ways that appear quite close to the vision of all Africans as so many units of labour at the disposal of the French colonial administration. Here I hasten to add that although the reactions of French women or African subjects to such objectification do not unfortunately figure in what follows, I certainly do not assume that they experienced these measures passively.

These points raise a number of interesting questions about how best to figure the relations between race and gender, and citizenship and subjecthood, in a French nation that was both republican and colonial in the early twentieth century. It is now common knowledge that French republicanism, from its inception in 1792 through the entire period of the Third Republic, was fundamentally grounded in gendered and racialised constructs of the nation and citizen.[1] The dynamic of republican nationalism drew upon the image of the individual white male citizen as the representative and protector of the nation. The nation itself was embodied in the female, whose principal role as *citoyenne* was 'mother of the nation'. To her fell the task of reproducing the unique French 'race' and those domestic institutions essential to the proper education of the future male citizen.[2] Working outside the home, then, was naturally suspect, since it could occur only at the expense of the 'race' and the nation. At times of perceived national decline, such as after the Franco-Prussian War and again after the First World War, women to a greater extent than men became the objects of special reforms designed to heighten fertility – to '*faire naître*' to borrow the phrase of the inter-war pro-natalists – and thus to regenerate the nation and preserve the race.[3]

What were the implications of these ideological constructs for the peoples inhabiting '*la plus grande France*'? Was the nationalist rhetoric of racial regeneration, and the intensified objectification of women that accompanied it in inter-war France, influenced, in fact perhaps determined, by an older and more extreme tradition of objectifying the other in colonies like French West Africa? The colonies by definition were an arena in which the human subject was conceived differently from within the *hexagone*. Only in France were men fully active self-determining subjects with a claim to citizenship; the African male was conceived as a passive subject of the state, and Africans were first and foremost "resource" races to be mobilised by the French at will.[4] Their lack of subjectivity was captured by a comparable phrase to the '*faire naître*' slogan levied in France in the 1920s and 1930s. In West Africa, a similar policy of race regeneration was called '*faire du noir*', a phrase obviously more pejorative and more racist than '*faire naître*'. How to understand the difference between these phrases, and how to read the language of race and its particular implications for women and the colonised in the discussion of health at home and overseas at the turn of the century and beyond, are issues to which I will return in my conclusion.

A hallmark of the Third Republic was an abiding concern with the biological regeneration of the nation. Several developments fed this concern early in the life of the Republic: defeat in 1870 and the outbreak of the Commune, both of which were blamed on the degeneration of the populace; the Pasteurian or bacteriological revolution, which in the 1880s dramatically changed the way doctors, hygienists, and politicians thought about disease by suggesting that it could be controlled and even prevented through vaccination coupled with improved salubrity; and the declining birth-rate, which made the preservation and improvement of France's population a matter of national security.[5] As early as 1874 the declining birth-rate led to the passage of the Roussel law, which sought to combat infant mortality by creating a system of medical supervision of children placed out to nurse.[6] The 1890s brought additional and broader reforms, this time in the realm of public health and medical care. For example, in 1893 a national medical assistance law was voted, guaranteeing in theory all needy citizens free medical care at home.[7] More innovative still were the changes occurring within the public health community. An increasingly professional group of hygienists, many of whom were doctors, saw themselves first and foremost as sanitary engineers who knew how to tackle and resolve health problems which had eluded their predecessors, and whose job it was to enforce uniform health standards throughout France. The reforms they sought included routine inspection of lodgings, the reporting of contagious diseases, mandatory disinfection and vaccination, the creation and enforcement of building codes, required permits for construction and habitation, wider jurisdiction over landlords, more precise definitions of insalubrity and clear lines of effective authority in matters of health.[8] These demands directly challenged existing ideas about privacy and property rights and threatened, if enacted, to expand vastly the power of the state over the individual.

Because of the perceived threat to liberalism, public health reform in France was limited before the First World War. Its most impressive achievement was the passage in 1902 of the first new hygiene bill since 1850, in which many, but certainly not all, of the demands of professional hygienists were met. Those measures which promised to lower mortality rates, thereby converging with national security objectives, were enacted. The 1902 bill set uniform standards of salubrity for all of France, stiffened penalties for infractions, and codified and updated regulations for the control and reporting of all contagious diseases. The legislation was, however, less impressive when it came to enacting the necessary means to enforce the new regulations. The conservative

Senate, always defensive of property rights, insisted that mayors, rather than professionals working exclusively for the state, be entrusted with the new health administration. As hygienists pointed out at the time, these mayors would have had to have been 'veritable heroes' to apply annoying and costly regulation to the constituency which elected them.[9]

At practically the same moment that the 1902 public health bill was passed in France, a social hygiene movement began to take shape under private auspices. In 1902, the director of the Pasteur Institute delivered a series of lectures entitled 'Hygiene Sociale,' and in 1904 a Social Hygiene Alliance was founded at the Musée Social. Social hygiene was an offshoot of the public health movement and in the years immediately preceding and following the First World War it was particularly influential. The specific agenda of social hygiene, at least at the outset, was not simply to preserve the race but to perfect it. Social hygiene 'envisages illnesses not in themselves but from the social viewpoint; that is from the point of view of their repercussions on society'.[10] In practice, this meant targeting, and preventing, three diseases in particular: the so-called social diseases of tuberculosis, alcoholism and syphilis. It also meant doing everything possible to increase the birthrate and lower infant mortality. Social hygienists thus added their voices to the chorus of those – radical republicans, women's organisations, physicians and eugenicists – who had been advocating maternal and child welfare programmes in France since the 1890s as a way of fighting depopulation. Their victory culminated in the 1913 passage of the Strauss law, extending maternity leave and benefits for the first time to all working women. The passage of this maternalist legislation revealed how compelling the demographic crisis had become to a significant number of social referees, and to legislators in particular, by the eve of the First World War.[11]

It was nevertheless only in the inter-war years that the Third Republic, reeling from the loss of over 1.3 million men and obsessed more than ever with depopulation, actively committed its resources to achieving both social hygiene objectives: the eradication of social diseases and the quantitative and qualitative improvement of the French population. In 1920, the government founded the first cabinet-level health ministry, the Ministère de l'Hygiène, de l'Assistance et de la Prévoyance Sociale (later renamed the Ministère de la Santé Publique.) 1920 also witnessed the creation of a national Ecole de Puériculture to teach mothers how to breast-feed and care for their newborns, as well as the passage of the famous July 31 law against abortion, and the advertising and sale of contraceptives. In 1922 a corps of visiting nurses was created whose mission was to teach French women basic hygiene in their homes.[12] In 1923, the teaching of puericulture was made mandatory for all school-girls. The following year the government created, with help from the American Rockefeller Foundation, the National Social Hygiene Office. One of the office's goals was

> the establishment in France and in the colonies of a continuous and methodical propaganda to the public, in order to make known the hygiene and prophylactic measures necessary for the maintenance of health, the fight against social diseases and the preservation of the race.

By 1931, the office was a well-financed, multi-faceted bureaucracy which helped coordinate the fight not only for a higher birth-rate, but also against venereal disease, tuberculosis and alcoholism, as well as cancer, typhoid fever, diphtheria, infant mortality and mental illness.[13] Finally, social insurance laws and family allowance laws were passed in 1930, 1932 and 1938 respectively, with the specific goal of combatting depopulation by providing monthly allowances for children. In addition, these laws guaranteed all women pre- and post-natal care. Such laws revealed the national importance now attached to the health of the mother and child in particular, and families in general.[14]

There can be little doubt that the inter-war programme of disease prevention, prophylaxis and repopulation represented a new way of conceptualising health care in France which appeared to put the greater public interest ahead of private interests. During these years French society became both more medicalised and maternalistic.[15] Doctors were no longer to wait for patients to come to them. Their job was to identify those persons who were contagious without even knowing it, to isolate or neutralise them, thereby protecting their families and society at large. Women, glorified as mothers more than ever in the anti-feminist backlash of the First World War, were to do their part by producing more, and healthier, children and by accepting the supervision by doctors and legislators of their reproductive and child-rearing functions. To accomplish these goals, state-sponsored propaganda and education were not enough. Medical personnel were to enter the households of the masses and make sure that the appropriate measures were being taken. Yet, for all the public health campaigns launched and new legislation passed in the inter-war years, the social aspect of this new approach to medicine must not be exaggerated. This at least is the argument of

William Schneider; in his book on French eugenics, Schneider maintains that, as memories of the war faded, the tendency was once again in France to view health and hygiene in France from the perspective of the individual, specific case, rather than from that of society or the race as a whole.[16] While this conclusion remains problematic when the case of women is considered, the notion that in France health care remained individualised in the inter-war years provides a useful point of departure for considering the rather different French policies of human *mise en valeur* applied in West Africa in this same period.

The interest in biological regeneration evident in France between 1890 and 1940 sheds light on how science and politics intersected in the metropole in the modern era. This intersection is even more starkly exposed in the French West African context, where health and demographic issues were always of concern to the French administration. More than any other overseas territory, sub-Saharan Africa had a reputation for insalubrity, which had to be overcome to attract French capital and a limited number of white settlers. In French West Africa, for example, regeneration of the inadequate local labour force wracked by disease was essential for extracting the colony's resources. The French estimated that there were only about 12 million inhabitants, whose health and fertility had further deteriorated since contact with Europeans. These considerations produced from the outset a discourse on developing their African human capital, reminiscent of the social hygiene movement in France.

French public health measures in West Africa can be divided into two periods: 1902–14, and the inter-war years. In the first period, the emphasis was primarily on making the colony salubrious for Europeans; after the war a new interest emerged in also addressing the medical needs of Africans. In both periods, however, health and hygiene issues were a central preoccupation. No sooner had the Government-General (founded in 1895) been reorganised in 1902, than it established as one of its principal departments a Service de Santé, almost twenty years before a comparable ministry was established in France. In 1904, the provisions of the 1902 metropolitan law on public health were applied to West Africa, but with important modifications.[17] Administrators in Africa were profoundly influenced by the discovery in 1899 that the two diseases perhaps most feared by Europeans – malaria and yellow fever – were mosquito-borne, and that these mosquitoes could only breed in small pools of stagnant water. This discovery revolutionised public hygiene in the colonies; instead of quarantining whole cities, the French now endorsed such preventive measures as eliminating all standing water, using screens in hospitals and homes to keep mosquitoes away from infected patients, and segregating the French and African populations.[18]

The 1904 decree reflected the new emphasis on prevention. Administrators were given powers far greater than their metropolitan counterparts to enter private and public dwellings, French or African, to regulate sanitary conditions and to punish all infractions. Even while acknowledging urban salubrity to be their first priority, however, the French admitted that their goal of improved public health would never be achieved until they had also developed a comprehensive health care programme for the 'decimated' and 'ravaged' African masses. Accordingly, in 1905 a Native Medical Assistance Service was founded to provide free medical care to the colonised and instruct them in general hygiene. Such ameliorating measures as up-to-date dispensaries, vaccination centres and hospitals were envisioned – and a few were actually built – before the First World War.[19]

Before the war, then, there was interest, but little urgency, in the issue of African health care and hygiene. The post-war years tell a different story. A change in both tone and policy emerge. This change can be partially attributed to the introduction of conscription in West Africa during the First World War, which for the first time revealed how 'ravaged' and 'decimated' the African populations were. In addition, the government was now determined to intensify cash crop production; the more fit and numerous their subjects, the greater the potential profits. These considerations led to an aggressive inter-war policy of social hygiene and '*médecine en profondeur*' the goal of which was, in the words of the French administration, the 'qualitative and quantitative development of our native races'.[20] As these words suggest, this new programme had much in common with what was happening in the metropole. It nevertheless differed in one respect: according to a ministerial circular of 1924, it focused on 'the treatment not of individuals but of the race'.[21]

The first sign of change in health care policy came in 1921, when the local administration acknowledged that, given its limited resources, it was impossible both to introduce better hygiene and to provide individualised medical care to their subjects. Priority would henceforth be given to what the French deemed the more urgent of the two: 'urban salubrity, better food, clothing and lodging, prophylaxis against the major endemic and epidemic diseases, and the fight against infant mortality'.[22] Important circulars throughout the 1920s and 1930s reiterated this preference for hygiene measures that aimed at the collectivity rather than the individual. 'It is from the viewpoint of public interest that the social question must be considered. In our colonies, should not a concern for public health . . . take precedence over the obsession for complicated treatments which an individual . . . might need?'[23] To 'increase and preserve the race', another official maintained, 'it is essential . . . not to try and combat . . . all causes of infant mortality, but to attack *les grands fléaux de la race* ('the great scourges of the race').[24]

Such 'preservation of the race' implied several new measures. Particular attention would be paid to extending medical care *en profondeur* to the rural masses. The preference in the 1920s was for *dispensaires-maternités* and mobile medical teams, rather than general hospitals devoted to caring for all the sick; hospital admissions actually declined in West Africa between 1926 and 1931, at a time when, thanks to the new *assurances sociales*, hospitalisation was on the increase in France.[25] The African dispensary and mobile units were to specialise in identifying and combatting the great endemic and epidemic diseases as well as promoting preventative hygiene and vaccination. New research laboratories for studying tropical diseases were built. As in France, a corps of visiting African nurses was created, with the mission to demonstrate proper hygiene in the home. Governors were to spend as much as 12 per cent of their budgets on the public health effort, and to start keeping demographic statistics. Special guidelines were issued to protect the health of African workers employed either by the colonial administration or by private companies.[26]

By the early 1930s, a particularly strong emphasis on lowering infant mortality among Africans also began to emerge, and with it maternalist health policies aimed for the first time specifically at women. 'I wish', the minister wrote, 'the Governor-General to personally take an interest in the development of assistance . . . which will profit children'.[27] The French trained more African midwives, built more maternity wards, began sending girls as well as boys to school and offered more extensive pre-natal and post-natal care in their clinics. As one administrator put it: 'it has been observed everywhere that the best way to have beautiful children is to care for ['*ménager*'] the mother;' and, he concluded, 'keeping young girls in school longer in order to teach them hygiene and puericulture can be extremely beneficial to the future of the race'.[28] However, a 1940 report noted that women were much more apt to let doctors examine their children than themselves.[29] By 1940, 130 *maternités* and 12 puericulture dispensaries had been built, and 800 consultation centres created.[30] Pre-natal consultations, of which records only began to be kept in 1929, increased from 6104 to almost 470 000 in 1937.[31]

In 1904, the Governor-General claimed that 'providing Africans with the care and medicine they needed' was one of the duties that republican France owed itself to fulfil as a civilised nation.[32] By the 1920s and 1930s, administrators changed their language and began referring routinely to their 'civilising work of sanitary protection and amelioration of the races'.[33] The crude term for this policy shift was *'faire du noir'*.[34] While social hygiene and related welfare measures in France in the same period, with their natalist and prophylactic preoccupations, might conceivably be described as a policy of *'faire du blanc'*, needless to say the term was never used. The closest policy makers at home came was to insist that *'il faut faire naître'*.

And just how close was that? At first glance, not really close at all. Whatever superficial coincidence in phraseology, the policies implemented made clear that in metropolitan France it was never forgotten, even at the height of the demographic crisis and despite the routine references to preserving and improving the 'race', that the population was made up of individuals. The colonised, in contrast, were defined first and foremost as members of a race.[35] A closer scrutiny, however, suggests that things are not so neat. For it cannot be forgotten that the individual in the metropole was itself a gendered as well as a racialised construct. In the late Third Republic's rapidly medicalising society, women as well as men may have felt that most of their particular health care problems were increasingly being addressed. This said, there can be no question that, because of their unique ability to give birth, women in at least one realm saw their own interests subordinated to the larger interests of society and the state to a larger degree than before the war. The maternalist *'faire naître'* discourse and policies of the inter-war years, which I have too summarily reviewed here, conceptualised French women not as self-determining individuals, but as so many wombs in the service of the nation. While men too saw some of their autonomy as individuals curtailed by this rhetoric and were seen increasingly as fathers first and foremost, their political rights were never threatened.[36]

This observation brings me back to the colonies, and more specifically to the exact nature of the relationship between the metropole and the empire, between citizenship and subjecthood, with which I began. Much of this chapter has been concerned with the differences between metropolitan and colonial approaches to health care and hygiene; but when gender and race are figured into the equation, an important similarity between the two contexts emerges. A concern with biological regeneration, coupled with new medical knowledge at home and in the colonies, led to the [further] objectification of a certain 'other' in the inter-war years – in France, of women, in French West Africa, of the colonised. While French women were conceived of primarily as mothers subordinate to the state – I use the term subordinate because they did not have the vote – African subjects were being viewed primarily as so many units of labour to be multiplied and improved for the benefit of Greater France.

It is not fair, of course, to push this analogy between the position of metropolitan women and that of African subjects in the 1920s and 1930s too far. Africans had always been objectified as subjects, and this now intensified. Even at the height of republican pro-natalism, however, French women continued to straddle two conditions. As producers of the French 'race' as nation they were deemed partial or not fully realised citizens, which entitled them to civil rights never given to Africans; but they also merged with the African resource 'races' because of this same reproductive vocation. Yet, when we look ahead just a few years to Vichy's notorious illiberal maternalism towards women, even that tenuous boundary is increasingly erased. Women under Pétain, in the words of historian Susan Pedersen, were 'endowed but unfree'. The inter-war colonial state discursively constructed Africans in much the same terms. This convergence suggests that perhaps the best way to describe the metropolitan–colonial relationship is one of symbiosis: while colonial and metropolitan social policies and rhetoric each had a racist and sexist logic, or illogic, of their own, they also reinforced and enabled each other in ways which deserve to be further explored.

Notes and references

I would like to thank Barbara Cooper, Eric Jennings and Tyler Stovall for their many helpful comments upon earlier drafts of this essay.

1. In the ever-growing literature on this subject, I have found the following particularly useful: L. Hunt, ed., *The French Revolution and Human Rights: A Brief Documentary History* (St Martin's Press, 1996); S. M. Singham, 'Betwixt Cattle and Men: Jews, Blacks, and Women, and the Declaration of the Rights of Man', in D. Van Kley, ed., *The French Idea of Freedom: The Old Regime and the Declaration of the Rights of 1789* (Stanford University Press, 1994); J. Landes, *Women in the Public Sphere in the Age of the French Revolution* (Cornell University Press, 1988); G. Fraisse, *Reason's Muse: Sexual Difference and the Birth of Democracy* (University of Chicago Press, 1994); J. Scott, *Only Paradoxes to Offer: French Feminists and the Rights of Man* (Harvard University Press, 1996); and P. Rosanvallon, *L'Etat en France* (Seuil, 1989).
2. On the sexual iconography of the French Revolution, see L. Hunt, *The Family Romance of the French Revolution* (Univeristy of California Press, 1992) and M. Gutwirth, *The Twilight of the Goddesses: Women and Representation in the French Revolutionary Era* (Rutgers University Press, 1992).

3. F. Boverat, 'Il faut faire naître,' *Revue de l'Alliance Nationale pour l'Accroissement de la Population Française*, 143, June, 1924, pp. 163–71.
4. On the objectification of Africans generally under colonialism, see M. Vaughan, *Curing Their Ills: Colonial Power and African Illness* (Stanford University Press, 1993). On the relationship between metropolitan citizens and colonial subjects, see F. Cooper and A. Stoler, *Tensions of Empire: Colonial Cultures in a Bourgeois World* (University of California Press, 1997). For the relationship between race, gender, and power in the French empire, see J. Clancy-Smith and F. Gouda, eds, *Domesticating the Empire: Race, Gender, and Family Life in French and Dutch Colonialism* (University Press of Virginia, 1998) and A. L. Stoler, *Race and the Education of Desire: Foucault's History of Sexuality and the Colonial Order of Things* (Duke University Press, 1995).
5. On these trends, see in particular A. Rabinbach, *The Human Motor: Energy, Fatigue and the Origins of Modernity* (Basic Books, 1993); P. Rabinow, *French Modern: Norms and Forms of the Social Environment* (MIT Press, 1989) and B. Latour, *The Pasteurization of France* (Harvard University Press, 1988).
6. A. Klaus, *Every Child a Lion: The Origins of Maternal and Infant Health Policy in the United States and France, 1890–1920* (Cornell University Press, 1993), pp. 56–62.
7. For background on the 1893 medical assistance law and its effects, see E. Ackerman, *Health Care in the Parisian Countryside, 1800–1914* (Rutgers University Press, 1990); J. Léonard, *Les Médecins de l'ouest au XIXe siècle*, 3 vols (Atelier Reproduction des Thèses, 1978).
8. L. Murard and P. Zylberman, 'De l'hygiène comme introduction à la politique expérimentale (1875–1925),' *Revue de Synthèse*, 3rd ser., 115 (1984), pp. 323–5; A.-L. Shapiro, *Housing the Poor of Paris 1850–1902* (University of Wisconsin Press, 1985), p. 135.
9. Shapiro, *Housing the Poor*, p. 150.
10. William Schneider, *Quality and Quantity: The Quest for Biological Regeneration in Twentieth Century France* (Cambridge University Press, 1990), pp. 54, 117; and also A. Carole, *Histoire de l'Eugénisme en France: Les Médecins et la procréation au 19e et 20e siècles* (Seuil, 1995).
11. Klaus, *Every Child*, p. 197; M. L. Stewart, 'Protecting Infants: The French Campaign for Maternity Leave, 1890–1919', *French Historical Studies*, 13, 1 (1983), pp. 79–105; S. Schafer, *Children in Moral Danger and the Problem of Government in Third Republic France* (Princeton University Press, 1997).
12. Y. Knibiehler, *Cornettes et blouses blanches: les infirmières dans la société française (1880–1980)* (Hachette, 1984), p. 147.
13. Schneider, *Quality and Quantity*, pp. 141–2.
14. S. Pedersen, *Family, Dependence, and the Origins of the Welfare State: Britain and France 1914–1945* (Harvard University Press, 1993), chs. 5 and 7.
15. F. Thébaud, *Quand nos Grand-Mères donnaient la vie: la maternité en France dans l'entre-deux-guerres* (Presses Universitaires de Lyon, 1986), pp. 27–47; K. Offen, 'Body Politics: Women, Work and the Politics of Motherhood in France, 1920–1950', in G. Bock and P. Thane, *Maternity and Gender Politics: Women and the Rise of European Welfare States, 1880s–1950s* (Routledge, 1991); M. L. Roberts, *Civilization without Sexes: Reconstructing Gender in Post-war France, 1917–1927* (University of Chicago Press, 1994); S. Reynolds, *Gender in Inter-war France* (Routledge, 1997); and S. Koven and S. Michel,

Mothers of a New World: Maternalist Politics and the Origins of Welfare States (Routledge, 1993).

16. Schneider, *Quality and Quantity*, pp. 117, 144; also see Thébaud, *Quand nos Grand-Mères*, pp. 29, 207; Rosanvallon, *L'Etat en France*, pp. 133.

17. Décret, April 14, 1904, *Journal Officiel de la République Française*, 17 April 1904, pp. 2398–9.

18. For a fuller discussion of hygiene measures in French West Africa, see A. L. Conklin, *A Mission to Civilize: the French Republican Idea of Empire in France and West Africa, 1895–1930* (Stanford University Press, 1997), ch. 2 and 7; B. Salleras, 'La peste à Dakar en 1914: Médina ou les enjeux complexes d'une politique sanitaire' (doctorat de troisième cycle, Ecole des Hautes Etudes en Sciences Sociales, Paris, 1984). For comparable measures in other colonies, see G. Wright, *The Politics of Design in French Colonial Urbanism* (University of Chicago Press, 1991).

19. Arrêté no. 131, 10 December 1904, *Journal Officiel de l'Afrique Occidentale Française (JOAOF)*, pp. 84–6. For a case study of health care in one colony, see D. Domergue-Cloarec, 'henceforth Politique coloniale française et réalités coloniales: l'exemple de la santé en Cote d'Ivoire 1905–1968' (thèse pour le doctorat d'état, Université de Poitiers, 1984).

20. Jules Carde, Conseil de Gouvernement, 5 December 1925, *JOAOF*, pp. 1036–7.

21. 'Instructions relatives au développement des services de médecine, hygiène et de assistance dans les Colonies,' ministre des colonies, 30 December 1924, *JOAOF*, p. 106.

22. Archives Nationales du Sénégal (ANS), circular no. 19, gouverneur-général to lieutenants gouverneurs, April 12, 1921.

23. Circular no. 279 bis s.s.m., gouverneur-général to lieutenants gouverneurs, 1 August 1930, *JOAOF*, pp. 697–706.

24. ANS, H 14, Rapport sur la mortinalité et mortalité infantile en AOF, August 1922.

25. 'Instruction relative à l'orientation et au développement des services d'Assistance médicale indigène en AOF,' gouverneur-général to lieutenants gouverneurs, 15 February, 1926, *JOAOF*, pp. 193–200; Archives Nationales, Section Outre-Mer (ANSOM), AP 3240, 'L'oeuvre sanitaire en AOF,' 31 December 1940.

26. Circular no. 279 bis s.s.m., gouverneur-général to lieutenants gouverneurs, 1 August 1930, *JOAOF*, pp. 697–706.

27. ANS, Circular, gouverneur-général to lieutenants gouverneurs, 19 December 1934; Circular, gouverneur-général to lieutenants gouverneurs, 6 August 1935.

28. ANS, 2 G 33–54, Rapport, Santé, 1934–5.

29. ANSOM, AP 3240, 'L'oeuvre sanitaire en AOF,' 31 December 1940.

30. Ibid.

31. ANS, 17G 96, Rapport, Assistance Médicale, 1937.

32. ANSOM, AP 3236, Ernest Roume, Discours, Comité Supérieur d'Hygiène et de Salubrités Publiques de l'AOF, 17 June 1904.

33. ANS, 2 G 33–54, Rapport, Santé, 1934–5.

34. J. Suret-Canale, *L'Afrique noire: l'ere coloniale 1900–1945* (Editions Sociales, 1962), p. 508; Jules Carde, Conseil de Gouvernement, 5 December 1927, *JOAOF*, p. 837.

35. Vaughan, *Curing their Ills*, pp. 1–28.

0t

36. Pedersen, *Family*, pp. 359–72.
37. S. Pedersen, 'Catholicism, Feminism and the Politics of the Family during the Late Third Republic,' in Koven and Michel, *Mothers*, p. 266. On Vichy and women, see also M. Hawthorne and R. J. Golsan, eds., *Gender and Fascism in Modern France* (University Press of New England, 1997) and M. Bordeaux, 'Femmes hors d'état français, 1940–1944', in R. Thalmann ed., *Femmes et fascismes* (Tierce, 1986), pp. 135–55.

11

'Negrophilia', 'Negrology' or 'Africanism'? Colonial Ethnography and Racism in France around 1900

Emmanuelle Sibeud

The 1900 Universal Exhibition can be considered, in view of the space allotted to the colonial pavilions, to be the first French colonial exhibition. The colonial section comprised numerous didactic items, with exhibits and erudite comments on people living under colonial domination, the burden of which was that the period of conquest was over and the time had come to move on to rational exploitation based on methodical inventory. Here we propose to look behind the scenes of this triumphant production, focusing on the particular case of Africa and Africans. The Universal Exhibition did not offer a comprehensive view but rather took a position firmly in the context of French metropolitan controversies and crystallised latent contradictions at the junction of the nineteenth and twentieth centuries. The fact is that colonial figures – administrators, officers and missionaries – had been drawing more and more precise pictures which differed greatly from the very general perspectives contributed by earlier explorers, and the period lends itself particularly well to examination of the changes in representations of Africa brought about by the colonial experience.

Colonial studies

Among the numerous scientific congresses held in conjunction with the exhibition, two at least were devoted entirely to colonial topics: the

156

Congrès International Colonial and the Congrès de Sociologie Coloniale. The former was concerned mainly with economic matters, while the latter laid the foundation for a new branch of learning, colonial sociology. In opposition to the principle of assimilation it advocated contracts of association, which were supposed to be more respectful of local customs.[1] In this sense colonial sociology could perhaps be seen as the well-spring of a new interest in colonised populations. But this view must be qualified. To begin with, the association-versus-assimilation controversy was largely Parisian and the eminent associationists of 1900 were self-styled ethnographers. Further, a scientific, ethnographically based representation of African populations had begun to emerge much earlier and outside the limits of the ideological debate.

In contrast with the capricious curiosity of Parisian journalists, there was in 1900 an active sector of non-professional savants (experts), colonial figures who had been collecting 'objective' data on African populations and sending them in the form of ethnographic notes to the best learned journals, both general-interest journals and those specialising in anthropology.[2] This scholarly activity resulted in numerous publications, detailed in the official bibliographies of French Africa published in 1912 and 1913.[3] It depended on networks linked to scientific establishments – centres of learning and learned institutions, such as the Muséum or the Ecole des Langues Orientales Vivantes – or to a particular personality, such as the director of the Musée d'Ethnographie du Trocadéro and professor of anthropology at the Muséum, Ernest-Théodore Hamy.[4] Collective effort was implied, each scholar donating his portion of knowledge to the group as a whole and benefiting in return from an assured position on the margin of French metropolitan networks. Scholarly affinities of this sort enabled colonial participants to develop what amounted to a strategy of distinction in relation to their prestigious forerunners, the explorers of the 1870s and 1880s.

François Clozel (1860–1915) was a colonial *savant* of this kind, inspired by Republican scientism and the constant toing and froing necessitated by a colonial career. His first achievement was the publication in the *Revue de Géographie* in 1891 of a *Bibliographie du Soudan* with more than a thousand titles.[5] The Comité de l'Afrique Française then recruited him as second-in-charge of the Maistre mission, which in 1893 opened the door to a career in the colonial administration.[6] At the same time he published an article on the Banziri population in the *Revue Scientifique*. This was in the form of a monograph and was based both on his travel notebook and on an exhaustive compilation of earlier travel notes, with numerous literary references to Ancient Greece and to Stendhal, as Banziri women, like their Italian sisters, had dark eyes.[7] In a sense the article bore more resemblance to travel narratives of the mid-nineteenth century, for example those of Barth, than to the more pragmatic accounts of exploration of the end of the century. However, apart from individual exploits, Clozel attached importance to professional and scholarly concerns. For instance, he drew attention to Banziri marriage rules and showed their endogamous basis by recounting the tribulations of an administrator in love. His learned contribution made use of both classical imagery and precise ethnographic inquiry and was not just the chance product of a surprise encounter with radically different societies. Offered as a gift to the learned community in metropolitan France, it was promptly taken to be a mark of high professional competence.

In 1891 the Société Africaine de France was founded. This was a venue for colonial representatives and businessmen and for a small group of ethnographers who had left the Société d'Ethnographie de Paris and put their ethnographic skills at the disposal of the colonial authorities. Their leader, Dr Eugène Verrier,[8] coined for their purposes the term *africaniste* with its current meaning of specialist in Africa, when he transformed the bulletin of the *societé* into the *Journal des Africanistes*. Unfortunately, the authorities were more interested in economic expertise and the ethnographers who struck a discordant negrophile note were soon sent back to the learned society they had left. The failure of these first 'Africanists' showed how very limited the tolerance of the associationists was. Ethnography was meant to supply them with arguments but it did not interest them as a science and they systematically rejected any scholars, colonial or metropolitan, who did not share their convictions. Thus by 1900 the current representations of African populations had already been affected by the experience of running the colonies, but the situation was rather that of a confused free-for-all with rival networks fighting over the tenuous claim to scientific legitimacy. The official partisan discourse of the Universal Exhibition sharpened these rivalries and led to decisive reclassifications.

The stereotypes of colonial sociology

In 1900 it was colonial sociology that seemed to carry the day in what was to be its first and last congress. The label is deceptive, the 'sociology' being much more of a racial psychology directly inspired by Gustave Le Bon. Its 'bible' was a work published in 1899 by Léopold de Saussure,

Psychologie de la colonisation française dans ses rapports avec les sociétés indigènes ('Psychology of French Colonisation in its Relations with Native Societies'), which gave a rather negative picture of 'natives'.[9] He saw them as masses characterised mainly by their status of subjection, or more precisely as races caught in separate and severely limited forms of evolution. In short, colonial sociology was circumstantial and partial in approach and a far cry from genuine contemporary social science, in particular the Durkheim school of sociology, or from the ethnographic studies undertaken by colonial *savants*.

Within these narrow horizons it was the missionaries who were habitually appealed to in reference to African populations, in particular Monseigneur Le Roy, superior of the important Congrégation des Pères du Saint-Esprit and an influential member of the Anti-Slavery Society. Bishop of Gabon from 1892–96, Mgr Le Roy had published a good deal, which enabled him to intervene with some authority and to contest in part the very negative image presented by Saussure and implicitly accepted by the congress. To Saussure's racist relativism he opposed, with verve and some humour, a conventional view of Africans as regenerated by their conversion to Christianity.[10] Because Catholic missionaries were assimilationist by dogma, they appeared to be the natural defenders of the African 'races' and the task of speaking for the latter was willingly left to them.

In 1900 the Anti-Slavery Congress was the only one that actually focused on Africa, but the representation it offered was doubly negative. It used pathos, presenting Africans as defeated populations, helpless victims of 'the leprosy of domestic slavery', if not of the slave traders; it also made use of outdated stereotypes such as cannibalism. French Catholic missionaries, for example, were asked to bring back images of Africa suitable for the edification of Christian masses in metropolitan France. They were not therefore reliable witnesses recounting what they had actually seen.[11] Mgr Le Roy's lecture 'L'Evolution de l'esclave dans les missions Africaines' ('The Evolution of the Slave in African Missions') was enthusiastically received because it restated all the conventional ideas:

in less than an hour we were made to believe we were ourselves explorers in Central Africa. We could see the villages in the bush poorly protected by wooden palisades against raids and fire, the fierce countenances of man-hunters, negroes dragged in chains far from their birthplace in long processions to the slave markets. We could see the unhappy mothers when the slave trader tore the baby

> from their breast to dash its head against a wayside stone so as to get rid of a useless load and not hamper the march of the captives . . . [12]

Missionary representations were clichés only somewhat qualified by personal experience. Added to anecdotes about cannibalism, which were favourites with both speakers and audience at the Congrès de Sociologie Coloniale, they finally sank to the level of caricature.[13] These images unfortunately reinforced colonial stereotypes. Where the missionaries saw pathos, colonial sociology saw monstrosity and the impossibility of assimilation. Léopold de Saussure even asserted that the 'negro race' spontaneously refused assimilation:

> Even from an anatomical point of view, the negro race is visibly at a much lower level of development. Negro brains are more grey in colour than those of other races. The virtually simian prognathism, the angle of the face, the section of the hair clearly differentiate it from the rest of humanity . . . in its own interest it is absurd to impose on it a civilisation it cannot assimilate and which is fatal for it . . . African blacks feel this and, at the approach of the white man, they resort to Mahometanism.[14]

This way of confusing 'negro race' and 'African blacks' shows how little the stereotypes prevalent in 1900 had to do with the more differentiated descriptions by explorers and even less with the body of knowledge amassed by colonial *savants*. As the rift widened, the old opposition between negrophiles and negrophobes once more reared its head. Some philanthropists and the new specialists on Africa took up the negrophile line to combat the caricatures bandied about by colonial sociology.

From raciology to Pan-Africanism

The totally negative view of the negrophobes was part of a process of denial which appears clearly when the article 'Africa' in the first edition of the Larousse Dictionary (published between 1864 and 1876) is compared with that in the second (1896–1906).[15] By 1900, Africa, conquered and dismembered, had become an object of contempt, even down to the very shape of the continent which inspired a value judgement other continents were spared:

> There is no comparison that can help us to describe the outline of Africa . . . What is to be noted above all is the thick massive nature of

its shape, which contrasts strikingly with the slender elegance of the shape of Europe, the most indented of all continents.[16]

Furthermore, the lively discussion on fetishism between an anonymous English traveller and Comoro, 'chief of a negro tribe of the White Nile', in the first edition had been replaced in the turn of the century edition by a horrifying enumeration of negative characters of the negro race borrowed from anthropology and ethnography.

In the absence of official institutions mediating between the learned circles and the general public, the data gathered by colonial *savants* could not effectively counteract this sort of thing. The Musée d'Ethnographie du Trocadéro, which opened in 1878, attracted numerous visitors every Sunday, but its budget was so ridiculously small it could do no more than present collections which colonial *savants* had themselves brought back.[17] Moreover, there were no longer any specialised ethnography periodicals in France other than the *Bulletin de la Société d'Ethnographie*, which took very little interest in Africa. Otherwise, there were only generalist publications like *L'Anthropologie*, in which the contributions of colonial *savants* were afforded very little space and their mere direct acquaintance with Africans could not stand up to comparison with the technical virtuosity displayed by Parisian anthropologists who were assiduous visitors to ethnographic exhibitions in metropolitan France.

In the meantime, the classical raciology inherited from Paul Broca was being contaminated by emerging anthropo-sociological theories.[18] At the end of a turbulent century, with demographers predicting the inexorable decline of Europe, the dividing line between racial studies by anthropologists and contemporary phobias became permeable. Africans were seen as savages and became the chief victims of the irrational return to a phantasmatic racial hierarchy:

The three basic races are the black, the yellow and the white. The melanian variety is the lowest of all and at the bottom of the scale the yellow race, apathetic and tending to mediocrity in all things, is the ideal element any civiliser would like to have as a base of society to constitute the common people and the lower middle class, but it cannot suffice to give society shape, verve and energy. The white race alone has the power to raise itself to the level of civilisation thanks to the power it transmits to others when it forms alliances with them; but in raising them it lowers itself . . . and the white race in its pure form is the tall, fair, dolicocephalic, blue-eyed one.[19]

The anthropo-sociologists were a minority, but the irrationality of their discourse finally discredited the notion of race, already threadbare after more than a century of methodological squabbling. As a result, anthropologists found themselves suddenly deprived of a basic tool and they were obliged to resort to an auxiliary science, ethnography, which they had left to travellers. Hence the compromise proposed by the librarian of the Muséum, Joseph Deniker, who published an anthropological textbook in 1900, entitled *Les Races et les peuples de la terre* ('The Races and Peoples of the World'), attempting somewhat clumsily to supplement the notion of race, which had become 'a matter of personal appreciation', by the no less vague notion of 'ethnic groups, constituted by language, religion, social institutions etc., held in common'.[20] This vagueness meant it was left to politics and controversy to find another type of answer.

To begin with, there were passionate denunciations of the abuses of colonisation which sought to counter the cynical pronouncements of the colonial congresses, but their success was limited. In 1901, a former navy physician turned journalist, Jean Hess, briefly published a journal, the *Magasin Colonial et des Voyages*, which vehemently denounced the abuses of colonial policy, 'the world of liars, thieves, and savage barbarians'.[21] He upheld indigenophile positions, views which were the logical product of his career as a successful colonial promoter of philanthropic-exotic travel. He had, in fact, made a name for himself as early as 1896 by publishing Yoruba legends gathered in the course of a mission to Central Africa, which he presented as constituting the 'bible' of an African people.[22] In 1898 he collected them in a work entitled *L'Ame nègre*, which takes up precisely the line of reasoning of the *Littérature des nègres* published in 1808 by the Abbé Grégoire:

> this simple translation has, I hope, made it possible to judge better how undeserved is the classification as barbarian and savage, of peoples who possess such literary monuments. When travellers are unable or unwilling to study the savage, they say the savage has no ideas. Others, more magnanimous, admit he has particular ideas but deny him 'general ideas'. My friend Mamadré, the good poet and singer of the pagan negro court of Oyo, was the equal of many a philosopher with general ideas.[23]

Modelled on the negrophilia of the beginning of the century, that is, on a pre-abolition type of discourse, these counter-arguments were clearly not adapted to the imperial realities of the turn of the century.

Jean Hess's orations contained, moreover, most of the contradictions inherent in French anti-colonialism before 1914. He outlined an association policy that was totally utopian, since it assumed complete respect for the colonised and ignored the relationship of domination. He constantly attacked official personalities of the *parti colonial*, the companies which held concessions in the French Congo and also the bespectacled scientists who imprisoned exotic beauty in barbaric instruments of measure. Jean Hess upheld the ideal of a civilising mission against the brutal pragmatism of contemporary imperial discourse and his negrophilia was based on an idealised view of Africans that had little to do with the real functioning of the colonies.

Another figure, more original than this fairly classical one, was that of the Haïtian lawyer Benito Sylvain, who spoke in the name of the negro race. Francophone, he belonged to the Antillaise élite that Paris welcomed but kept on the fringes. In 1893 he joined the Société d'Ethnographie de Paris, which had opposed Broca's raciological anthropology since 1859 in the name of a rather vague spiritual philosophy. A year later, with a group of Haïtian students, he founded a Comité Oriental et Africain to denounce the colonial exploitation suffered by Africans and also the fallacies of anthropometrics which classified races to suit the interests of the colonisers. He did not condemn colonisation out of hand, but asserted that the civilising mission was an indispensable compensation without which domination had no legitimacy. Finally, he was to be seen in the biennial anti-slavery congresses, which suggests he was attempting to mobilise all potential defenders of the 'negro' race. But in 1900 the end result was bitterly disappointing: he had failed everywhere. The anticolonial declarations of the Comité Oriental et Africain dealt a death blow to the Société d'Ethnographie, which faded out of existence between 1900 and 1903. Furthermore, the Anti-Slavery Society, the only such philanthropic society in France, took an active part in the Congrès de Sociologie Coloniale through the participation of Mgr Le Roy. It declared that forced labour was the first step to civilisation. Thus, Benito Sylvain was very much alone when in 1901 he defended his law thesis on *Le Sort des indigènes dans les colonies d'exploitation*. ('The Fate of the Natives in the Colonies of Exploitation'). However, although he abandoned the attempt to make himself heard in France, he was active in other places, notably in the mainly Anglo-Saxon Pan-Africanist movement.[24] This change of direction points up the failure of the only consistent attempt at a renewal of French negrophile action at the end of the nineteenth century.

Enter the negrologists

Finally, it was the colonial *savants* who put an end to the stalemate between outdated 'negrophilia' and racist stereotypes by proposing a positive scientific 'Africanophilia'. They intervened in the favourable context of the vigorous reaction of the Durkheimian school of sociology against all biological reductionism and an even broader mobilisation of intellectuals in the wake of the Dreyfus Affair. Their arguments in favour of Africans echoed those of Mauss, who claimed in 1901 that there is no such thing as an 'uncivilised' people, or Célestin Bouglé, who in 1904 took the defence of 'la Démocratie devant la Science'.[25]

In actual fact, the colonial *savants* did not have much connection with Mauss or Bouglé, but by speaking up in reaction to the aggressive claims of colonial sociology they showed they were of the same intellectual ilk. They were intransigent positivists who challenged both racial stereotypes and negrophile oratory because they were based on generalisations; instead, they restricted their remarks to the populations with which they had been in close contact and which they had studied for years. So they characterised individual African cultures but did not concern themselves with the general notion of a 'negro soul'. The title of the work published in 1902 by Dr Barot, physician to the colonial troops, was eloquent: his intention was to illustrate the 'intellectual value of blacks', but he limited his remarks to the 'Soudanese soul' (*L'Ame soudanaise*). He attacked the deceptive representations that were used to amuse the general public: 'who know nothing but caricatures of Negroes – the unfortunate feathered grooms business houses use for advertising – or what they see in immoral fair exhibits where specimens of the human race are shown between performing dogs and anatomic collections'. But he also criticised the attitude of the philanthropists who saw Africans through 'the eyes of slave-traders'.[26] In brief, he challenged static representations which did not take any account of knowledge acquired in the field. Based on images justified by experience as well as by republican conviction, Africanophilia deliberately moved away from negrophilia, opposing real Africans to the phantasmatic figure of the 'Negro'.

There was another level of reaction on which explicit scientific claims came into play. In 1901, Maurice Delafosse published a lengthy comparative study of the Liberians and the Baules, in which he took up a position equidistant from both negrophobes and negrophiles, which he defined as the objective position of the *négrologue* ('negrologist'): 'I would like to ... introduce into the study of Negro peoples ... the scientific point of view, that is, [a point of view] neither sentimental, nor utilitarian. In a word I would like to be neither negrophile nor negrophobe but merely negrologist, if I may be forgiven for coining the term.'[27]

Delafosse had a thorough knowledge of both populations. He had been vice-consul of France in Monrovia in 1897–8 and had served for a long period in Baule country. He chose these peoples because they illustrated respectively a process of acculturation based on an inconsistent assimilation policy (Liberians) and a society of 'savages', refractory towards colonial domination but culturally autonomous. He answered both the negrophiles, by showing the social and political fiasco of Liberia, and the negrophobes, by showing the strength and consistency of Baule culture. His article in fact provided a model for 'negrology' based on a rigorous scientific protocol. Its object of study was individuals and cultures, more real than the races of classical anthropology, and this was another way of defusing the debate between negrophobes and negrophiles. Also, he argued that familiarity with the object of study did not impair judgement but was a necessary condition for objective knowledge. Delafosse defended himself against any possible reproach of excessive sympathy for the Baules, and based the legitimacy of his observations on his knowledge of the language and long-term contact which enabled him to compare them:

> I did not just pass through Baule: I stayed there twice, forty-two months in all, I travelled everywhere, visited most of the villages, lived the life of the natives outside the colonial posts, on the track, or on stopover in the villages, eating and drinking the same food and drink, sleeping in their huts, listening to their discussions and their family squabbles, watching their games and their dances, listening to their songs and their legends, taking part in their celebrations, their mourning, their religious or funeral ceremonies, arbitrating their disputes...I must add that from my second year in Baoulé I hardly ever used an interpreter in my private relations with the natives, having learnt to speak and understand their language almost as fluently as my own.[28]

In fact he enunciated the basic rules for ethnography, which was to be reorganised on the basis of fieldwork. The term he coined did not gain favour, but the positive militant Africanophilia he represented created an opening for gradually emerging 'Africanism' in France.

The beginning of the century saw a historical break in the way the French represented African populations. The emergence of 'a-scientific' racism and the doubts of classical anthropology spurred the colonial savants to decisive action. From the 1890s, a rift had appeared between popular stereotypes and the factual knowledge of the colonial *savants*, but the need to defend Africans against the prejudices of colonial sociology provided Africanists with an opportunity to speak out. Africanism was the direct heir of this scholarly protest. Hence arose a fundamental ambiguity: the *savants'* Africanism replaced the negrophile movement, which had failed to update its thinking in France, and, although it defended the dignity of Africans, it also spoke in their stead and postponed all possibility of real dialogue to an indeterminate future.

Notes and references

1. At the same time, colonial governments in French Africa began to publish official records of indigenous customs such as F. J. Clozel and R. Villamur, *Les Coutumes de la Côte d'Ivoire* (Challamel, 1902).
2. For example, the *Revue Scientifique*, which regularly published résumés of lectures given at the Muséum, or the *Revue d'Ethnographie*, founded in 1882, by the director of the Musée d'Ethnographie du Trocadéro and replaced in 1890 by the more comprehensive *L'Anthropologie*.
3. E. Joucla, *Bibliographie de l'Afrique occidentale française* (E. Larose, 1912) and G. Bruel, *Bibliographie de l'Afrique equatoriale française*, (E. Larose, 1913).
4. N. Dias, *Le Musée d'Ethnographie du Trocadéro* (CNRS 1991), p. 224. The Muséum is now just a natural history museum, but then it included anthropological collections, which were hived off in 1937 to form part of the Musée de l'Homme.
5. *Revue de Géographie*, 1890, vol. 2 and 1891, vols 1 and 2.
6. François-Joseph Clozel (1860–1915),one of the last administrators who had been an explorer. His career was impressive: governor of Côte d'Ivoire from 1903 to 1907 then of Haut-Sénégal-Niger from 1908 to 1915, Governor-General of French West Africa from 1915 to 1917. After 1902, when his responsibilities made fieldwork impossible, he became 'patron': in 1903 he commissioned the first compendium of native customs (Côte d'Ivoire) and in 1915 founded the Comité des Etudes Historiques et Scientifiques de l'Afrique Occidentale Française.
7. F.-J. Clozel, 'Les banziris', *Revue Scientifique*, 2 September 1893, no. 10.
8. Eugène Verrier (1824–1910), obstetrician, had been a member of the Société d'Ethnographie since 1885. In 1888 he made a first unsuccessful attempt to launch a Société Africaine in liaison with the Société d'Ethnographie. In 1891, he sought the patronage of elected representatives of the *parti colonial*, who soon completely took over the Société Africaine de France and turned it into one more pressure group. Verrier was probably marginalised as much because of his political (Fouriérist) ideas as for his long-winded philanthropy.
9. L. de Saussure, *Psychologie de la colonisation française dans ses rapports avec les sociétés indigènes* (F. Alcan, 1899). The family name is prestigious: he was the son of the naturalist Henri de Saussure and younger brother of Ferdinand. Gustave Le Bon was his main theoretical reference.
10. He observed, for example, that 'missionaries are not ideologists roaming the land, gospel in one hand, cross in the other, converting peoples. They are a bit more down-to-earth than that', *Congrès de Sociologie Coloniale. Procès-verbaux des Séances*, Paris, 1900, p. 378. And he caricatures Saussure's racial

relativism in order to refute it as '[when] the poppy flowers [are] red the negro's morals reach full bloom in cannibalism', ibid., p. 379.

11. F. Raison-Jourde, 'Image missionnaire française et propagande coloniale', in N. Bancel, P. Blanchard, L. Gervereau, eds., *Images et colonies. Iconographie et propagande coloniale sur l'Afrique française de 1880 à 1962* (BDIC-ACHAC, 1993), pp. 50–7.

12. Mgr A. Le Roy, 'L'evolution de l'esclave dans les missions africaines', in *Comptes-rendus des séances du Congrès International Antiesclavagiste de 1900* (Société Antiesclavagiste de France, 1900), p. 193.

13. For instance, the sly answer of an old African chief when an administrator banned cannibalism: 'You're the strongest; we won't eat it any more; but it wasn't bad; you never tasted it,' reported by the governor De Lamothe, *Congrès de Sociologie Coloniale. Procès-verbaux des séances*, Paris, 1900, p. 384.

14. De Saussure, *Psychologie de la Colonisation*, p. 233.

15. *Grand Dictionnaire Larousse*, published between 1864 and 1876, *Le Nouveau Larousse Illustré*, 1896–1906, p. 108.

16. H. Froidevaux, H. Maindron, R. Verneau, 'Afrique', in *Nouveau Larousse Illustré*, vol. 1 (Larousse, 1896–1906), p. 108.

17. Dias, *Le Musée*, p. 252.

18. Cf. C. Blanckaert, 'Le système des races', in I. Poutrin, ed., *Le XIXe siècle* (Berger-Levrault, 1995), pp. 21–41.

19. H. Muffang, 'Avant-propos du traducteur', in O. Ammon, *L'Ordre social et ses bases naturelles. Esquisse d'une anthroposociologie*, translation by H. Muffang (Fontemoing, 1900), p. ix. Muffang was a disciple of Georges Vacher de Lapouge and, from 1890 to 1899, he also was in charge of an 'anthroposociological' section within *L'Année Sociologique*. The confusion between racial hierarchy and social stratification is typical of anthroposociology which played on the contrast between an immutable 'biological order' and contemporary social disorder.

20. J. Deniker, *Races et peuples de la terre. Eléments d'anthropologie et d'ethnographie* (Schleicher Frères, 1900), p. 3.

21. Cf. Jean Hess, 'A propos de Saïd Ali. Un sultan dépossédé. Un exemple de notre colonisation par le mensonge, le vol et la violence', *Le Magasin Colonial et des Voyages*, no. 2 (15 juin 1901), p. 120.

22. Dossier Jean Hess, Archives Nationales de France, Paris, F[17] 2975.

23. J. Hess, 'Une bible nègre. Les mythes et l'histoire du pays Yorouba', *Revue de Paris*, 1 February 1896, p. 616.

24. He was in London in 1900, at the first Pan-Africanist congress, where he represented all the African populations under French domination. The francophone black élites, especially West Indians, were very few in number in comparison with the anglophone élites, which was part of the reason his attempt to make himself heard was unsuccessful.

25. M. Mauss, 'Leçon inaugurale du cours d'histoire des religions des peuples non civilisés (27 janvier 1902)', *Revue de l'Histoire des Religions*, vol. 45 (1902), pp. 36–55; C. Bouglé, *La Démocratie devant la science. Etudes critiques sur l'hérédité, la concurrence et la différenciation* (F. Alcan, 1899).

26. Dr Barot, *L'Ame soudanaise. Essai sur la valeur intellectuelle des noirs* (Pages Libres, 1902), p. 4.

27. M. Delafosse, 'Les Libériens et les Baoulés. Nègres dits civilisés et nègres dits sauvages', *Les Milieux et les Races*, 2 (February 1901), p. 102.

28. Ibid., p. 111.

12
Direct or Indirect Rule: Propaganda around a Scientific Controversy

Véronique Dimier

A fact that observers have long neglected is that colonial issues no longer belong to national politics. International censure turns its gaze upon us more than ever. Thus all nations concerned with our material and moral results can arbitrate between us. Through this arbitration, colonising nations risk being subject to local and international sanctions, the significance of which cannot be ignored. Their servitude is to legitimate themselves each day by their actions and to restore continuously their power and authority.[1]

Much has been written by colonial historians and anthropologists about the differences between the colonial administrations of France and Great Britain as practised in their tropical African dependencies. In particular, there was the famous controversy which occurred on the subject during the 1960s between Michael Crowder, a British historian, and Hubert Deschamps, a French historian and former colonial administrator.[2] In fact, this controversy was not new. In the 1930s a similar debate took place between French and British specialists in colonial administration.[3]

From the British side, the French system was seen as a very centralised, unified and bureaucratic system, the aim of which was the assimilation of native people, and whose method was direct rule, namely the destruction of native authorities and their replacement by French officers. The main task of these officers was then to act as the typical civil servants of the bureaucratic state as envisaged by Max Weber.[4] They would mainly enforce the law prescribed by Paris regardless of a native society's customs and particularities. If they happened to use the local chiefs, they would merely nominate them according to their loyalty

168

and turn them into French civil servants. By contrast, the British system was regarded as very decentralised, pragmatic and based on indirect rule. Through its native policy, it aimed to respect native customs as long as they were not opposed to British conceptions of civilisation. It also tried to respect the real native chiefs chosen by their people, and rule through them by means of persuasion, advice and education. For British analysts, these basic differences were based on the political culture of each country.[5] The French were republican, that is more ideological and contemptuous of traditions and local autocrats. Moreover, the French state had been built through a process of assimilation and centralisation. The British, on the other hand, had a political culture made up of liberalism and conservatism. With their respect for tradition, they were more likely to accept the aristocratic chiefs and customs of the native societies. Besides, the system of indirect rule was especially adapted to their decentralised state and pragmatic character. This was the British interpretation of the differences between French and British ways of governing dependencies. French interpretations apparently saw less contrast. On the French side of the Channel, there had never been one single position on the matter, but for some French analysts it was clear that these differences were largely overstressed. When confronted by foreign opinion they tended to argue that in practice both systems were based on the pragmatic and decentralised system of indirect rule and on a native policy respectful of native customs. They agreed that some differences existed; for example, in some French parts of Africa the chiefs were left with fewer financial and judicial powers than their counterparts in Nigeria, for example. However, even on this point, they always found excuses, saying that this situation was not intended by the French, but was caused by circumstances, lack of native treasuries or organised native institutions. In any case, if there were differences between the French and British systems, they were more of degree than of kind.[6]

Unlike most historians, we will not try here to solve this controversy. We will not try to see which of these comparisons is well grounded as far as the real practices of colonial administration and government are concerned. We will rather try to answer the following questions: who made these comparisons, what precisely was their object, and why did the French and British disagree on the matter; in other words, what was at stake? This will lead us to consider the specific conceptions of colonial administration that were held and promoted by a certain French and British élite. We will see then how this image was used for propaganda in the new process of legitimisation of empire generated by the League of Nations, in a context of the longstanding rivalry between France and Great Britain.

A science of colonial administration

Curiously, comparisons like those of the British kind set out above were first made by the French themselves. At the end of the nineteenth century, colonial theoreticians such as Jean-Marie de Lanessan, Jules Harmand and Joseph Chailley-Bert used to praise the decentralised and pragmatic British system in India, especially its respect for native customs and institutions.[7] It was a model to be followed by French colonial administrators whose tendencies towards centralisation, bureaucracy and assimilation were much criticised. When British officers like Lord Cromer or Lord Lugard began to have some interest in the foreign colonial experience, they tended to draw the same comparisons, introducing only a few subtle distinctions.[8] In the 1920s and 1930s, however, these kinds of comparisons were increasingly disputed on the French side, while in both countries comparing French and British colonial administrative systems became the privileged field of various specialists in colonial administration.[9] Only two will be considered here: Henri Labouret, director (together with Lord Lugard) of the International Institute of African Languages and Culture, teacher of African languages and cultures and of comparative colonial administration at the Ecole Coloniale in France (1926–45), and Margery Perham, research lecturer in colonial administration (1935) at Oxford University, then reader in colonial administration and director of the Institute of Colonial Studies (from 1939 to 1948). Both Perham and Labouret played an active role in the training institutions and programmes meant for colonial administrators: the Ecole Coloniale in France and the Colonial Administrative Service courses, organised in Oxford and Cambridge from the end of the 1920s. In this capacity, the two specialists sometimes met[10] and they also both contributed substantially to the development and teaching of a 'science of colonial administration'.[11] The implementation of native policy and colonial administration had to be studied through their day-to-day workings, that is mainly at the local level where native policies were carried out, and where the colonial administrators dealt directly with native societies. Methods and results were then to be analysed in the different colonies. The approach had to be comparative; one had to compare the colonial principles and practices of the different colonial powers. For Perham and Labouret, the main field of study was tropical Africa, and especially West Africa. Thanks to her Rhodes Trust Travelling

Fund, Perham went there between November 1931 and April 1932 to study British colonial administration, and as part of her journey she visited the French Cameroons.[12] Labouret was a former colonial administrator in Côte d'Ivoire. Later on in 1934, as a teacher at the Ecole Coloniale, he went to the French Cameroons for six months for fieldwork on native societies and colonial administration, funded by the Ministry of Education and the International Institute of African Languages and Culture.[13] Nevertheless, despite visiting the same colonies and despite agreeing on what they were comparing, they drew different conclusions. Margery Perham tended to see many differences, giving a scientific basis to the comparisons formerly drawn by Lords Lugard and Cromer. In contrast, Henri Labouret tended to see only nuances and emphasised the similarities, especially when addressing an international audience.

Principles of native policy

Considering the disagreement between Labouret and Perham, one may wonder whether it was not due to some misunderstanding regarding the meaning of the concepts used and praised: those of native policy and indirect rule. After analysing their discourse, one concludes, however, that their definitions of these concepts, and more generally their conceptions of colonial government, were quite similar. Concerning native policy, it is worth noting that the concept was ill-defined in both France and Great Britain. It meant, broadly, to respect native cultures and institutions as long as they were not opposed to British or French conceptions of civilisation, and to develop native societies on their own lines (*l'évolution dans la tradition*), which was a very ambiguous aim in itself. Indeed, it was particularly imprecise as to the kind of society and government which could eventually evolve from such a process. As a result, it could be, and was, interpreted differently by different people according to the way in which they considered the relationship between European civilisation and African cultures. For those Social Darwinists who were persuaded that culture was something genetic, untransmittable from one people to another, it meant leaving native societies as they were, to evolve according to the harsh law of nature. For those evolutionists who still regarded colonisation as a civilising mission, and progress as a law of history, it was a necessary step in the impending evolution towards the kind of society already reached by Europeans. Considered in this way, the ultimate aim of British native policy was not different from that of assimilation.

Finally, there were those who were more influenced by the functionalist theories of the inter-war period, who considered colonisation as a more or less destructive cultural contact for native societies, and who began to recognise the value of the latter. For them, indirect rule aimed at mitigating this clash of cultures and at finding a new *modus vivendi* made up of African native and European elements. Of course, this mixture could vary greatly from one person to another according to his or her conception of what part of tradition should, or could, be kept and what should, or could, evolve. Among these different interpretations, those of Perham and Labouret were apparently closer to the latter position, but their views did not diverge radically from those of the evolutionists either.[14] What was clear in their concept of native policy was the methods it implied for the rule of 'native races', that is the type of government it embodied. One may thus wonder whether the specificity of British native policy compared with that of assimilation did not rest on its methods rather than on its aims.

Indeed, in French discourse, assimilation meant the imposition on 'native' societies of a law which was regarded as universal. It was then linked to an idea of government based on coercion and grounded in purely philosophical or legal considerations.[15] By contrast, the native policy they envisaged was rooted in more subtle forms of government and was supposed to proceed mainly from knowledge of 'native societies'. In a way, it was very close to the idea of '*gouvernementalité*' as defined by Michel Foucault.[16] One has to govern not by force or rule of law but by using patience, diligence and knowledge, by taking into account people's will, fears and interests in order to use them and reach the objectives desired; one has to influence rather than coerce, and act on societies through diverse social policies. In this sense, the colonial state was not merely meant to keep order and justice through the use of force and the rule of law. It was also to become an agent of social welfare, acting through a certain art of government. This role was to be filled first by its local agents, the territorial administrators (that is the *commandants de cercle* or district officers), who had day-to-day contact with the 'native' societies and consequently the best knowledge of them.

British and French conceptions of the role of colonial administrators

An examination of the courses and writings of both Perham and Labouret seems to suggest that these colonial administrators were easier to define by what they were not: civil servants of the rational-legal type of administration described by Max Weber, mere wheels in a very centralised, hierarchical and bureaucratic system in which authority rests mainly on the rule of law, and where the centre defines precise goals and methods, produces legal, impersonal and constraining rules, and controls their application at all stages of the hierarchy.[17] What they *were* is more difficult to grasp. As territorial agents, they had no specialised functions; they were supposed to assume simultaneously the manifold tasks of tax collectors, magistrates, accountants, superintendents, masons or architects. As time went on, some of these tasks were given to specialist technical services, but colonial administrators retained strict control of their work. This was essential if they wanted to keep their main responsibility: to apply locally native policy as defined by central governments in Paris, London or in the colonial capitals. The word 'apply' is perhaps not appropriate here. Indeed, according to Labouret and Perham, they were supposed instead to 'adapt' it to local circumstances and customs. They had to make the general law of the imposed colonial state compatible with the particulars of native societies. In this sense, they were as much the representatives of the colonial state to the indigenous population as the representatives of the indigenous population to the central government.

This meant that the provisions of native policies had to be general enough to allow for different interpretations according to circumstances, and that the system had to be very decentralised, leaving the local administrators with great responsibilities and powers. And indeed, the system envisaged by Margery Perham and Henri Labouret left much initiative to the men on the spot. At worst, decrees and circulars could be ignored when they were too numerous or impossible to adapt to local societies. As a result the incentives for colonial administrators to act were to be found less in orders issued by the central state than in their own drive for initiative and action, their common sense, their will, character and sense of duty: in sum, their personal qualities. Similarly, as no control from above was regarded as desirable, everything was to rest on their self-control, morality and personality, as well as their faith in the goals and plans of the colonial ministry – what we may call an '*esprit de corps*'. Good recruitment and regular education in the principles of colonial government and native policy were thus essential to the good working of the system. Even more important were administrators' knowledge of 'native' society and their closeness to the 'native' rulers.

Indeed, as a second aspect of their task, they also had to work in close cooperation with the leaders of the 'native' communities such as the chiefs and councils of elders. This was called 'indirect rule'. In Labouret and Perham's view, existing authorities had to be maintained and allowed to rule their people according to tradition. Everything should be done through 'native' administration and 'native' authorities. They had to be left responsibilities and the power of initiative in financial, judicial and executive matters. This was, however, within the limits of French and British sovereignty. The colonial administrator's task was then to convince them to help with implementing native policy and to educate them in better government, which meant more efficient and humane government. In this sense, the term *'commandant de cercle'* used to describe the French local administrator was ill-suited to describe his methods. He would not command, he would not give orders. Like the district officer of the British empire envisaged by Perham, he would rather persuade, control and try to gain the confidence of the 'natives' through the confidence of their rulers. Force was not ruled out as a means to maintain French and British sovereignty: chiefs who were reluctant to follow the advice of the colonial administrators could even be deposed, but only in the last resort. In this system, the traditional instruments of the bureaucratic state – the law and the coercive means to enforce it – were to be avoided where possible. Everything was to rest rather on personal relationships and compromises as well as mutual respect and confidence. And in these specific relationships, the only things which were of real use for the colonial administrator were his personal qualities or rather gifts: patience, tact, the capacity for exerting influence, knowledge of local languages and customs, sympathy with the 'native' societies. Of course, to be able to carry out his task properly, since the colonial administrator often had to reside in districts as large as those of the African colonies, this meant touring. Visiting each village, he was supposed to enquire about people's desires and grievances, to enter the life and soul of each tribe, to honour each chief and get him to back colonial native policy. In these dealings with the local elites, his method itself could not be described clearly. It was very varied, resorting to diplomatic or pedagogic means, or even to a sixth sense. Depending on the loyalty of the chief and his subjects, and on the degree of 'evolu-tion' undergone by local societies, it ranged from mere advice to strict control. As Perham recognised, this control itself was not easily measured: 'even those exercising it would give different calculations'.[18] The same was true for the powers left to the chiefs in judicial and financial matters, for example. At best they could have their own treasuries and courts, whose decisions and sentences were submitted to the colonial adminis-trator's approval. At worst they would merely levy taxes and assist the colonial administrators in trying cases. Between both these extremes lay a wide range of possibilities.

Whatever these variations, some fixed rules had to be respected by colonial administrators. The leaders they dealt with had to represent African societies accurately and be their legitimate rulers. Indeed, they were supposed to be active agents and not mere executive officers of the colonial administrator. As such, they had to be representative enough to convey their people's will and inform the colonial administrator of it, as well as having enough authority over their people to persuade them to collaborate with him. As democratic representation through the normal process of election was seen as unsuitable for such societies, the most representative leaders were considered to be the emirs, chiefs or councils of elders, those chosen by the people according to their traditional customs, whether these customs were of a democratic or an aristocratic kind. Picked in such a way, they had to be given official recognition by the colonial authorities. In this sense, the French, republican or not, were no less respectful of African aristocratic chiefs than the British.[19] Indeed, what was essential was not so much the traditional and aristocratic aspects of the chief but his supposed position as native representative.

In conclusion, one may say that Henri Labouret and Margery Perham's conceptions of colonial administration were very similar, especially on two important points. First, the enforcement of native policies was mainly dependent on the administrator, his qualities, his capacity for exerting influence, his personal relationship and compromises with the local society's elite. For this reason, and because the colonial administrator was not a mere agent of execution whose behaviour was crystal clear to the eyes of the centre, the system lacked the transparency and regularity of the Weberian bureaucratic system. This is why it was so difficult to prove that its principles were followed in practice, and why it was so easy for it to be a matter of controversy.

Second, the very features which made colonial administration more personal also made colonial domination more human and less oppressive. Considered from the point of view of liberal democracies, colonial domination was in every respect a form of subjection, even if the situation was considered temporary. With Labouret and Perham's figure of the colonial administrator at its heart, the system took on a more liberal aspect. Native policy might be decided by the colonial state and not by the 'native' societies themselves, but it was still supposed to be adapted to these societies, and not merely imposed. When applying it, local administrators had to take into account the will, interests and customs of the colonised peoples. With their true representatives, they had to make the compromises on which a fruitful and indispensable cooperation could be based. Thus through these compromises, 'native' society, far from being passive, was already taking part in its own government. For some people, the system of indirect rule was even considered to be a substitute for liberal western democracy. In 1927, Donald Cameron, then governor of Tanganyika, called it a 'democratic' system.[20] As a later report on the British Cameroons made for the Trusteeship Council of the United Nations put it, the system 'is really one with the old and tried idea that the government of the people should be for and by the people'.[21] Similar statements are to be found on the French side.[22] A 1951 report concerning the status of the chiefs in French colonial administration presented the system as one of the means to reach the objectives written down in the preamble to the 1946 constitution, that is to help people to rule themselves democratically.[23]

French and British rivalry around the League of Nations process

Considered in this way, the system became very popular in French and British official circles in the inter-war period.[24] Such popularity may explain why some French specialists like Henri Labouret tried so hard to prove that it was implemented in practice in French tropical Africa. Nevertheless, it cannot account for his disagreement with Margery Perham. In so far as this disagreement does not come from some mis-understanding as to the meaning of indirect rule and native policy, one wonders if it is not linked to strategic considerations lying behind their scientific discourse – more specifically, the new process of legitimisation engendered by the League of Nations' mandate system in the 1920s.[25]

The League set up in the covenant (clause 22) some common prin-ciples, officially accepted by the mandate powers, by which one could judge their government of native peoples in their mandated territories, but also by extension in their dependencies. As a supra-national organ-isation, the League did not have any means of enforcing these principles or any sanctions to impose if these principles were infringed. Neverthe-less, the system made moral sanction and criticism easier, all the more so because these could be made publicly in a political forum: the Permanent Mandate Commission. Also, the mandate powers had to prove regularly to this commission that they were governing their territories according to the principles by which they had agreed to abide. And the proofs given were not to be mere political statement and intentions. There had to be real evidence, practical results and facts, presented in an annual report which had to answer the questionnaire devised by the commission. In a way, the process of legitimisation became as much the politicians' business as that of 'specialists in colonial administration'. It is worth noting that Labouret and Perham were both more or less directly connected with the League of Nations. As part of their research work and courses they both spent time looking through the mandate commission's minutes and reports. Margery Perham even went to Geneva, and was later presented by Lord Lugard as a potential successor to Lord Hailey, the British representative to the commission (1936–1939). Henri Labouret worked in the Direction des Affaires Politiques at the French Colonial Office, where he was responsible for the mandate territories (1926–7).

This could have led to greater cooperation between scientists and politicians of both countries, and cooperation was indeed the aim presented at each official meeting between French and British representatives.[26] In fact, the opposite seems to have prevailed during the inter-war period. The new legitimacy process led to a kind of rivalry between France and Great Britain, with each country trying to prove to the world its goodwill in following the League of Nations' principles. This tacit rivalry increased a tension which was permanent between France and Great Britain at this time, and which gained in momentum with German colonial claims during the 1930s.[27] In the context of these claims, foreign criticism, expressed either from a rival or a neutral power, became much feared in both countries. At the same time, the emergence of nationalist movements also increased British and French vulnerability. Criticism could lead to unpredictable consequences, as Albert Sarraut recognised.[28] Thus one understands the great efforts made by French and British theoreticians, scientists and their respective governments to prove that their colonial administrations were abiding by the League of Nations principles.

One could say that these principles were quite imprecise, potentially leading to different interpretations. They sanctioned the idea that colonies were not mere properties to be exploited, but were inhabited by peoples whose 'well-being and development form a sacred trust of civilisation'. The main objective of the mandate governments was then to ensure this well-being. As to the form of this government, it could be summed up in the word 'tutelage'. In short, experienced nations had to rule those people who were 'not yet able to stand by themselves under the strenuous conditions of the modern world'. Their rule could vary according to the degree of evolution of the people concerned and different types of mandates were devised to reflect this. The B mandates – Cameroon, Togo, Tanganyika and Ruanda-Urundi – were supposed to be administered more or less directly. But the term 'not yet' also meant that this administration would not be for ever, and that the mandate powers had to educate the people in the mandate territories in self-government, whatever its form. In this sense, mandate rule had to be more educational and liberal than repressive and authoritarian.

Still, different interpretations were possible concerning the methods to be used. Education could take the form of the progressive introduction of democratic elections, or it could be translated into methods similar to those of indirect rule. Looking through the Mandate Commission's minutes, one quickly realises that the second interpretation did in fact prevail among its members. One may guess that the prestige of Lord Lugard, the so-called inventor of indirect rule and British representative to the commission from 1922 to 1936, had something to do with it. Moreover, the system was officially given recognition by the commission in 1927 after a brilliant intervention at the eleventh session by Donald Cameron, another theoretician of the system and then governor of Tanganyika.[29] In these circumstances, to present French colonial administrators as incapable of indirect rule, as the British did, was in fact to accuse them of not being able to rule in a liberal and educational way or to abide by the League of Nations principles. One also understands why some French observers were not so happy with British comparisons. The minutes of the Mandate Commission debates show that a controversy similar to that involving Labouret and Perham took place between French and other representatives, especially the British.[30] In both cases, the disagreement about possible differences or similarities between systems of colonial administration dealt with a specific mandate – the French Cameroons – and gained momentum in the 1930s, at a time when Germany was claiming back her former colonies, especially the French Cameroons.[31]

In France, official positions towards these claims had always been very clear: no territorial concessions could be envisaged. But on the British side, opinions seem to have been more balanced. Some in colonial circles did not rule out such a possibility as a last resort to appease German ambitions.[32] As French territories were those wanted by the Germans, it is not difficult to guess that they would be the first ones to be conceded. In both countries, however, debates went on regarding alternative solutions. Unsurprisingly, Perham and Labouret took an active part in them.[33] In 1938, the Royal Institute of International Affairs, in co-operation with the Centre d'Etude de Politique Etrangère in Paris, set up a joint study group on two subjects: the German claims and the colonial policies of different colonial powers.[34] Both Henri Labouret and Margery

Perham were members of these groups.[35] Following several meetings and discussions, the French group came to the conclusion that there may be some differences in policy – though more studies were needed to establish these – but that, whatever the differences, they did not prevent some form of collaboration between them in order to confront German ambitions.[36]

On the British side, opinions were different. In a comment to the joint study group, Margery Perham was particularly doubtful as to whether such collaboration was appropriate:

Do we think that by working more closely together (France and Britain) we could define and justify our trusteeship in the eyes of our subjects and the world? This would be difficult as, having visited French Cameroon, I should think the people there would as soon have the Germans as the French . . . I should guess from a number of indications that the one certain opinion held by the Africans (the tribesmen not the educated élite), wherever they can compare administration across frontiers, is that they prefer our rule to the French.[37]

Such considerations were not actually new. Lord Lugard had been very critical of German ways of ruling colonies, accusing them of destroying the chiefs, or of using them as mere agents of their despotic authority.[38] He also reproached the French in similar fashion.[39] In these circumstances, it is no wonder that the latter were not especially reassured by British opinion and comparisons, and were so eager to prove that they could respect indigenous customs and rule through the chiefs as well as the British.

The reaction of the French government to the publication of a book by Robert Leslie Buell, who was a Professor at Harvard University, is significant in this respect. The book, entitled *The Native Problem in Africa*, provided scientific justification for arguments similar to those that had been developed by Margery Perham and Lord Lugard.[40] Having got wind of Buell's study before its publication, the French Colonial Ministry asked Henri Labouret to make a report on it. His comments were particularly fierce: he described the book as a 'tendentious charge against French colonial administration' which, according to him, aimed at 'making an impression upon a foreign opinion which was ill informed'.[41] Labouret's comments were serious enough to persuade the French Colonial Minister, Léon Perrier, of the 'importance of this issue' and of the 'bad opinion of our empire' that such a book, 'covered by the moral authority of Harvard', would generate around the world.[42] He contacted the French Foreign Minister and asked him to put pressure on the American and Harvard authorities to prevent the book from being published or a least to make some changes in it.[43] Unfortunately for the French, his action failed: the book was published and even used in the Permanent Mandate Commission to criticise the French government.[44] Later propaganda through Henri Labouret's books did not work either. The 'English' view prevailed and nowadays France is still remembered for its policy of assimilation and direct rule.

Notes and references

1. A. Sarraut, *Grandeur et servitude coloniales* (Sagittaire, 1931), pp. 120–1.
2. M. Crowder, 'Indirect Rule. French and British style', *Africa*, 34, 1964, pp. 197–204; H. Deschamps, 'Et maintenant Lord Lugard?', *Africa*, 33, 1963, pp. 294–305.
3. M. Perham, 'France in Cameroon: the Exercise of a Mandate', *The Times*, 17 May 1933; 'A contrast of policies', *The Times*, 18 May 1933, in M. Perham, *Colonial Sequence, 1930–1948* (Methuen, 1967), pp. 68–76; H. Labouret, 'French Colonial Administration', in *Oxford University Summer School on Native Administration* (Oxford University Press, 1937), pp. 63–4; H. Labouret, 'Protectorat ou administration indirecte, direct or indirect rule', *Afrique Française*, 6, May 1934, pp. 289–92.
4. M. Weber, *Economie et société* (Plon, 1971).
5. M. Perham's archives, Box 230, File 7,1937, fragments of lectures on native administration given at Oxford for the cadets, p. 21.
6. H. Labouret, *Le Cameroun*, Centre d'Etude de Politique Etrangère, travaux des groupes d'études, publication no. 6 (Hartman, 1938), p. 24.
7. J. Chailley, *L'Inde britannique. Société indigène, politique indigène: les idées directrices* (A. Colin, 1910); J. Chailley-Bert, *La Colonisation de l'Indochine* (A. Colin, 1892); J. Harmand, *Domination et colonisation* (Flammarion, 1910); J.-M. de Lanessan, *L'Indochine française* (F. Alcan, 1889).
8. Lord Cromer, 'The Government of the Subjected Races', *Edinburgh Review*, 7 (1908), p. 127 ; Lord Cromer, *Modern Egypt*, VII (Macmillan, 1908); Lord Lugard, *The Dual Mandate in British Tropical Africa* (Blackwood, 1922), pp. 59–60, 228–9.
9. One of the first to challenge this kind of comparison was M. Delafosse, a former colonial administrator in French West Africa and teacher of African languages and cultures at the Ecole Coloniale (1909–26): M. Delafosse, 'Politique coloniale. Pour ou contre la décentralisation, L'excès en tout est un défaut', *Dépêche Coloniale* (1 August 1923); M. Delafosse, 'Menus propos', *Dépêche Coloniale* (9–10 August 1925); M. Delafosse, 'Propos et opinions', in M. Delafosse, *Broussard ou les états d'âmes d'un colonial* (Larose, 1922) p. 150.
10. Labouret was invited to a summer school for colonial administrators organised by Perham in 1938 to give a paper on 'French Colonial Administration', published in *Oxford University Summer School on Native Administration* (St Hugh's College, 3–17 July 1937), op. cit.

11. H. Labouret, *A la Recherche d'une nouvelle politique indigène dans l'ouest africain* (Editions du Comité de l'Afrique Française, 1931), pp. 95–6 ; H. Labouret, 'A la recherche d'une politique coloniale', *Le Monde Colonial Illustré*, 82, June 1930, p. 133; M. Perham's archives, Box 230, File 7, 1937, fragments of lectures on Native Administration given at Oxford for the cadets, 1937, p. 15; Box 231, File 12, 1941, notes for a series of 6 lectures on administration prepared in 1941 but intended for Hilary term 1942, p. 9; Box 236, File 3, 1949, notes for lecture on development and practice of British colonial government given in Hilary Term, p. 8.

12. Her impressions of the French Cameroon are to be found in her articles, 'France in Cameroon: the exercise of a mandate', *The Times*, 17 May 1933, 'A contrast of policies', *The Times*, 18 May 1933. See also her diaries in: M. Perham, *West African Passage* (Peter Owen, 1983) pp. 175–210.

13. This study was published four years later in: H. Labouret, *Le Cameroun*, Centre d'Etude de Politique Etrangère, travaux des groupes d'études, publication no. 6, op. cit.

14. H. Labouret, 'La colonisation, fait social', *Le Monde colonial illustré* (November 1936) 242 ; H. Labouret, *Paysans d'Afrique occidentale* (Gallimard 1941); M. Perham's archives, Box 232, File 5, 1943, lecture on Africa given to Army officers at Chatham House in May, p. 30; Box 229, File 11, 4 undated and unidentified lectures on indirect rule and the colonisation of Africa possibly intended for the courses of cadets at Oxford 1936–37, p. 7; Box 230, File 16, 1938, lecture on 'Problems of Race and Government in Africa' given in Michaelmas term 1938.

15. Labouret, *A la Recherche d'une nouvelle politique indigène*, pp. 12, 31; Labouret, 'A la recherche d'une politique coloniale', p. 133; M. Perham, 'France in Cameroon: the contrast of policy', *The Times*, 18 May 1933, in *Colonial Sequence*, p. 76.

16. M. Foucault, 'La gouvernementalité', *Actes*, 54, summer 1986, pp. 6–14.

17. M. Perham's archives, Box 229, File 3, 1933, lecture on Africa given to the Raleigh Club, Oxford, 5 March, at Rhodes House; Box 229, File 4, 1933, lecture on 'The Political Officer as an Anthropologist' given at the LSE, on 2 May; Box 229, File 5, 1933, 4 lectures on native administration in British Tropical Africa given in Trinity Term at Oxford; M. Perham, *Native Administration in Nigeria* (Oxford University Press, 1937); M. Perham, *Major Dane's Garden* (Rex Collings, 1926); M. Perham, *Lugard* (Collins, 1956), 2 vols; H. Labouret, *A la Recherche d'une nouvelle politique indigène*; H. Labouret, *Le Cameroun*; H. Labouret, 'Question de politique indigène africaine. Protectorat ou administration directe' *Outre Mer*, 1 (March 1929), pp. 80–94.

18. Perham, *West African Passage*, p. 71.

19. Labouret, *A la Recherche*, p. 42; H. Labouret was on this point much influenced by J. Brévié and J. Van Vollenhoven, both governors-general in French West Africa: J. Van Vollenhoven, 'Circulaire sur les chefs indigènes', 15 August 1917 in *Une Ame de chef* (Imprimerie H Diéval, 1920), pp. 194–5; J. Brévié, 'Circulaire du 27 septembre 1932 sur les chefs' in *Circulaires sur l'Administration et la Politique Indigènes en Afrique Occidentale* (Imprimerie de Gorée, 1935), p. 37.

20. Minutes of the Permanent Mandate Commission, 8th meeting, 11th session, 27 June 1927, C 348. M 122. 1927 VI, p. 62.

21. *Report of His Majesty's Government in the United Kingdom of Great Britain and Northern Ireland to the General Assembly of the United Nations on the adminis-tration of Cameroon under UK Trusteeship for the year 1948* (London: HMSO, 1949), p. 40.

22. See for example M. Delafosse, 'Pour les indigènes, ceux dont il faut demander l'avis', *Dépêche Coloniale*, 24 September 1924.

23. Rapport fait au nom de la Commission de la Législation, de la Justice, des Affaires Administratives et Domaniales, sur les demandes d'avis transmises par le Président de l'Assemblée Nationales (à l'Assemblée de l'Union Française) relatives au Statut des Chefs coutumiers en AOF, AEF, Cameroun et Togo, par Jousselin, séance du 27 novembre 1951, Annexe no. 275, *Journal Officiel de l'Assemblée de l'Union Française*, Documents, pp. 314–5.

24. For the French side, see V. Dimier, 'Une analyse de l'administration coloniale signée Broussard', in J. L. Amselle, E. Sibeud, dir., *Maurice Delafosse. Entre Orientalisme et Ethnographie: l'Itinéraire d'un Africaniste (1870–1926)* (Maison-neuve et Larose, 1998), pp. 21–38.

25. For more information concerning the Mandate system, see *Le Système des Mandats, Origines Principes et Applications* (League of Nations publication, no. 89, 1945).

26. Speech by Leo Amery, secretary of state for the colonies, in a dinner offered by l'Union Coloniale Française, 2 June 1927, on his visit in France, in *Le Monde colonial illustré*, 46, 1927, p. 146; Speech by A. Sarraut, Minister for the Colonies, at a dinner offered by the African Society on 23 May 1933, on his visit to London, in 'The Society Dinner to the French Minister for the Colonies', *Journal of the African Society*, 32 (July 1933), pp. 220–35.

27. P. D. Essomba, 'Le Cameroun entre la France et l'Allemagne, de 1919 à 1932' (thèse de doctorat, 3ème cycle (Histoire des relations internationales), Université des Sciences Juridiques, Politiques et Sociales de Strasbourg, 1984).

28. A. Sarraut, *Grandeur et servitude coloniales* (Sagittaire, 1931), pp. 120–1.

29. 'Rapport sur les travaux de la Commission lors de sa 11ème session, 20 juin–6 juillet 1927', *Journal Officiel de la Société des Nations*, October 1927, sent to the Council 8 September 1927, pp. 1259–60; Minutes of the Permanent Mandate Commission, 8th meeting, 11th session, 27 June 1927, C348 M122, 1927, VI, p. 58–72.

30. Minutes of the Permanent Mandate Commission, 10th meeting, 9th session, 14 June 1926, C 174. M 144, 1926, VI, pp. 62–3, 78; 20th meeting, 9th session, 21 June 1926, C174, M144, p. 141; 28th meeting, 22nd session, 24 November 1932, C 772. M 364. 1932 VI, pp. 204–7 ; 2nd meeting, 30th session, 27 October 1936, C 500. M. 313. 1936 VI, pp. 22–3, 29–34; 'Rapport annuel du gouvernement français sur l'administration sous mandat des territoires du Cameroun, pour l'année 1936' (Paris, Imprimerie Lahure), p. 42.

31. For more information on the German Claims see P. D. Essomba, 'Le Camer-oun entre la France et l'Allemagne'; G. Maroger, *La Question des Matières Premières et les Revendications Coloniales. Examens des Solutions Proposées*, Centre d'Etude de Politique Etrangère, Travaux des groupes d'études, publica-tion no. 4 (P. Hartman, 1937); *Peaceful Change: Colonial Question and Peace. A survey prepared under the direction of E. Moresco* (vice-president of the Council of Dutch India), (International Institute of Intellectual Co-operation,

League of Nations, 1939); Royal Institute of International Affairs, *Germany's Claims to Colonies*, Information Paper no. 23 (Oxford University Press, May 1938). See in particular: Foreign Office papers, 371/19925, Document 663, Memorandum on the ex-German colonies in Africa, by W. Ormsby-Gore, January 1936. W. Ormsby-Gore was appointed Secretary of State for the Colonies in May 1936.

32. Ibid., pp. 55, 57–8.
33. H. Labouret took part in the 10th International Studies Conference which took place in Paris in June–July 1937. His book on Cameroon was published and used as a report for this occasion. Cf. *Peaceful Change, Procedures, Population, Raw Materials, Colonies: Proceedings of the 10th International Studies Conference*, 28 June–3 July 1937, op. cit. He also published a number of articles on the subject, for example: 'Opinion britannique et revendications coloniales allemandes', *Afrique Française*, November 1936, pp. 571–5; 'Les revendications coloniales allemandes. L'opinion anglaise', *Afrique Française*, January 1937, pp. 16–19 ; 'Le problème colonial et la paix dans le Monde', *Afrique Française*, March–April 1938, pp. 120–4. M. Perham was also much interested by the German claims: see her articles published in *The Times*, 10, 11 and 12 February 1936, 'Our Task in Africa', in *Colonial Sequence, 1930–1949*, pp. 141–54.
34. The work of this joint study group led to two publications in English: Royal Institute of International Affairs, *The Colonial Problem. A Report by a Group of Members of the RIIA* (Oxford University Press, issued under the auspices of RIIA, 1937); Royal Institute of International Affairs, *Germany's Claims to Colonies*, Information Paper no. 23.
35. M. Perham's archives, Box 674, File 2, Anglo-French relations, RIIA Study, 1938–1939. See also the journal of the Centre d'Etude de Politique Etrangère, *Politique Etrangère*. See especially no. 3 of June 1938, p. 301; no. 6 of December 1938, p. 643; no. 3 of June 1939, p. 347; no. 4 of August 1939, p. 470.
36. M. Perham's archives, Box 674, File 2, Item 2: 'La politique coloniale et la collaboration franco-anglaise', mémoire préparé par un groupe de membres du Centre de Politique Etrangère et du Centre d'Information Documentaire pour être soumis à un groupe de membres du RIIA, Paris, April 1938.
37. M. Perham's archives, Box 674, File 2, Item I, p. 14: 'Anglo-French Study: Colonial Policy and Colonial Claims', comments by M. Perham, 6 September 1938.
38. Lord Lugard, 'Address to the Colonial Probationers', *Cambridge University Colonial Services Club Magazine*, 1, 1931, p. 6.
39. Lugard, *The Dual Mandate*, pp. 228–9.
40. R. L. Buell, *The Native Problem in Africa* (Macmillan, 1928).
41. Papers of the Colonial Ministry, Direction des Affaires Politiques, Box 28, H. Labouret, 'Note for the Minister' (not dated) about Buell's work.
42. Papers of the Colonial Ministry, Direction des Affaires Politiques, Box 28, letter from L. Perrier to Jouvenel, 13 June 1927; letter from L. Perrier to minister for foreign affairs, 29 June 1927.
43. Ibid.
44. Rappard, representative of Switzerland, minutes of the Permanent Mandate Commission, 2nd meeting, 15th session, 1 July 1929, C 305. M 105. 1929 VI, pp. 20–3.

13
Representation or Recuperation? The French Colonies and 1914–1918 War Memorials

William Kidd

In 1993 and 1996 respectively, France erected memorials to the Jewish victims of the 'rafle du Vel d'Hiv' (16 July 1942) and to her Algerian war dead (1954–62). Largely unremarked between these events was the bronze group unveiled on the seafront at Fréjus in 1994 to the 'Black Army' which fought for the mother country in two world wars and whose members, in Léopold Sédar Senghor's injunction to the passer-by, 'fell as brothers that you might remain French' ('*sont tombés fraternelle-ment unis pour que tu restes Français*'). The choice of location was doubly appropriate, Fréjus having been since 1915 the main entry-point and metropolitan HQ for colonial troops from French Equatorial and French West Africa (AEF and AOF) as well as Indochina. Detachments of the latter built the Hông-Hien pagoda there in 1917, which was used as a garrison place of worship and has latterly become a garrison memorial ('*lieu de mémoire*'). Coincidentally but not inappropriately, Fréjus was also the summer residence of Gallieni, before Mangin the best-known commander of the colonial troops, whose wife was from the town.

Apart from its belatedness, a number of features of the new memorial command attention, of which the most important is that, unlike others erected after 1919 *and still extant*, it portrays the group of soldiers in their unambiguous '*négritude*'. Another point of note is the potential irony generated by the contrast between the description of these troops 'fraternally united', overcoming their own local/regional/tribal/cultural differences to come to the aid of their French brothers, and the historical practice of their colonial masters which was to divide and rule. And it is doubly ironic that by 1994 the Var, formerly part of the historic 'Midi rouge' (red South), had become securely part of a 'blue' political map in which the overlap between the neo-Gaullist Rassemblement pour la République (RPR) and the Front National, anti-immigrant sentiments and nostalgia for empire are defining characteristics.

To what extent do such memorials offer a socio-cultural and icono-graphic paradigm of the evolving colonial relationship? What values are encoded or occluded? This chapter addresses these and related questions using illustrations from France and overseas, and, by way of contrast or corroboration, references to other iconographic or literary material from a relevant colonialist or post-colonialist perspective.

This study is research-led, and forms only a small part of a larger analysis of French commemorative practice since 1870. Two introductory remarks may therefore be helpful. First, by representation I mean sculpted memorial figures, not abstract configurations such as the outline of Korea used to commemorate the French battalion in the UN forces in 1953. These figures may be realistic or allegorical, though both modes can and do coexist on certain memorials: the stone soldier, to take an obvious example, must be realistic enough to be identified and, for the grieving survivors, to be *identified with*, while at the same being capable of symbolising other values. Second, research in the colonial field is constrained by difficulty of access to the memorials, whether by reason of distance, post-independence neglect or deliberate destruction by the liberated territories. Many memorials have however survived and, *'par un juste retour des choses'*, have been relocated in France. In this respect, Alain Amato's *Monuments en Exil* is an invaluable source.[1] Also useful, and an indication of the extent to which 'the paths of memory' (*'les chemins de la mémoire'*) have gained widespread official acceptance, is the recent series of illustrated brochures published under that title by the Ministry for War Veterans and Victims (Ministère des Anciens Combattants et des Victimes de Guerre), two of which are devoted to colonial army 'monuments and burial places'.[2]

The majority of post-1919 memorials erected in the colonies reflected metropolitan practice and cultural norms: they were often serially produced by French firms converting from wartime production, bought from catalogues, imported and installed by local architects or masons. These included models by C. Pourquet and E. Benêt (Fonderies Durenne), as well as the so-called 'Poilu de Jacomet', marketed in bronzed cast iron (3500 francs) or bronzed cement (1800 francs), and protected by an 'exclusive monopoly for France, Algeria, Alsace-Lorraine, the Colonies and Belgium' (in that order).[3] Common in France, a 'Jacomet' found its way to Mondovi (Algeria), another model to Saint-Pierre-la-Réunion. Iracoulo and Sinnamary (French Guyana) chose a *'poilu* advancing with the flag' and an allegorical Victory supporting a dying *poilu* respectively, while in Cayenne an incongruous but typically Gallic cockerel is guarded by four 1914–18 trench mortars. Some of these cast infantrymen such as the example at Pointe-Noire (Guadeloupe), were given a coat of French 'blue horizon' uniform paint, a practice unusual though not unheard of in France itself.[4] A minority of original memorials were the work of local, indigenous craftsmen such as Ebstein and the Algiers-born H. M. Galy, who created a stone group for Basse-Terre (Guadeloupe). But these were to some extent overshadowed by – and not markedly different in inspiration from – commemorative works commissioned from French artists of national or international reputation such as Bouchard and Landowski, whose work is considered below, or Sarrabezolles (Siddi Bel Abbes) and Réal del Sarte (Jemmappes, Saint-André de la Réunion).[5] In most cases, these memorials alternated between 'a vigorous naturalism deployed in narrative mode' – at Hamman-Bou Hadjar, a massive stone *poilu*, task completed, lays down his military pack and equipment – and equally predictable allegorical tropes: at Philippeville, the troops offer up prayers to a winged victory.[6] They also included replicas of that most traditional patriotic icon, Joan of Arc, in whom religious symbolism recalled the missionary aspects of the colonial project whose commemorative apogee was Dakar cathedral, Notre-Dame des Victoires, inaugurated in 1936 'to the memory of Africans who died for France'. Less grandiose and more secular memorials included Ebstein's soldier protecting a grieving widow at Sétif (Algeria), a similarly veiled figure at Pointe-à-Pitre (Guadeloupe), and the classically garbed 'Nike' at Case Pilote (Martinique) penning in stone the epitaph 'Honour to our glorious dead'.[7] Berthe Girardet, one of the few women sculptors involved in this field,[8] and creator of the temporary ossuary at Douaumont, produced a relief for Do Neva (New Caledonia). A replica of Moreau-Vauthier's bronze commemoration of the 'Black Army', cast by Durenne and erected at Rheims, was exported to Bamako (Mali).[9] At Saint-Laurent-du-Maroni (Guyana), the memorial is a typically European obelisk topped with an urn and decorated with the Croix de Guerre and the colonial anchor, symbol of the so-called '*troupes de la marine*', their original appellation. Another obelisk surmounted by a Croix de Guerre commemorates the fallen at Abidjan (Côte d'Ivoire).[10]

Two further examples from Martinique, Trinité and Le Lorrain,[11] confirm the essentially nationalist nature and function of commemorative practice. The former has a '*poilu* defending the flag' of a type produced and marketed from Paris by the Marbreries Générales, and bought by scores of 'communes' from the Moselle to the Charente. The 'Pro Patria' engraved on the plinth (a standard abbreviation of the Horatian 'Dulce et decorum est pro patria mori') underlines, paradoxically, its unambiguously French, that is, 'Latin', character. At Le Lorrain a work, which on this occasion might be that of a local artist, combines the soldier figure in colonial whites, wearing uniform and pith helmet, and the winged allegory, bearing victor's laurels.[12] Readable in a number of ways, the 'angelic' aspects of this figure and a Christian cross underline the transcendental thrust of the memorial: what is being transcended is, of course, the local specificity of the dead combatants: like the imagined native soldier in Apollinaire's wartime poem, the figure in stone might have uttered:

> I'm a French soldier and so they turned me white
> Sector 59 I can't say where
> But why is it better to be white than black?[13]

It is true that troops from the so-called 'old colonies' in the Caribbean (Guyane, Réunion, Guadeloupe, Martinique) had quasi-metropolitan status and were incorporated into 'white' colonial regiments, unlike those from AEF and AOF, Madagascar, Somalia, Nouméa and Indochina, so one could find a spurious justification for the 'whitening' ('blanchissage') memorially effected. Colonial regiments raised in Algeria in 1914 also included significant numbers of recruits of European origin, given the circumstances in which the area was developed, notably after 1870 and the influx of settlers who had elected not to remain, for example, in German-annexed Alsace-Lorraine. It is nonetheless the elision of difference, and notably physical/racial difference, which most strikingly characterises these memorials, whichever part of the overseas territories they represent. The singularity of the colonial experience – perhaps better described as its 'otherness', to avoid a falsely unified view of its diversity (as distinct from the France–colonies divergence) is monumentally and memorially denied: these soldiers are iconographically French.

At Boufarik, Bouchard's 'Chasseur d'Afrique' offered the image of a soldier in regiment marching uniform more redolent of the nineteenth-century conquest of Algeria than the twentieth-century realities of the Western Front. This was a revealingly anachronistic representation – what better idiom to emphasise the colonised nature of the dead soldiers? – and a tragically appropriate one for Albert Camus's immigrant father and countless others, killed at the Marne in September 1914, 'dressed in smart shining colours, straw hats on their heads, red-and-blue targets you could see for hundreds of metres'.[14] On the other hand, only a tiny handful of memorials expressed the reality of war, whose sanitisation, the transformation of the 'fields of horror' into 'fields of Honour' was a standard, perhaps inevitable, feature of commemorative practice.[15] With colonial memorials, more than one form of reality is being occluded: the French colonies *were France*, though only Algeria was divided into *départements* as if they were part of the metropolitan territorial entity, and France was the '*patrie*' for which the colonial troops laid down their lives and on whose soil some had never before set foot: 'when my father was called up, he had never seen France. He saw France and was killed.'[16]

When colonial diversity is memorially represented, it is usually in the side panels of the monuments, in reliefs showing exploits of colonial and French communities joined in particular engagements, or the traditionally recuperative form of the mobilised and mobilising group. Again with the sole exception of Moreau-Vauthier's 1924 group, to my present knowledge only Favre's memorial for Mostaganem, which shows two *tirailleurs algériens*, departed from what seems to have a standard rule of thumb: where only one figure was possible or desired, that figure, symbolic or realist, was in French idiom; where more than one was chosen – two and often three – one could be in ethnic idiom. Ebstein's memorial at Tlemcen (1925) consists of a female allegory in the Republican idiom of Delacroix and Rude, winged and sword-bearing, rallying a helmeted *poilu* and turbaned *tirailleur sénégalais*, trampling the inevitable spiked Prussian helmet underfoot![17] The memorial at Oran (Pommier, 1927) featured a similar group, inclusive, homogenising, above all unifying '*la plus grande France*'. The Marseilles memorial 'To the heroes of the Army of the East and Distant Lands' offers a good metropolitan example of the same type. Here we see the classical device of the triumphal arch inscribed on one side with Moorish crescent and star with grouped figures at the base of each upright representing different types of colonial unit (pith-helmeted *fusillier-marin*, turbaned *tirailleur*) and an allegorical female figure symbolising victory, the Republic, and the more abstract qualities of élan, duty and sacrifice.[18] The latter is similar in turn to that used at Fort-de-France by Bouchard, whose public sculptures included the provisional '*Poilu libérateur*' erected on the Esplanade in Metz (1919–22), the war memorial at Dijon, and the colonial war memorials already mentioned, as well as medals struck for the Marseilles colonial exhibition in 1922, and for the Citroën Trans-Saharan Rally of the same year.[19] Bouchard's career is emblematic in more ways than one of the coherence of France's post-war colonial 'project' as mediated in the links, largely unquestioned at the time, between art, commerce and ideology.

The 'monument to Franco-Moroccan fraternity' was inaugurated at Casablanca in July 1924 by a local chieftain and by Lyautey, spokesman of French colonial practice between the wars.[20] Its two equestrian figures, a French cavalryman and a white-robed spahi, invite the reading that this is the noble, free being of the desert meeting his equal and the two combining to do battle against the common enemy. Even in the colonial theatres, however, where they distinguished themselves (Macedonia, Egypt), the cavalry were the marginal forces of the First World War, and this memorial is a statement about municipal and artistic pretention as well as fundamentally colonialist in its assumptions. It is true, as Annette Becker, points out, that 'some Arab inscriptions resemble quotations from Lyautey and Joffre',[21] while the dates 1914–18 and 1332–1337 acknowledge the Muslim calendar. But that duality and apparent equality merely reinforce and in no way subvert the interpretation proposed: these memorials work within a colonialist frame of reference, reproduce a culturally 'safe' iconographical lexicon, familiar in pictorial form in the military-colonial representations which began to circulate during the period of colonial conquest from 1830 to the 1880s and became common currency during the Third Republic through colonial exhibitions, official and semi-official publications, geographical magazines and illlustrated 'reportages' such as 'Regards sur l'Afrique'.[22] The same comment could be made about Landowski's Algiers memorial (1928), in which a 'lying figure' is borne aloft by three horsemen (of the Apocalypse?) whose classical features and proportions evoke an antiquity which belongs within the colonialist discourse of denial – denial of the cultural specificity and ethnic '*mixité*' of the populations who fought and died.[23] Significantly, Landowski himself claimed that the Casablanca memorial had been inspired by a precise 'classical' memory, the sight of two mounted shepherds greeting one another in the Roman countryside.[24]

The invariably European idiom used in representations of colonial troops contrasts however in one respect with an area of representation in which their ethnicity was not only respected but exploited: in France itself, the coloured soldiers were encapsulated in a double-image as likeable, unsophisticated but intrinsically noble, that is, harmless but educable savages lending an exotic and unthreatening element to entertainments and official presentations – the '*ballet noir et blanc*' at the Exposition Coloniale of 1931, for example – and to commercial advertising. The famous 'Banania' advert springs to mind, as do less well known but more revealingly racist adverts for soaps and bleach,[25] which corroborate the black/white symbolism underlying Apollinaire's verse, namely that the colonial soldier was white when needed, black when required, lending an extra dimension to the poster of the *tirailleur*, smiling, childlike, over the statement: 'Before I was a negro, now I am French.' One has only to compare this with a contemporaneous advert for a different brand of bleach, the patriotically named '*Coq gaulois*' used by 'Tiger' Clemenceau to administer a graphically vigorous hair rinse to ... the defeated kaiser, for the complexities of discourse in such representations to become apparent. In fact, as recent commentators have argued, discourses and representations can be inscribed within a strategy of reinforcing ideological control at a point when post-war tensions (revolt in the Syrian protectorate, war in the Moroccan Rif in 1925) were beginning to emerge:

> The First World War was characterised by the production of images designed partly to promote assimilation, but inspired in fact by propaganda directed as much at the indigenous French as at the colonial populations who were beginning to escape from metropolitan control. There was, then, a growing mis-match between the iconography of colonialism and the appearance of the first cracks in the colonial edifice.[26]

For non-domestic consumption, the colonial troops were packaged as fearless and terrifying adversaries whose legendary ferocity was exploited by French military propaganda and accredited, rightly or wrongly, by the German troops themselves as '*les Sénégalais! Hirondelles de la mort!*' ('swift harbingers of death'). The memorial plaque on the wall of a Southern barracks in Perpignan, showing a cruelly stylised *tirailleur* head, and the well-known 'without fear and without pity' memorial in the Moroccan cemetery at Vimy underline the contribution of these troops recorded elsewhere by Gallieni, or Mangin, chief 1914–18 exponent of the 'Black Army'. Magnified in the phantasmatic no man's land which existed between the disinformation of official communiqués and the rumour-mill of the trenches so characteristic of all the First World War armies on the Western Front (Highland troops, (Frauen von Hölle: the 'kilted devils'), and the Gurkhas have been similarly mythified), the *tirailleurs sénégalais* acquired a more problematic reputation during the post-armistice and pre-treaty militarisation of the Rhineland (1919–20) and subsequent occupation of the Ruhr, when not altogether unfounded fears of miscegenation – some 400 children were born to local women and coloured troops[27] – and underlying racism produced a predictable backlash. The latter included a poster campaign in the name of 'German women protesting against the coloured occupation of the Rhine' (*'Protest der deutschen Frauen gegen die farbige Befatzung am Rhein'*).[28]

Erected by an unhappy coincidence in 1924, when the new Herriot cabinet ordered withdrawal from the Ruhr and adopted a policy of rapprochement, Moreau-Vauthier's memorial 'To the Black Army' at Rheims was demolished by the Germans in 1940, in a gesture whose inspiration requires no further comment than to recall the propaganda images of *'die barbaren'* filmed by Wehrmacht photographic units for newsreel audiences in the 1940s and seen again in *Le Chagrin et la Pitié*. In fact, in France itself, representations of the coloured troops formed part of a construct of colonialist attitudes, and rested upon assumptions about power relationships and ultimately, ambivalence. On the one hand, there was what one commentator on the Josephine Baker phenomenon has called the

> huge disparity between the image of the young black American woman so enthusiastically adopted by Parisians, and the paternalist attitude of the French towards the natives who so obediently contributed to towards the construction of 'their' colonial Empire.[29]

On the other, there was Lyautey's expressed anxiety that by 1930 France had become too dependent on colonial troops for a large proportion of her regular army (150 000 out of 537 000), and the 'dangers represented by the presence on French soil of such a large number of colonial *'indigène'* regiments'.[30] Such anxiety is doubly revealing. Partly a reflection of the country's acute demographic situation – colonial fertility was seen as helping to offset the declining French birth-rate – and one of a number of factors which produced the defensive 'Maginot Line' psychology, it was also based on an underlying fear of subversion, analogous perhaps to Weygand's anxiety during the battle of France in May–June 1940 that certain units were undependable and that a popular uprising in Paris was to be guarded against. Moreover, the iconographic glorification of the attacking qualities of the *tirailleurs sénégalais* was in symptomatic contradiction to the dominant military thinking of the period as epitomised by Gamelin, Weygand's predecessor as commander-in-chief, unable to 'break the mould' of 1914–18 and still, like Joffre (and Gallieni, then military governor of Paris) before him, under the lingering illusion that he might stop the invader on the Marne.

Following the Second World War, during which colonial forces were the object of racial atrocity at the hands of the invaders[31] and once again made a disproportionate contribution to French fortunes, notably in the ranks of the Free French forces, commemorative and iconographic assumptions continued to follow largely metropolitan practice. Existing 1914–18 memorials underwent modification to accommodate the dead of the second conflict, usually by the incorporation of the dates 1939–1945 and enlarged or additional name plaques. Restored and repositioned after the Second World War, the previously cited example at Le Lorrain (Martinique) was further enhanced by the addition of crossed rifles, a tricolour flag and a fountain with, of all things metropolitan, ornamental lions as water spouts. In fact, the imperial dislocation, signs of which had been visible before 1939, had been dramatically accelerated and was brought to its logical conclusion by colonial conflicts in Indochina (1947–54) and Algeria (1954–62). Already problematic, many memorials in the former colonies were sacrificed to the iconographical requirements of the new post-independence regimes; the Algiers memorial was covered in concrete; others were repatriated at the behest of local regimental associations and '*ancien combattant*' groups in France. The twin horsemen of Casablanca were reinaugurated in 1965 at Senlis, garrison for France's last overseas regiment, disbanded in 1964, while the Philippeville memorial went to Toulouse, Mostaganem to Montpellier, Oran to Lyon, Hamman-Bou Hadjar to Fréjus, and Tlemcen to Saint-Aygulf, a part of Fréjus which since 1961 has been home to a large *pied noir* exile population. And Fréjus is of course where we came in, with the memorial to the 'Black Army' (1994).

Created by the sculptor Yvon Guidez at the behest of the 'Amis du Musée des Troupes de Marine', this memorial was in part inspired by the Moreau-Vauthier group preserved in replica at Bamako.[32] In fact, the composition is less massively compact than the original, the five figures arranged more freely in two groups at different levels facing into the town with their backs to the (disembarkation) beach. On a low forward plinth, two uniformed and helmeted figures appear to make a slight bow in a form of arrival-greeting, but the overall structure and handling of the memorial prevents this from seeming unduly submissive. A second plinth supports a further group of three military figures, a flag-bearer and two infantrymen in less formal pose, one of whom, his arm raised, is captured in an almost dancing rhythm, underlining the kinetic aspect of the memorial which can be seen from all sides. Indeed one of the soldiers represented, in his Second-World-War-style woollen cap, appears equally redolent of the coloured Amercan GI as of the archetypal *chechia'd tirailleur*, offering thereby a wholly unintentional homage to another liberating army and beyond that, to the celebrated '*Lafayette, nous voilà!*' of 1917. Cast in Poland with a dedication by Senghor, it was inaugurated by former defence minister François Léotard, president of the UDF and still at that point mayor of Fréjus. Léotard was a longstanding local campaigner against the Front National in an area which, as the March 1998 regional elections showed, remains politically disputed territory. His patronage of this unequivocal homage to the 'Black Army' may also be seen as belonging to that political context.

Notes and references

1. Editions de l'Alanthrope, 1979.
2. Issued by the Délégation à la Mémoire et à l'Information Historique, 37 rue de Bellechasse, Paris.
3. P. Rivé, A. Becker, O. Pelletier, D. Renoux et C. Thomas, eds., *Monuments de Mémoire. Monuments aux morts de la Grande Guerre* (La Documentation française, 1991), p. 141.
4. See A. Becker, *Les Monuments aux morts* (Errance, 1988), pp. 116–8 and illustration, p. 128.
5. See M. Lefrançois, 'La sculpture coloniale: une leçon des choses?', in *Coloniales 1920–1940*, Catalogue de l'Exposition tenue au Musée Municipal de Boulogne-Billancourt du 7 novembre 1989 au 31 janvier 1990, pp. 29–43.
6. Ibid., pp. 39–40.
7. *Monuments de mémoire*, p. 189.
8. Ibid., pp. 262 and 264.
9. On one of their number, see H. E. Beale, 'Women and First World War memorials in Arles and la Provence mistralienne', *Modern and Contemporary France*, 7, 2 (May 1999), pp. 209–24.
10. I am indebted to Tony Chafer, University of Portsmouth, for a photograph of this memorial.
11. Photographs by Paul Parker, Stirling University French Photographic Archive (SUFPA).
12. Le Lorrain, previously called Grande Anse, was renamed during the First World War. I am indebted to Richard Burton, School of African and Asian Studies, University of Sussex, for this information.
13. 'Les soupirs du servant de Dakar', in Case d'Armons, *Calligrammes*, Apollinaire, *Oeuvres Poétiques* (Gallimard, 'Bibliothèque de la Pléiade', 1965), pp. 235–6; also quoted in Becker, 1988, p. 128.
14. A. Camus, *Le Premier Homme* (Gallimard, 1994), p. 70.
15. These issues were addressed by Antoine Prost in his classic three-volume study, *Les Anciens Combattants et la société française, 1914–1939* (Presses de la Fondation Nationale des Sciences Politiques), 1977, and in the abbreviated monograph published by Gallimard and Julliard, coll. Archives, in 1977. W. Kidd, 'Les monuments aux morts pacifistes et la culture populaire, 1919–1939: image inversée ou miroir brisé?', paper delivered at the 1997 French Studies Conference, offers a number of case studies.

16. Camus, *Le Premier Homme*, p. 278.
17. Photographs: Alan Rodney (Conseil Supérieur de la Recherche et de la Technologie, Paris).
18. Photographs: Greg Reade (SUFPA).
19. *Coloniales 1920–1940*, p. 41.
20. See M. Lefrançois's piece on Landowski in *Monuments de Mémoire*, pp. 221–5.
21. See Becker, 1988, p. 118.
22. In R. Bachollet, J.-B. Delost, A.-C. Lelieur, M.-C. Peyrière, *NégriPub* (L'image des noirs dans la publicité) (Somogy, Editions d'Art, 1987), p. 65.
23. P. Dine, *Images of the Algerian War. French Fiction and Film, 1954–1992* (Clarendon Press, 1994), pp. 157–9 and *passim*.
24. *Monuments de Mémoire*, p. 222.
25. See *NégriPub*, pp. 17, 22 and 92–100.
26. See *Images et Colonies*, edited by P. Blanchard and A. Chatelier (Achac/Syros, 1993), p. 24.
27. Ibid., p. 146.
28. *NégriPub*, p. 135.
29. Ibid., p. 136.
30. Quoted by D. David, 'France: la puissance contrariée', in *La France en Question* (Gallimard/Limes, 1996), pp. 19–36.
31. The memorials to colonial troops killed in France in 1940 are outside the scope of the present study. See S. Barcellini and A. Wieviorka, *Passant, souviens-toi! Les Lieux du souvenir de la seconde guerre mondiale en France* (Plon, 1995), pp. 62–5.
32. I am indebted to M. Roland Halin, *directeur de cabinet* at the Mairie in Fréjus, for a copy of the commemorative brochure from which these and other details are drawn.

14
Defending the Empire in Retrospect: The Discourse of the Extreme Right[1]

Christopher Flood and Hugo Frey

The past in the present

During the campaign for the European election of 1999 the Front National (FN) listed Charles de Gaulle, grandson of *the* General Charles de Gaulle, second on its list of candidates. This choice was described in the FN's newspaper *National hebdo* as being motivated by the fact that the general's conception of French sovereignty within a Europe of nations was shared by the FN.[2] On the other hand, it was stated that the grandson's candidature was also intended to symbolise national reconciliation and the gathering together of French people on behalf of their country. In this context national reconciliation evidently implied that the party itself should serve as an example, since the general had long remained an object of loathing among the extreme right after he had negotiated the independence of Algeria in 1962. The bitterness and resentment had been particularly acute among the former European inhabitants of Algeria who had been forced to take refuge in France, where many of them now voted for the FN.

De Gaulle's presence on the list was only part of the symbolic picture. In tenth place was Sid Hamed Yayahoui. An FN regional councillor, he was a son of the senator and mayor of Sidi Bel Abbès who had been assassinated by the FLN in 1962. Were he to be elected, it was said that he would represent all the *harkis* and *pieds noirs* whom France had forgotten. The implication was not only that there was solidarity between loyal Arabs who had fought for France and white former settlers, but also that the FN was not racist and that its draconian policies on immigration were not aimed indiscriminately at all Arabs. Twentieth on the list was Huguette Fatna. Described rather patronisingly as 'coffee-coloured' and

195

'patriotic in the way that people are in the little versions of France at the ends of the world', she represented the DOM-TOMs.[3] Her presence reinforced the message that the FN was not racist or sexist and suggested that right-minded native peoples in the remaining overseas territories were, or should be, contented with France's continuing rule. But three other names on the list carried a sinister symbolism: Jean-Jacques Susini had been a leader of the OAS struggle to keep Algeria French; Roger Holeindre was a former OAS activist; and Jean-Baptiste Biaggi had campaigned against Algerian independence.

These anecdotal details illustrate the fact that the historical memory of the Empire and of decolonisation, especially that of Algeria, remains very much alive among members of the extreme right. Although the extreme right had been slow to espouse the imperialist drive fostered by Jules Ferry and his successors from the 1880s onwards, by the mid-twentieth century loyalty to the empire had long been a central tenet of ideological faith for most of its publicists.[4] Whereas their predecessors had once regarded the creation of the empire as an expensive distraction from the real business of restoring France's position within Europe, particularly in relation to Germany, the colonies had come to be perceived by extreme right-wing nationalists as essential attributes of their country's status as a great power. In the decades following the Second World War, with France's international standing already diminished, they believed that the growing threats from native liberation movements in the colonies should be resisted with the utmost vigour. This was true of Algeria above all, because of its geographical proximity, the number of settlers there and its particular status as a notional part of France. Opposition to withdrawal from Algeria had, in any case, been an issue around which extreme right-wingers could coalesce and seek to build support, during a period when they were attempting to escape the political impotence to which they had been condemned in the wake of the post-war purges of former Vichyites and collaborationists.

Although the distant war in Indochina attracted far less attention than the Algerian conflict was to do, the surrender of Dien Bien Phu and the loss of Indochina in 1954 had been perceived as dreadful blows, even by those who had not followed the war closely. Raoul Girardet, a veteran of the extreme right as well as a distinguished historian, recaptures the sense of anguished bewilderment, when he recalls how the capitulation had reawakened his memories of France's collapse in 1940:

> Dien Bien Phu was a decisive shock. Humiliation again, defeat, the
> columns of prisoners, the flag being lowered, loyal dependents being

abandoned. Memories of the armistice, the barracks at Fontenay-le-Comte and the retreat came back to me with the same feeling of rage and helplessness.[5]

As Girardet had shown at the time in his own articles for the neo-Maurrassian review *La Nation française*, and in his eventual commitment to the OAS, the loss of Indochina had made the defence of Algeria imperative in the eyes of the extreme right. It is important to remember that in 1954 support for maintaining French sovereignty over Algeria had extended across the political spectrum except to the extreme left, but that it gradually eroded thereafter, whereas the extreme right remained committed to maintaining French control there. Indeed, many extreme right-wingers had supported resistance and even rebellion in the face of political attempts to negotiate independence.[6] In the aftermath, associated once again with a failed cause, tainted again by charges of fascism, racism and violent activism, the extreme right suffered a further period of political eclipse until the FN began to achieve a measure of electoral success in the mid-1980s, building its policy platform around issues which were often closely linked to the consequences of decolonisation.

Thus, although the imperial past has not been among the most prominent topics in the publications of the FN, it is evoked directly or indirectly in many contexts. The same is true of extreme right-wing publications not tied to the FN such as *Enquête sur l'histoire*, a glossy magazine which draws its contributors primarily, though not exclusively, from the extreme right under the editorship of Dominique Venner, himself a veteran of the OAS and a progenitor of the intellectual New Right.[7] In fact, there is continuity of interpretation in many areas from the arguments produced by extreme right-wingers during the heated debates over colonialism and decolonisation in the 1950s through to the retrospective interpretations offered today. Furthermore, during the period since decolonisation extreme right-wing writers have asserted that the meaning of the imperial era has been grotesquely misinterpreted by communist, socialist, centrist and Gaullist publicists for their own political reasons, and that these distortions dominate public understanding of a crucial aspect of French history. For example, in his preface to an issue of the FN's theoretical magazine *Identité* on the subject of past and present forms of imperialism, Le Pen argued that the west had come to view the imperial past through a screen of propaganda and masochism. Current orthodoxy made colonialism a dirty word, synonymous with exploitation and oppression. Anyone who challenged the claim that all of the problems of the former colonial territories today were consequences of the previous period of colonisation was subjected to charges of heresy, he asserted.[8]

Le Pen's stance was a familiar one. Extreme right-wing publicists have habitually sought propagandistic advantage by presenting themselves as martyrs in the defence of truths which other political groups have attempted to hide. Nevertheless, in this instance he was not simply striking a pose. Extreme right-wing writers have seen the retrospective defence of the empire as a duty towards the past, both in the name of historical accuracy, as they see it, and in the name of fidelity to a cause for which they themselves (in the case of older members) or their predecessors struggled. Conversely, they have considered that political groups to the left of them are the descendants of those which were responsible for the tragic and avoidable loss of the empire. These are highly charged emotional and ideological issues which feed into the collective identity of the extreme right and the transmission of shared values which are grasped as being distinct from, and opposed to, those held by other political groups.

The colonial past is also a matter of significance because of its connection with important areas of foreign and domestic policy in the present. Besides the fact that France still possesses scattered territorial remnants of the empire, it also has close, if sometimes uncomfortable or embarrassing, relations with many of its former colonies, including Algeria. On home soil, it has to deal with the complexities of a multi-racial, multicultural society arising from the presence of a large immigrant population drawn in part from those territories. Postcolonial issues are therefore of vital concern to the extreme right. We have given a detailed analysis elsewhere of extreme right-wing thinking on postcolonial matters.[9] The remainder of the present chapter focuses primarily on the extreme right's retrospective representations of the conduct of French imperialism and the process of decolonisation. Post-colonial questions will be taken into consideration relatively briefly to round out the discussion at the end.

Acquiring and holding the empire

There are, of course, different nuances of thought within the extreme right on the subject of colonialism. The majority of writers on the subject follow the line which developed increasingly among adherents of the nationalist right from around the turn of the nineteenth century onwards, as they found reasons for endorsing the possession of empire. Catholic traditionalists had been attracted by the notion that the cross could follow the flag and vice versa. In a counterpart of the republican, universalist ideology of the *mission civilisatrice*, they could even believe that France had a providential vocation to spread Christian culture to the heathen, by force where necessary, and beyond that, to bring the benefits of higher forms of organisation and economic development. These thinkers, as well as others whose arguments did not depend on providentialist, religious justifications, could also legitimise France's acquisition of colonies in the light of racial-determinist or Social-Darwinist assumptions concerning the natural dominance of the more intelligent over the less intelligent or the more highly evolved peoples over the less highly evolved. Contrary to republican ideologues, they did not preach an egalitarian, democratic creed but assumed a need for hierarchical order in the colonies, just as they believed in authoritarian government at home. However, since the colonies themselves were not, in fact, governed in a democratic, egalitarian way, but were administered under a regime of Jacobin/Napoleonic centralism and of a form of assimilationism which stopped short of being emancipatory for the vast majority of natives, whatever the Republic might claim as its long-term objectives, the ideological difference could be subsumed for practical purposes.

On the other hand, there had been an internally diverse minority of extreme right-wingers, including theorists such as Gustave Le Bon and Léopold de Saussure, whose views on race, culture or government, without necessarily challenging the legitimacy or the desirability of imperial rule in itself, led them to believe that the best way to conduct it was by delegating power back to native elites and, more generally, allowing the territories to follow their own customs and traditions, in so far as these were not too barbaric and did not threaten France's interests. Marshal Lyautey, a royalist in the service of the Republic, had been a practitioner of this type of approach during his period as resident-general of the Moroccan protectorate from 1917 to 1925.[10]

At the time of the debates over decolonisation during the 1950s, most defenders of the empire still held to various versions of the right or duty to bring civilisation to less developed societies. For example, many of the recurrent themes can be found in a tract produced for the national conference of the neo-fascist Jeune Nation group in 1954 – after the fall of Indochina and anticipating the struggle for North Africa – which announced that the sole criterion for possession of territories was the process of civilisation applied to them and the effort put into the process.[11] According to this view, some peoples were builders of civilisa-tions whereas others were not. It was claimed that France had opened up uninhabited lands, pacified and administered territories which had never been coherently governed, playing a constructive, creative role. Those who were capable of building had the right to do so, and what Frenchmen had built by their toil and their intelligence, they had a right to keep. Here, then, the notion of bringing civilisation was underpinned by the right to hold it by force if necessary.

Much the same attitudes are apparent in retrospective accounts today, although there is little inclination to engage in philosophical discussion of the legitimacy of acquiring colonies by military means. It is rare to find expressions of Social-Darwinist, Catholic-providentialist or other historicist justifications of the right to empire, although Le Pen and his close associate, Jean-Claude Martinez, have been exceptions.[12] Most writers have simply taken the empire as historical fact, while emphasising the benefits brought by French colonialism, in contrast to the situation of those regions before the advent of French control or after France's withdrawal. It can be acknowledged that there was considerable slaughter and that military repression of uprisings was a feature of the imperial world, but this has not been approached from the standpoint of moral condemnation. At worst, excesses have been viewed as episodic, negative aspects of what was nevertheless a largely positive balance sheet. Indeed, there is a tradition of admiration for the courage and self-sacrifice of the French forces in opening up and holding the colonies, with little real backing from the parliamentarians at home. Descriptions are often couched in the language of epic and adventure, but also in terms of cherished extreme right-wing values of discipline, obedience and unity under firm leadership. Dominique Venner, for example, argues that the prowess of French military officers was often essential in winning the respect and loyalty of native chiefs, who viewed this type of valour as a mark of superiority.[13] And the popular historian of colonialism Pierre Montagnon (ex-paratroop officer, ex-OAS) epitomises the same perspective on the empire when he remarks that colonisation was primarily a matter of hard-fought military conquest. 'Along the way there were strong men. There were leaders. Leaders who could create events and shape fate,' he observes, adding later, 'The men on the ground were the real builders. On rare occasions they were supported by policies'.[14]

The army's role in the wars of decolonisation is also defended. At the time, extreme right-wingers' support for the army had contrasted with their contempt for most of France's civilian politicians. Defence of the military had not only involved praising its successes and finding mitigating circumstances for its setbacks – often in terms of the inadequacy of resources granted by the government – but also of denying or minimising atrocities. For example, Michel Déon had hailed the achievement of winning a war against terrorism and revolutionary subversion in Algeria without using degrading methods.[15] Similarly, in more recent extreme right-wing writings there is often an implicit or explicit argument that the army conducted itself with honour and restraint in Algeria, despite the horrific actions of the Front de Libération Nationale (FLN).[16]

Furthermore, notwithstanding complaints that much of it had been left too late owing to the weakness of colonial policies under the Third Republic, there has been real pride in the material development of the colonies. The construction of railways, roads and other infrastructure, the development of natural resources, such as the oil and gas in the Sahara, the medical services, the educational effort and even some aspects of the administration have frequently been cited as elements of an impressive legacy bequeathed to Indochina and Algeria in particular.[17]

Betrayers and defenders of France's honour

Why, then, was the empire lost? Perhaps the most sophisticated explanation is given by Pierre de Meuse in the 1994 issue of *Identité* devoted to old and new forms of colonialism.[18] His argument is broadly in line with those of earlier thinkers who argued against the assimilationist conception of the civilising mission and/or against the centralist approach to colonial administration. It also develops points made more recently by the maverick New Right theorist Alain de Benoist in his book *Europe, Tiers monde, même combat*.[19] The underlying assumptions derive from the deterministic conceptions of culture and ethnicity which the New Right has substituted for the older, less publicly acceptable discourse of racial inequality. De Meuse presents the causes of the loss of the colonies in terms of the pernicious effects of republican ideology, coupled with a centralist approach to colonial administration. His contention is that the universalistic doctrine of rights, democracy and equality preached by republicans was entirely spurious because it assumed that only one model of society was valid: it took no account of the fact that collective identity is a product of shared culture and that cultures which are fundamentally different from each other should be maintained as separate as possible in order to avoid destabilising, socially damaging effects. According to this argument, republican ideology was not merely invalid from a theoretical standpoint. It did not accord with the practice of colonial government which undermined native customs, beliefs and practices but did not fulfil the unrealistic, culturally alien aspirations which were propagated among sections of the local populations which received French education. Even the dedication of French teachers can be viewed as disruptive and ultimately destructive from this standpoint. Writing in *Enquête sur l'histoire*, Jean-François Gautier makes an analogous critique of the medical services in so far as they not only disrupted native populations' traditional cultural practices, but also paved the way for the appalling demographic and economic imbalances of the postcolonial period through reduction of mortality rates.[20] In this sense, French colonialism prepared its own downfall. It was the fault of the Enlightenment ideological legacy on the left, but de Meuse also reproaches the majority of the extreme right for having failed to develop its own distinctive approach on the basis of respect for the specificity of every culture.

Whether or not they endorsed this viewpoint, most extreme right-wingers had a more prosaic perspective on the causes of France's enforced departure from Indochina and Algeria, the two main battlegrounds of decolonisation. The reasons have been seen to lie in two major areas. First, the subversive influence of left-wing notions of the right to self-determination was coupled with the communists' translation of the concept of class struggle and revolution into the colonial context as a doctrine of emancipation of oppressed peoples from the exploitative rule of capitalist imperialism. This propaganda had not only played its part in stirring dissent both in the colonies themselves and within France, where agitation by the PCF and its intellectual fellow-travellers had helped to undermine the resolve of successive governments of the Fourth Republic.[21] On the other hand, the extreme right's habitual contempt for parliamentary politicians made it easy to blame politicians for their failure to give adequate support to the army in Indochina and Algeria. However, given the subsequent course of events, de Gaulle's treachery and duplicity were even more heinous, since he had come to power with support from many on the extreme right precisely because he had given the impression that he would stand firm. Furthermore, extreme right-wing writers have argued that the military conflict had been won, but that this victory was irrevocably undercut by de Gaulle's announcement that the people of Algeria would be allowed to decide their own future. The road to Evian was a road of ignominy, followed by the final betrayal of European Algerians, *harkis* and other loyal Arabs.[22]

In recent years, as the inclusion of de Gaulle's grandson in second place on the FN's Euro-election list signified, there have been signs that a more measured perception of the General has been spreading within some extreme right-wing circles. In fact, there have been pointers to a desire for the FN to assume his mantle, in so far as he can be construed as a precursor of some of the extreme right's current positions, or at least to claim to replace the Rassemblement pour la République (RPR) as the defender of a neo-Gaullian aspiration to national independence and an assertive role for France as an international actor. With regard to de Gaulle's handling of Algeria, the incipient shift of perspective has been aided by more recent claims that his policy was intended to sever a link which would otherwise culminate in mass migration of Maghrebis into France. In this respect his aims can be construed as understandable but misguided and subsequently shown to have produced precisely the opposite of the intended effect.[23] In any case, whatever his motives, his methods are still regarded as disgraceful and dishonourable.

As we have already mentioned, many of the older intellectuals and political activists on the extreme right today participated in the events surrounding decolonisation. Some committed themselves to the clandestine struggle in the OAS, having previously served in the armed forces. Others had been civilians who worked for the OAS or belonged to political groups which were sympathetic to the aims of the OAS, whether or not they approved of its methods. For many, this has not become a cause of shame. Even when it is acknowledged that the slaughter was ultimately futile and that misjudgements were made along the way, the characteristic stance has remained one of defiant pride. This is illustrated, for example, by the continuity of tone between a large collection of articles and testimonies edited by Philippe Héduy in 1980 under the title *Algérie française 1942–1962* and an extensive dossier on the OAS and the Algerian war contained in one of the issues of Dominique Venner's magazine *Enquête sur l'histoire* in 1992.[24] Héduy, like Venner, served as a soldier in Algeria and was subsequently a member of the OAS.

The recurrent thesis underlying the contributions to both collections was that the organisation had come into existence because the *pieds noirs* and loyal Arabs of Algeria were being betrayed by those who had promised repeatedly that France would never hand over this part of its sovereign territory to the butchers of the FLN. Thus, according to this interpretation, the OAS was defending France's national honour by attempting to force de Gaulle and his government to meet solemn national obligations. The OAS had been obliged to employ terrorist means because it was fighting against an enemy who had successfully employed terrorism in pursuit of a revolutionary war which had broken the determination of French politicians and the people of metropolitan France. In other words, although the means were savage, the ends were redemptive in the eyes of extreme right-wing defenders of the OAS.

Neither collection dwells on the fact that many of those killed at its hands were innocent civilians, but both are at pains to point out the full horror of the massacres committed by the FLN before and after independence. Equally, the viciousness of the organisation's actions is implicitly mitigated by references to the clandestine activities of the *barbouzes*, portrayed as a gang of thugs, in many cases professional criminals, who would stop at nothing to carry out the will of those who had betrayed the country.

Bitterness over the betrayal of Algeria is counterbalanced, therefore, by the claim to have fought the good fight. The memory of those who lost their lives, and above all those who were executed, provides a gallery of martyrs, with Colonel Jean Bastien-Thiry pre-eminent among them for the altruism of his motives, the power of his eloquence in the courtroom and his refusal to plead for a pardon. The sacrifice of these former soldiers, as well as the lesser, but still severe, penalties inflicted on other ex-officers, such as Generals Salan and Jouhaud or Colonels Denoix de Saint Marc and Argoud, serves the representation of the OAS as the true continuation of the military struggle which had been abandoned by the state.

The consequences of failure

Among adherents of the extreme right the bitterness of betrayal and defeat has had a corollary in the perverse gratification of being able to claim that events have proved them right. France's withdrawal from most of the former colonies can be taken to have precipitated decades of decline and decay in those territories. France's departure from Indochina, followed by partition, the Vietnam War, then the establishment of communist regimes made the obvious case for drawing a contrast between the relative peace and prosperity achieved under French rule before the rise of insurgency and the ruination of Vietnam, Laos and Cambodia after that time.[25] Similarly, the FN's leading specialist on Africa, Bernard Lugan, has tirelessly pointed to the pattern of catastrophic overpopulation, economic collapse, chronic misgovernment and vicious civil wars in the post-colonial African states. However, Lugan does not accept that France is to blame for the fate of its former colonies. On the contrary, France should not have accepted the burden of guilt which the partisans of decolonisation had placed on the country. Far from exploiting the colonies, France had left them relatively prosperous, or at least with far better material conditions than they would otherwise have had. In any case, drawing on the work of the economic historian Jacques Marseille, Lugan argues that although a small number of individuals or companies had made large profits from investing in the overseas territories, the overall economic cost of the empire had been far greater than the benefits. That being the case, there was and is no need for France to bear the white man's burden by giving aid, unless there is an obvious return for France itself. [26]

In any case, Lugan and others have argued that aid policy can easily be damaging to the recipient countries.[27] In Africa the errors can be explained in terms of ideological factors. Preaching the gospel of loathing for France's imperial past, the communists, followed later by the socialists, alongside a host of Third-Worldist pressure groups, have continued to use France's alleged guilt as an exploitative imperialist power to push successive French governments into pursuing ill-conceived, incompetently executed policies of *coopération*. These policies have had disastrous effects through the siphoning of vast sums of money to corrupt élites in the former colonies, while the mass of ordinary people have been reduced to desperate levels of subsistence. The damage has been compounded by the economic dislocation of these countries through varying mixtures of ideological contamination, adoption of inappropriate socialist or liberal models of development, misgovernment, cultural disorientation, external interference, the creation of an aid-dependent mentality and the consequent inability to compete in world markets. Furthermore, under Mitterrand's presidency, French interference in the government of these territories became a hallmark of the Socialist Party's policy as it coerced them in the name of universal rights and equality to adopt western-style democratic regimes which ran directly contrary to traditional customs and social divisions, thereby promoting murderous inter-ethnic conflicts. Worse still, it is assumed, the United States, having hypocritically done all that it could to undermine the French empire in the post-war decades, has been working to supplant French influence in pursuit of its own goal of world domination.[28]

The adverse consequences of decolonisation can be said to have extended to France itself. Massive immigration into France from the former colonies, especially the African territories and above all the Maghreb, can be presented as the other side of the disastrous decline of the former colonies. The allegedly relentless, overwhelming influx of immigrants is often labelled as 'colonisation in reverse' ('*colonisation à rebours*'), to evoke the historical link and to imply that the process of settlement is a more or less deliberate attempt at domination in revenge for the past.[29] While extreme right-wing writers will admit that temporary immigration by individual workers was of value up to the end of the colonial period, the continuation of immigration to France since that time, establishing patterns of permanent settlement, family regrouping, illegal entries and applications for asylum, can be understood as the source of a wide range of economic, social and cultural ills. The issue of swamping is, of course, very frequently linked to claims concerning the levels of violence and juvenile delinquency in the ghettos which allegedly make them into no-go areas for the police. This factor has offered the FN grounds for arguing that the internal security of 'immigrant-saturated' areas of France should be treated as part of France's military defence.

Furthermore, there is the 'threat' of militant Islam. At the time of decolonisation extreme right-wing writers often represented defence of the empire as part of the global struggle to defend Europe, or western civilisation, against communist barbarism. Colonial liberation movements were portrayed as willing or unknowing instruments of the Soviet quest for international power.[30] The external conspiracy was linked to France's internal politics by the nefarious activity of the PCF and its fellow-travellers in their campaigns for decolonisation, among other subversive pursuits. More recently the threat of global hegemony has been attributed to the United States, seconded by the European Union and aided within France by a vast range of client groups, including the major parties. However, Islamic fundamentalism is viewed by the extreme right as another source of external and internal danger, with France and its overseas interests as obvious targets for attack, given the French colonial past and the installation of a large Islamic community in France since the time of decolonisation. Extreme right-wing intellectuals can explain the rise of militant Islam in parts of the former empire as an understandable assertion of collective identity in reaction against French, and more generally western, values. However, against multiculturalists and integrationists who claim that Islam can be tolerated in France like any other religion, publicists such as Le Pen, Pierre Vial, Max Cabantous, Jean-Yves Le Gallou and Pierre Milloz argue from historical and current examples that Islam has been in permanent conflict with Europe since the time of its emergence in the seventh century, despite periods of calm.[31] In terms of foreign and security policy, the Islamic threat can be interpreted as a dimension of the emerging North–South polarisation between rich nations with ageing populations and impoverished nations undergoing demographic explosion. Not all Muslim immigrants are portrayed as radicals but they are considered to form a vast pool of potential recruits for an extension of the holy war and revenge for the past crimes attributed to the former colonial overlords.

Conclusion

With an eye to the future, by the early 1990s the FN had developed a range of policies which would allegedly rebuild France's strength and status in the world.[32] Some elements of this platform are well known. The repatriation of vast numbers of immigrants and systematic political, economic and cultural discrimination against others is an important part of it. Outside France, it entails a clearly instrumental approach to overseas aid, tying it to the halting and reversing of migration on the one hand and the promotion of French business and security interests on the other. Within the wider framework of a drive to extend French influence wherever possible in the international sphere according to a neo-Gaullian conception of national grandeur, it is intended that the remaining fragments of the empire should serve as a springboard for the expansion of French commercial and strategic interests in the southern hemisphere. As a sop to the New Right critique of centralism and to the defence of cultural identities, the FN offers a neo-associationist model of three autonomous regional groupings under decentralised government which would respect local traditions.

Of course, all this is likely to remain hypothetical for the foreseeable future, given the improbability of a government dominated by the FN or the rival Mouvement National (MN). And besides, despite the rhetoric of national assertiveness and rediscovery of international power, the programme does not amount to very much, except in the repugnant, and probably impracticable, policy of mass repatriation of several million people. If anything, it indicates recognition of the limits of France's resources and freedom of action.

On the other hand, the retrospective defence of the colonial past is of real importance. Whatever the future of the FN, the MN or any other extreme right-wing party, the intellectual culture of the extreme right is unlikely to wither away after standing the test of two centuries. Like any other political sub-culture, that of the extreme right feeds on historical myths (not in the crude sense that the accounts are necessarily false, but that the selection and interpretation of facts is heavily coloured by ideology) as well as other types of political discourse. Like the story of Vichy, it is one in which the extreme right emerged on the losing side. Like the story of Vichy, it involves claims that the actions of the extreme right at the time have been the subject of outrageously distorted historical accounts by political enemies whose views are taken as unimpeachable truth. The collective sense of injustice is itself a powerful factor binding together those who consider themselves victims (directly or by vicarious identification). But whereas the extreme right has difficulty in making the story of Vichy into an inspiring epic of heroism – except in the sense that it can be presented as a narrative of stoical endurance and sacrifice for patriotic reasons – that is not true of decolonisation, as we have seen. On the contrary, being prepared to fight to the very end for one's country at the risk of one's life conforms to one of the cultural stereotypes of romantic heroism. And whereas Vichy turned its back on the Republic which had engendered it, the defence of the empire, and particularly of Algeria, is easier to represent as fidelity to what had been accepted by successive regimes and nearly all currents of political opinion up to the moment when it was abandoned for reasons of expediency rather than conviction. After all, the last defenders of French Algeria had sought to identify themselves with the Resistance, however spuriously. When and if the process of decolonisation is placed under the same microscopic examination as the Vichy period has been during the last twenty years, it is to be expected that the extreme right will defend its version of history vigorously.

Notes and references

1. The use of the label 'extreme right' throughout this chapter is for convenience. It is not intended to suggest that the extreme right is a single, ideologically homogeneous grouping. The label is justified here because a range of concerns and positions are, nevertheless, shared between representatives of different currents of thought.
2. J.-M. Le Pen, 'Les 87 candidats présentés par Le Pen', *National hebdo*, 20–26 May 1999.
3. Ibid. ('couleur café' and 'patriote comme on l'est dans les petites Frances du bout du monde').
4. On the extreme right and colonialism, see for example, R. Girardet, *L'Idée coloniale en France de 1871 à 1962* (La Table Ronde, 1972); G. Pervillé, 'L'Algérie dans la mémoire des droites', in J.-F. Sirinelli, ed., *Histoire des droites en France* (Gallimard, 1992), vol. 2, pp. 621–56; M. Michel, 'La Colonisation', in Sirinelli, *Histoire des droites*, vol. 3, pp. 125–63; M. Heffernan, 'The French Right and the Overseas Empire', in N. Atkin and F. Tallett, eds., *The Right in France, 1789–1997* (Tauris, 1998), pp. 89–113.
5. R. Girardet and P. Assouline, *Singulièrement libre: entretiens* (Perrin, 1990), p. 133.
6. See S. Berstein, 'La peau de chagrin de "l'Algérie française"', in J.-P. Rioux, ed., *La Guerre d'Algérie et les Français* (Fayard, 1990), pp. 202–17.
7. On Venner, see his memoirs, *Le Coeur rebelle: guerres d'Algérie* (Les Belles Lettres: 1994); and on his ideological activism in the wake of the Algerian war, J. Algazy, *La Tentation néo-fasciste en France 1944–1965* (Fayard, 1984), pp. 264–87; A.-M. Duranton-Crabol, 'Du combat pour l'Algérie française au combat pour la culture européenne; les origines du Groupement de Recherche et d'Etudes pour la Civilisation Européenne (GRECE)', in J.-P. Rioux and

J.-F. Sirinelli, eds., *La Guerre d'Algérie et les intellectuels français* (Complexe, 1991), pp. 59–78.

8. Le Pen, 'Le sinistre mea culpa de l'homme blanc', *Identité*, 22, Spring/Summer 1994, p. 3.

9. C. Flood and H. Frey, 'Questions of Decolonisation and Postcolonialism in the Ideology of the French Extreme Right', *Journal of European Studies*, 28, 1/2, (1998), pp. 69–88.

10. For a sympathetic biography of Lyautey by an extreme right-wing author, see J. Benoist-Méchin, *Lyautey l'Africain ou le rêve immolé* (Perrin, 1978), especially pp. 233–307 on his time in Morocco; and G. Comte, 'Lyautey l'énigmatique', *Enquête sur l'histoire*, 8 (autumn 1993), pp. 53–8.

11. F. Sidos, 'Mouvement jeune nation', typed statement for national conference of Jeune Nation, 'Peuple de France et d'Outre-mer', Paris, 22 May 1954 (Bibliothèque Nationale).

12. Le Pen, 'Le sinistre mea culpa de l'homme blanc'; J.-C. Martinez, 'Conclusion', in Association pour le Respect des Lois de la République/J.-C. Martinez, ed., *La Nouvelle-Calédonie: la stratégie, le droit et la République* (Pedone, 1985), pp. 209–11.

13. Venner, 'Les derniers féodaux' and 'Une poignée de capitaines', *Enquête sur l'histoire*, 8, autumn 1993, pp. 4–5, 62–8; and his 'C'était le moment d'avoir vingt ans', ibid., 2, spring 1992, pp. 38–43.

14. P. Montagnon, *La France coloniale I. La Gloire de l'empire* (Pygmalion, 1988), p. 482.

15. M. Déon, *L'Armée d'Algérie et la pacification* (Plon, 1959), p. 109.

16. See for example, R. Girardet and P. Vidal-Naquet (interviews with Daniel Bermond), 'La Torture', *L'Histoire*, 140 (January 1991), 104–7; Girardet and Assouline, *Singulièrement libre*, pp. 139–43; D. Venner, 'Exactions et tortures, *Enquête sur l'histoire*, 2, spring 1992, p. 18; P. Pellissier, 'Les paras en première ligne', ibid., 15, winter 1996, p. 49.

17. See for example, J.-P. Angelelli, L'entre-deux-guerres', in P. Héduy, ed., *Algérie française 1942–1962* (Société de Production Littéraire, 1980), pp. 65–8 (and other articles by M. Weckel, G. Barbet, P. Goinard, X. Yacono *et al.* in parts 2 and 3); R. Holeindre, *L'Asie en marche* (Laffont, 1983), pp. 157–8; B. Lugan, *Afrique: de la colonisation philanthropique à la recolonisation humanitaire* (Christian de Bartillat, 1995), pp. 42–6.

18. P. de Meuse, 'Le colonialisme: enfant de la gauche', *Identité*, 22, spring/summer 1994, pp. 5–8, 34.

19. A. de Benoist, *Europe, tiers monde, même combat* (Laffont, 1986).

20. J.-F. Gautier, 'Hippocrate sous les tropiques', *Enquête sur l'histoire*, 8, autumn 1993, pp. 59–61.

21. For example, M. de Saint Pierre, 'Les complices du FLN', in Héduy, *Algérie française*, (Société de Production Littéraire, 1980), pp. 342–4; G. Chambarlac, 'Tueurs et porteurs de valises', *Enquête sur l'histoire*, 15, winter 1996, pp. 52–4.

22. See, for example, A. de Sérigny, *Echos d'Alger II: l'abandon* (Presses de la Cité, 1974); A. Argoud, 'La guerre d'Algérie ou l'accélération de la décadence', in Héduy, *Algérie française*, pp. 362–3; J.-C. Pérez, *Le Sang d'Algérie (histoire d'une trahison permanente)* (Eds du Camelot et de la Joyeuse Garde, 1992); P. Montagnon, 'Une guerre de huit années (1954–1962)', *Enquête sur l'histoire*, 2, spring 1992, pp. 11–24.

23. On de Gaulle's misjudged attempt to avoid Colombey-les-Deux-Eglises becoming Colombey-les-Deux-Mosquées, as he is reported to have said to Alain Peyrefitte, see F. Quesnay, 'La tragédie algérienne', *Enquête sur l'histoire*, 14, summer 1995, pp. 59–61; B. Cabanes, 'Un problème pour la France', ibid., 15, winter 1996, pp. 70–3. Already, in *Enquête* 2, Venner had remarked that his view of de Gaulle had become more nuanced with time, though he was still sickened by his duplicity over Algeria (pp. 4–5). The dossier which forms *Enquête* 14, devoted to 'De Gaulle et le gaullisme', attempts a degree of balance by including some writers sympathetic to de Gaulle and others deeply hostile.

24. Héduy, *Algérie française 1942–1962*; *Enquête sur l'histoire*, 2, spring 1992.

25. For example, in Holeindre, *L'Asie en marche*, pp. 157–69.

26. See P. Lugan, *Afrique*, pp. 42–6; 'Un empire ruineux', *Enquête sur l'histoire*, 2, spring 1992, pp. 72–3; see also, unsigned, 'Colonisation, décolonisation: le bilan', *Identité*, 22 spring/summer 1994, p. 12.

27. P. Lugan, *Afrique, bilan de la décolonisation* (Perrin, 1991); 'Décolonisation: un cadeau empoisonné', *Identité*, 22, spring/summer 1994, p. 9; D. Lefranc, 'Le tiers monde à libérer', ibid., pp. 13–17;'Les nouvelles africolies', interview with Philippe de Baleine, *Paris-Match*, 24 August 1995; P. Bonnefont, 'Les pièges de la coopération', *Enquête sur l'histoire*, 8, autumn 1993, pp. 74–5.

28. See, for example, P. Gannat, 'Le nouveau visage du colonialisme', *Identité*, 22 spring/summer 1994, pp. 18–21; General J. von Lohausen, 'Main basse sur l'Europe', *Eléments*, 84, 1996, p. 41; and his *Les Empires et la puissance: la géopolitique aujourd'hui* (Labyrinthe, 1996); and the dossier of articles, 'L'Amérique, adversaire des peuples', in *Identité*, 23, July–September 1996, pp. 3–21.

29. For examples of the usage, see P. de Meuse, 'Le colonialisme, enfant de la gauche'; B. Cabanes, 'L'immigration: un problème pour la France', *Enquête sur l'histoire*, 15 (1996), p. 72. Venner is more explicit when he argues in *Le Coeur rebelle*, p. 12: 'Future historians will note that the twentieth-century invasion of France and Europe by African Muslim crowds began in 1962 with the French surrender in Algeria.' Jean Raspail's fictional treatment of the theme of unarmed invasion by immigrant hordes in *Le Camp des Saints* (3rd edn, Laffont, 1985) is widely cited in extreme right-wing publications as prophetic.

30. A recurrent theme in, for example, Marshal Juin and H. Massis, *L'Europe en question* (Plon, 1958); and Déon, *L'Armée d'Algérie*.

31. Articles by Le Pen, Vial, Cabantous, Le Gallou and Milloz in the dossier, 'Le réveil de l'Islam', *Identité*, 6, March/April 1990, pp. 3–23; see also (unsigned), 'Dreux en voie d'islamisation', *National Hebdo*, 18–24 April 1996. The dossier, 'L'Europe et l'Islam', forming the greater part of *Enquête sur l'histoire*, 15, Winter 1996, follows similar themes.

32. Set out in Front National, *300 Mesures pour la renaissance de la France* (Editions Nationales, 1993).

15
Putting the Colonies on the Map: Colonial Names in Paris Streets

Robert Aldrich

Over the last decade the study of 'realms of memory' has been a grow-ing field, pioneered by Pierre Nora's magisterial *Les Lieux de mémoire*.[1] Statues, *hôtels de ville* and *monuments aux morts*, the church and the café, as well as famous edifices such as the Bastille and the Eiffel Tower, have attracted attention as sites in which the French preserve and continu-ously reinterpret their memory of the past.[2] But what about colonial memories? Nora's collection includes only one piece on the empire, Charles-Robert Ageron's essay on the Exposition Coloniale of 1931. Is France's colonial memory so slight? Edward Said, among others, argues that colonial references are omnipresent in British and French art and literature, politics and daily life.[3] However, Antoine Raybaud answers negatively to the question: 'Does France have a colonial memory?' Raybaud speaks about a collective 'forgetting' of the colonial past, even an 'amnesia' regarding the empire, a 'disinheritance' apparent in 'artistic and monumental memory'.[4]

The extent to which the colonial past is preserved in France – whether or not the French choose to recognise or remember it – can be seen in the visible traces of the overseas empire in the landscape. In Paris, they are numerous, though not always well known. These include vestiges of the colonial exhibition in the western part of the Bois de Vincennes – the old Musée Colonial, a statue formerly called 'La France colonisatrice', as well as the pavilions of Cameroun and Togo, now turned into a Buddhist centre. At the eastern end of the forest is the old colonial botanical garden (with monuments to colonial soldiers). The mother-house of the Société des Missions Etrangères in the Rue du Bac, the former Ecole Coloniale on the edge of the Luxembourg Gardens, the headquarters of the old Banque d'Indochine in the Boulevard Haussmann and the former colonial ministry in the Rue Oudinot testify to the 'uses' of colonies. Orientalist painting is displayed at the Musée d'Orsay and the new Musée des Années Trente (in Boulogne-Billancourt), weaponry and uniforms at the Musée de l'Armée, ethnographic art – much of it colonial booty – at the Musée de l'Homme, the Musée National des Arts d'Afrique et d'Océanie (itself the former Musée Colonial) and in other collections. Statues of personalities important in the history of the French empire stand in Paris streets. The Paris Mosque was built in honour of loyal service by Muslim troops in the First World War.[5] Marshal Lyautey is buried in the Invalides, and other colonial figures are interred in Père-Lachaise cemetery.[6]

One approach to the colonial inheritance is street names, a way in which a city or nation enshrines its past and, in general, civic or national identity. Many names are more or less accidental, especially those inherited from the Middle Ages, referring to the particular trade or profession practised there or recording a landowner's name. Others are purely descriptive, indicating that a street is broad or bent, situating it in relation to a river, park or hill or a city hall, train station, hospital or similar public building, or showing that a road is on the way to another destination. Names bestowed more intentionally sometimes evoke a certain atmosphere, as when names of flowers or trees are given to streets in newly developed urban areas. Yet many names are bestowed for clearly political reasons. Naming of streets honours famous sons (and, more rarely, daughters), but also provides a history lesson to residents and visitors. The lesson usually teaches a traditional version of history bespeaking civic or national pride. Names articulate national aspirations and ideals (such as 'republic' or 'nation') and evidence dominant ideologies. Streets far more frequently bear the names of famous figures – monarchs, prime ministers, senior military officers – than more ordinary folk; even names now utterly obscure were accorded to honour some contemporary figures hailed for worthy accomplishment. Political and military figures hold pride of place in nomenclature, though individuals from fields such as scholarship or the arts are also honoured. Streets named after individuals commemorate either the victorious or those whose bravery in defeat, untimely death or martyrdom accorded them hero status. Others commemorate battles, cities or regions or abstract concepts considered significant.

In Paris the first half-hearted efforts to systematise street names occurred in 1660, but not until the 1770s was a concerted attempt made to do so, particularly by bestowing the names of famous historical figures on streets.[7] The Revolution abolished royalist, religious and noble names, but few new names survived the Napoleonic period and Restoration. Napoleon was a great namer, giving the names of battles and generals to an enormous number of streets. Succeeding regimes proved less radical in rebranding, though purges occurred after the end of the Second Empire and the Vichy regime. The extension of Paris, especially with Haussmann's annexation of suburban communes in 1860, required a vast list of new names. Paris covered 3370 hectares at the time of the Revolution, 7802 hectares in 1860; the 20 *arrondissements* comprised 10 450 hectares by the late 1950s. The number of public streets increased from 1070 in 1789 to 5218 by 1957.[8]

Street-naming constitutes a type of propaganda as authorities, by bestowing particular historical names, write an official view of the past onto the landscape. Ceremonies accompanying street-naming, the positioning of signs or commemorative plaques, and the erection of statues or other monuments, re-enforce the didactic design implicit in nomenclature. Great political changes generally inspire renaming of streets: after revolutions, names from old regimes often disappear, and after successful wars of independence, colonial names are erased. Names of previously neglected or repudiated heroes are resurrected, while those of hated recent rulers are banished, to present a revised version of history.

Colonial appelations are a clearly visible category of street-names in all European countries which ruled overseas empires. Having conquered the world's second largest empire, France's street names generously recall overseas ventures. Numerous municipalities have streets named for such famous colonial figures as General Faidherbe and Marshal Lyautey, Cardinal Lavigerie and Albert Camus, and the explorers Cartier, La Pérouse and Savorgnan de Brazza. In Bordeaux, over three dozen street names come from the colonies, including references to areas in which Bordeaux merchants were particularly interested – the Rues Madagascar, Fort-Dauphin, Majunga and Tamatave underlining the importance of France's Indian Ocean possessions – and to local figures (such as the merchants Hubert Prom and Emile Maurel) active in colonial affairs. Rochefort pays particular homage to the native sons Pierre Loti – one street is named after him, another after his novel *Aziyadé* – and William Ponty, an administrator in Africa. Cities with fewer colonial connections have few streets with colonial names; Dunkirk, for instance, only has streets named after the eighteenth-century corsair Jean Bart, who was born there, the explorer Kerguelen, whose wife came from the city, and Faidherbe, who owned a house nearby.[9]

The empire in the streets of Paris

As befits the capital, the street names of Paris provide a virtual inventory of French history, including colonial history.[10] With few attempts to 'purify' the city of now dubious or simply obscure references, thirty years after France's retreat from its last major colonies, Paris's streetscape continues to bear witness to the colonial past. About 275 streets of some 5400 in the twenty *arrondissements* bear names of people or places linked directly with the colonies.[11]

All eras in French expansion are recalled. The Rue Bérite derives from the Phoenician name of Beirut, conquered by crusaders in 1110, and the Rue Damiette refers to an Egyptian city taken by St Louis in 1249. Conquest of 'New France' is well covered with names of explorers of Canada and the settlements they founded. A street was named for Admiral de Coligny, killed in the St Bartholomew's Day massacre, who tried to colonise Brazil and Florida in the mid-1500s. A number of names commemorate France's ill-fated attempts to carve out an empire in India in the 1600s and 1700s, and successful colonisation in the West Indies. Names commemorating Napoleon's campaign in Egypt are almost as common as the sphinxes which ornamented streets in a wave of 'Egyptomania': Aboukir, Alexandrie, Caire and Pyramides commemorate battles, while Caffarelli, Decrès, Desaix, Dupetit-Thouars, Emériau, Friant, Kléber and Lannes honour officers who served in Egypt.[12] Streets named after Geoffroy de Saint-Hilaire, Champollion, Gaston Maspéro and Prisse d'Avennes recall scholars of Egyptology, a field born in the wake of Napoleon's occupation.

The largest number of names reflect the 'new' empire of the nineteenth century, with allusions to non-colonial overseas exploits as well. These include the Crimean War (the Rue Eupatoria, after a city taken by the French), actions of French troops in Mexico (the Rue Borrégo was named after a battle, the Rue du Général-Détrie after an officer) and the Opium War (the Rues de Pali-Kao and Pékin). The Rue du Nil was named a couple of years before the opening of the French-built Suez Canal, and the name Suez itself was given in 1884 (the same year that a street was named Panama in honour of another, ill-fated, project). The canal's engineer, Ferdinand de Lesseps, was honoured with a street name five years later. The Villa Saïd, named by its founder, one of the canal-builders, honoured the khedive who had encouraged de Lesseps.

Explorers from all periods and areas are represented in Paris streets. Pioneers of North America – Samuel de Champlain, Jacques Cartier and Robert Cavelier de La Salle – are memorialised, as are those who reconnoitred the South Seas in the Rues Bougainville, La Pérouse, Dumont d'Urville and Freycinet; Francis Garnier is a rare Asian explorer honoured. Africa has its share, with streets named after Brazza, Foureau, Gentil, Monteil, Flatters and René Caillié; ironically, Caillié's street is far from the Rue Tombouctou, named after the city he was the first Frenchman to reach. Even polar exploration is not forgotten: there is the Rue du Pôle-Nord and a street named after René Bellot, who died in a British polar expedition.

After explorers came conquerors, and they are legion on the Paris map. La Boudonnais, active in the Indian Ocean, Bugeaud, who 'pacified' Algeria, General Dodds, who took over Dahomey, the triumvirate of conquistadors famous to schoolchildren in the colonial era – Faidherbe, Gallieni and Lyautey – all have streets, as does the legendary Commandant Lamy. Streets even bear the names of less successful conquerors: Montcalm, whose defeat evicted France from Canada, and Dupleix, who failed in a bid to wrest India from the British. Later officers who spent part of their careers overseas – Generals Gouraud and Catroux, Marshals de Lattre de Tassigny, Franchet d'Espérey, Leclerc and Juin – have streets named after them. Several groups of soldiers boast streets: the Rue du Bataillon du Pacifique, named for Oceanic volunteers in the First World War, the Rue de la Légion Etrangère, the Square des Combattants en Indochine and the Place des Combattants en Afrique du Nord. The French Navy has streets and squares honouring Admirals Bruix, Cloué, Courbet and other commanders.

Government figures connected with colonialism also appear in Paris's streetscape. Chasseloup-Laubat, a nineteenth-century minister of the navy who promoted overseas expansion, Guizot, the minister who advocated acquisition of *'points d'appui'* around the globe, Jules Ferry, Paul Deschanel and members of the *parti colonial* (colonial lobby), including Chailley, Leroy-Beaulieu and Paul Bert, are remembered. So, too, are colonial governors, among them Clauzel (Algeria), Moll (Chad), Rousseau (Indochina) and Ballay (Guinea).

Streets bear names of writers and scientists linked to the colonies: Ernest Psichari, a leading colonialist novelist in the early twentieth century, Algerian-born Albert Camus, New-Caledonian-born Francis Carco, Guadeloupean-born Saint-John Perse and the Réunion-born Leconte-de-Lisle have given their names to streets, as have Pierre Loti and Victor Segalen, the memoirist of the Antilles, Père Labat, and such scholars of Orientalism as Etienne Burnouf. Michel Adanson, an eighteenth-century botanist, gave his name to a Paris street and to a species of baobab. Figures associated with the Jardin des Plantes are remembered in streets neighbouring the garden. Streets also have the names of artists associated with the colonies: Delacroix gained early fame for paintings of Morocco, and Gauguin is best known for images of Tahiti; streets are named for the Orientalist painters Léon Bonnat, Alfred Dehodencq, Eugène Fromentin and Alexandre Decamps.

Missionaries also have their place in the nomenclature. The Rue de Babylone was named in 1673 in memory of Bernard de Sainte-Thérèse, founder of the Société des Missions Etrangères, titular bishop of Babylon; there is also a Rue des Missions Etrangères. The Rue du Cardinal-Lavigerie was named after the founder of the Pères Blancs, the Rue Charles-de-Foucauld after the martyred hermit of Tamanrasset. The Rue Albert-Schweitzer honours a later religious and humanitarian figure celebrated for his medical work in Gabon. The Rue de l'Abbé-Grégoire commemorates a Revolutionary-era campaigner for slave emancipation.

Some of these streets received their names soon after the deaths of those honoured: de Lesseps and Marchand were unusual in having streets named for them while they were still alive.[13] Generally, only those who perished tragically were immediately honoured. One of the quickest 'consecrations' came for Antoine Mizon, a now little-remembered figure who travelled with Brazza, explored central Africa and served as French Resident in Madagascar and administrator of Mayotte; he had just been named governor of Djibouti when he died in a shipwreck in 1899, and his name was given to a street the same year. (General Mangin, who promoted the use of the '*force noire*' in the army, was also honoured in the year of his death.) Henry de Bounazel – now also unknown, but one of the last soldiers proclaimed a conquering hero – won his street name in 1934, a year after he was killed fighting in Morocco. The Rue Flatters was named three years after Paul-Xavier Flatters was killed fighting Tuaregs, and the Rue du Commandant-Lamy was named in 1900, immediately after Lamy had been killed warring against the African leader Rabah. Brazza's name was awarded to a street in 1907, two years after he died, somewhat mysteriously, on the way home from a mission to Africa. In these cases, street-naming paid homage to men 'in the news' cited for bravery and martyrdom. In other cases, names were given relatively rapidly to honour national heroes: a street was named after the abolitionist Victor Schoelcher the year following his death in 1893, and one was named after Félix Eboué, one of the first colonial governors to rally to de Gaulle, two years after his death in 1946. Gallieni had to wait two years to be posthumously commemorated, Lyautey four years.

Certain periods have been rich in colonial street-naming, corresponding to both the growth of Paris and the degree of colonialist ardour.

After Haussmann's enlargement of the city, over 30 colonial names were apportioned between 1863 and 1869 (including 13 in 1864 and a similar number in 1867). The late 1870s and early 1880s saw a wave of colonial naming – 12 streets in 1877, 9 in 1884 – responding to revived imperialist interest in the age of Jules Ferry. The next round of colonial naming came during the 'new' imperialism, with 35 names given between 1890 and 1914. The years from 1929 to 1936 saw 26 streets labelled with colonial names. The period, punctuated by the colonial exhibition (and numerous new names in the vicinity of the fair), represented the apogee of official pro-colonial feelings; and this round of naming paid tribute as much to the *idée coloniale* as to particular people or places. Finally, 15 new names were given between 1976 and 1984, a post-colonial naming relating to Paris's recovered municipal unity and authority, but also seeming to 'tidy up' the map by acknowledging neglected individuals or places (Brazzaville, Québec, Acadie) and recognising soldiers who had served in North Africa (and the French battalion in UN forces in the Korean War).[14]

Streets are named after most of the colonies, from the Rue Pondichéry to the Rue de la Guadeloupe, the Rue Gabon to the Rue Taïti [*sic*]. Place names record particular locales but were often given in commemoration of battles or soon after conquests: the Rue d'Alger got its name in 1832, the Rue d'Annam and Rue de Cambodge in the 1870s, the Rue de Casablanca in 1913. Tardily, the Rue de Tanger was named in 1864 in commemoration of the French bombardment of the city two decades earlier; the Rue Sidi-Brahim was named, in 1904, after a battle against Abd el-Kader in 1845. A few were presciently named before takeover: the Rue de Liban in 1867, the Rue de Madagascar in 1884. Others, by contrast, were named long after French withdrawal, such as the Rue Port-au-Prince (1961), and the Place d'Acadie (1984).

The *plan de Paris* provides a geography of the empire. Algeria is particularly well represented: Sahel, Alger, Algérie, Constantine, Guelma, Mazagran, Mouzaïa, Laghouat, Oran, Saïda, Tlemcen, Sidi-Brahim, Kabylie and Atlas. In honour of the Maghrebin protectorates streets are called Maroc, Casablanca and Tanger, and Tunis, Tunisie, Bizerte and Sfax. The Indian Ocean gave Paris the Rue de Madagascar, the West Indies streets named for the Antilles, Guadeloupe, Martinique, Guyane and Port-au-Prince, the Pacific Taïti and Nouvelle-Calédonie. Sub-Saharan Africa is recalled with the Rues Soudan, Tombouctou, Brazzaville, Congo, Gabon, Dahomey, Niger and Sénégal. From the Far East come the Rues de l'Indochine, Cambodge, Laos and Saïgon. Almost all of the colonies are honoured, except those which emerged as separate entities in the last decades of colonisation (there is no Rue Mauritanie); also unremembered are the smallest outposts, such as the Comores, Mayotte, Djibouti, Wallis-et-Futuna and Saint-Pierre-et-Miquelon, apparently too unimportant to be recorded on the Paris landscape.

Yet many street names (colonial or otherwise) are very obscure: the Rue Allard was named after a forgotten French general killed in India in 1839, the Rue Bobillot after a sergeant and amateur playwright who died in Hanoi in 1885. Some are coincidental with imperial links – the Rue de Bizerte was named in 1907 after the Tunisian port city and French military base because the architect of a building in the new street was born there. A few are curious: the name of the *Astrolabe*, one of La Pérouse's ships in the Pacific, was given to a cul-de-sac. Some are even misleading: the Rue de la Colonie, according to Stéphane, was named not in connection with the empire but because of the presence there of a 'colony' of rag-pickers. The streets called Liban and Niger were officially named for a mountain range and a river rather than the territories. The Rue Négrier does not honour a slave-trader but an unfortunately named general who served as interim governor of Algeria in 1837.

Location of street names depends on urbanism – especially the opening of new streets – and the decision of authorities. The 'colonial' map of Paris is suggestive of the ways colonies are remembered. The historic centre of Paris, the four *arrondissements* of the centre right bank, contains almost no colonial names. The Rue Flatters is the only one in the Latin Quarter, but five clearly colonial names appear in the sixth *arrondissement*, near the Ecole Coloniale. The seventh *arrondissement*, replete with ministries, honours a larger number of colonial figures, as does the neighbouring *quinzième*. The wealthy eighth and ninth *arrondissements* are barren of colonial names, but the fashionable *seizième* is rich with them: Bugeaud, Marchand, Dumont d'Urville, La Pérouse, Leroy-Beaulieu, Lyautey and other marshals. This exclusive district boasts the names of explorers, conquerors and colonial promoters, as does the *septième*.

The largest number of colonial names is probably found in the *douzième*, immediately bordering the Bois de Vincennes where the 1931 exhibition was held.[15] Working-class north-central and north-eastern *arrondissements* also have many colonial names, generally of places – Guadeloupe, Louisiane, Martinique, Oran and Tombouctou in the *dix-huitième*, Algérie, Indochine, Kabylie, Maroc and Tanger in the *dix-neuvième*, Cambodge, Liban, Sénégal and Tlemcen (as well as, un-tropically, Terre-Neuve) in the *vingtième*. Many African, West Indian and Maghrebin migrants thus now live in streets which carry the names of their ancestral homelands, while aristocratic and bourgeois Parisians are more likely to live and work in *beaux quartiers* with streets named after French conquerors and administrators of empire. The correlation is not perfect, but does appear more than random.[16]

A number of 'colonial' names belong to practically invisible streets or squares: few Parisians think of particular segments of the Boulevard Saint-Germain as the Place d'Acadie or the Place du Québec, or recognise the Place des Antilles, part of the larger Place de la Nation. No one lives on the Rue de la Légion Etrangère, which intersects parkland and highways at the Porte d'Orléans, nor in squares named after the soldiers in Indochina and Algeria. Indeed almost none of the 'colonial' streets contains a major public building.

Someone walking around Paris is often not aware of the origin of street names, although signs do provide prompts. For instance, the Avenue du Général Lemonnier, dividing the Tuileries gardens, has a plaque explaining that on 10 March 1945, when captured by the enemy at Lang Son in Indochina, Lemonnier 'twice refused to sign a capitulation and chose to be beheaded rather than lose his honour'. More discreetly, the marker on the Rue Bugeaud identifies only a 'French marshal' and says nothing about his role in the conquest of Algeria.

Such signs indicate the ambivalent attitude towards the colonial past manifest in the French landscape and memory. If missionaries and administrators, sailors and soldiers, scientists and writers are memorialised, no streets recall colonial business – there is no Rue des Messageries Maritimes or Place de la Banque d'Indochine. More tellingly, no street is named for the *pieds noirs*. Only two streets seem to be named after colonial women: the Impasse Eugénie-Eboué, after the wife of Governor-General Eboué, the Rue Juliette-Dodu after a Réunion-born heroine of the Franco-Prussian War. (The Rue Joséphine was named for the wife of a landowner.)

Also missing is recollection of indigenous people. The French would have been unlikely to name streets after El Hadj Omar, Samory or Ataï, who fought against French expansion, but even those who ultimately accepted colonial rule, like Abd el-Kader or Queen Pomaré, go unmemorialised. No streets have been named for such prominent and francophile leaders as Léopold Sédar Senghor or Félix Houphouët-Boigny, much less for more militant opponents of French imperialism such as Ho Chi Minh. Eboué and his wife, the *métis* General Dodds and Alexandre Dumas are the only *gens de couleur* to whom Paris renders homage. Although many colonial promoters are honoured, anti-colonialists are not. The only anti-colonial leaders commemorated are South American rebels against the Spanish (Simon Bolívar), a Greek campaigner against the Turks (Botzaris) and Mahatma Gandhi. The street named for the journalist Albert Londres is as close as Paris gets to remembering a French anti-colonialist (and the name was only given in 1984). The Rue Schoelcher nevertheless honours the legislator credited with the definitive abolition of slavery in the empire. In the post-colonial era, city councillors have not engaged in 'politically correct' labelling of streets in honour of anti-colonialists or victims of colonialism. A group of West Indian students did try, unsuccessfully, to secure a change of name for the Rue Richepanse, named after the general sent to Guadeloupe in 1802 to put down rebellion and re-establish slavery there.[17]

Authorities have been reluctant to give names to prominent places to recollect the end of empire, a painful experience for the French. Two examples provide proof. Near the old Musée Colonial is the Square des Combattants d'Indochine, a pretty little *espace vert* marked with only one discreet street sign. The square is dominated by a large gilded statue sculpted for the 1931 exhibition – whether the juxtaposition of 'La France colonisatrice' with the Square des Combattants en Indochine, honouring those who fought a losing battle to retain France's Far Eastern empire, is appropriate or ironic is left to the beholder. Meanwhile, the Place des Combattants en Afrique du Nord is one of Paris's least appealing public spaces, a traffic-choked and graceless square outside the Gare de Lyon. Many soldiers departed for the Algerian front from this train station, but the commemoration seems slight and embarrassed: only one sign even notes the name of the *place*, symbolic of the tortured memory of the Algerian War in France.

Streets and political memory

The simple existence of a street name does not necessarily suffice to trigger association with an historical figure, place or event. Parisians and tourists rushing about their daily business pay little attention to street names except for their utilitarian purpose as addresses. Many are undoubtedly oblivious to the meaning of most names, though they do show enough passing fascination to buy a ten-franc guide to street names sold by the homeless. Despite widespread ignorance of it, the colonial patrimony in Parisian street names nevertheless remains significant for at least three reasons.

First, national and municipal authorities intended to mark the city with colonial references, just as they labelled streets with names of prominent politicians, eminent cultural figures and honoured foreigners.[18] They wished to bring the empire home, erect visible signs of France's overseas domains and, thereby, inculcate respect for France's colonial mission, remembrance of its heroes and their achievements, and association with the cities and countries of *la plus grande France*. Just as with colonial exhibitions and conferences, posters and advertising, these efforts aimed to provoke popular imperialism, instil colonial pride, secure devotion to the colonial cause and inspire colonial vocations. Street-naming was symbolically an attempt to inscribe the far-flung empire on the map of the capital.

Secondly, distribution of the street names reveals some of the pre-occupations of empire. The 'old' empire in the Americas gave way, in names and history, to the new empire of Africa and Asia. North Africa, best commemorated, was the most treasured outpost; the most distant and less useful outposts are seldom represented. Military figures who conquered and ruled France's possessions were most prominent in the colonial pantheon and so in street names. Colonised people – signally absent in street-names – were seen to play background roles in the colonial venture behind triumphant explorers and soldiers, missionaries and administrators. If the list of names commemorating colonial people and places is bewildering to present-day Parisians, that mirrors the vague and imprecise knowledge that many French citizens had of the cities, jungles, deserts and islands over which the flag flew.

Few names commemorate figures whose entire life was spent in the colonies or in colonial activities, though there are exceptions. *Métropolitains* who are honoured were despatched to the empire as explorers, military officers, governors or missionaries. Those born in the colonies only achieved great renown when they 'made it' in Paris: purely colonial *notables* are not recognised in Paris. The names of individuals recollected in Paris, moreover, are associated with the early stages of conquest and 'pacification'; fewer names are associated with later stages in imperial history. The end of empire was less glorious, or less worthy of commemoration, than the beginning. Streets named after Albert Schweitzer, Marshal Juin and Albert Camus are almost the only ones dedicated to figures of the post-Second-World-War period; those three were honoured, respectively, for humanitarian, military and literary accomplishments rather than specifically colonial contributions. Colonisation not decolonisation is imprinted on Paris's map.

About 5 per cent of the streets of the twenty *arrondissements* have names which refer directly or indirectly to the overseas empire. From one standpoint, that small number indicates the limited role that the empire played in metropolitan France. Names were generally given to outlying *arrondissements* (the *douzième, seizième, dix-huitième*) rather than to central ones. Failure to give a colonial name to a truly major street, though colonial names were bestowed on so many smaller ones, confirms that the empire seldom stood at the centre of French public life. However, that proportion of colonial street names is far from trivial. One study has calculated that 7.6 per cent of Paris's street names are those of authors (including scholars and scientists), a figure which puts the amount of space devoted to colonial names in a different perspective.[19]

The third reason that colonial street names are significant is that they remain one of the clearest reminders, at least for those who choose to recognise them, of France's colonial past, perhaps a warning against historical 'amnesia'. In a France still trying to assimilate its colonial inheritance – memory of the colonial wars, often difficult political relations with former colonies, immigration of large numbers of Africans and Asians, the issue of national identity in an increasingly multicultural society and in the context of unifying Europe – the names of Paris streets represent an enduring symbol of the entangled history of France and its colonial domains.[20]

Notes and references

1. P. Nora, ed., *Les Lieux de mémoire* (Quarto edition, Gallimard, 1998 (1st edn 1984–6)).
2. See for example H.-J. Lüsebrink and R. Reichardt, *The Bastille: A History of a Symbol of Despotism and Freedom* (Duke University Press, 1997).
3. E. Said, *Culture and Imperialism* (Chatto & Windus, 1993).
4. A. Raybaud, 'Deuil sans travail, travail sans deuil: la France a-t-elle une mémoire coloniale?', *Dédale*, 5–6, spring 1997, pp. 87–104.
5. For further discussion of this, see the chapter by Neil MacMaster in this collection.
6. The present paper is part of a long-term project on material 'traces' of colonial history in France. See R. Aldrich, 'Vestiges of the Colonial Empire: The Jardin Colonial in Paris', in R. Aldrich and M. Lyons, eds., *The Sphinx in the Tuileries and Other Essays in Modern French History* (Department of Economic History, University of Sydney, 1999), pp. 194–204.
7. D. Milo, 'Le nom des rues', in Nora, *Les Lieux de mémoire*, pp. 1887–1918.
8. Ibid., p. 1912.
9. R. Galy, *Les Rues de Bordeaux* (Les Editions de l'Orée, 1978); R. Allary, *Histoire des rues de ma ville: Rochefort* (n.p., 1977); J. Foort, *Glossaire des rues de Dunkerque* (n.p, 1976).
10. Milo emphasises that in street names Paris is exceptional; the capital has 'tout et trop', in Nora, *Les Lieux de mémoire*, p. 1890.
11. B. Stéphane, *Le Dictionnaire des noms de rues* (Mengès, 2 edn, 1984), and J. Hillairet, *Dictionnaire historique des rues de Paris* (Minuit, 1985) are the major sources for this paper; also indispensable has been the *Plan de Paris par arrondissement* (A. Leconte, 1992 edition). The exact number of 'colonial' streets is impossible to determine. Presidents, prime ministers, marshals,

generals and admirals often played a major role in colonisation – Jules Ferry and Charles de Gaulle are prominent examples – but street names in their honour were not given solely on account of colonial deeds. Similarly, painters and writers such as Malraux and Delacroix were not honoured primarily for their views of the colonies. My count includes those who were born or died in the colonies, and those largely associated with colonial ventures.

12. See J.-M. Humbert, *L'Egypte à Paris* (Action Artistique de la Ville de Paris, 1998).

13. Marchand, after his return from Fashoda, lived in the street bearing his name.

14. Paris also pays tribute to non-French explorers (the Rues Christophe-Colomb, Vasco-da-Gama and Magellan) and some British and other colonialists and their territories – with streets named after Livingstone, Captain Scott, the Boers, Transvaal and Botha.

15. See C. Hodeir and M. Pierre, *L'Exposition Coloniale 1931* (Ed Complexe, 1991).

16. Streets in communes adjacent to Paris have their share (though not a particularly generous one) of colonial names. Kléber, Gallieni, Faidherbe, Lyautey, Eboué reoccur with regularity. Colonial place names are less common, though Aubervilliers and Montreuil remember Nouvelle-France, Saint-Mandé has a Boulevard de la Guyane and Le Kremlin-Bicêtre a Rue de La Réunion; there is a Rue du Congo in Pantin, and a Rue de Tunis in La Plaine-Saint-Denis. Boulogne-Billancourt boasts a Rue Koufra (named after Marshal Leclerc's oath), as well as a street named after the tennis star Roland Garros, who was born in Réunion. Ivry-sur-Seine and Malakoff have a Rue du 19 mars 1962 in honour of end of the Algerian War. Somewhat surprisingly, traditionally communist communes do not have streets named after anti-colonialists or colonial nationalists, despite a plethora of other 'leftist' names (notably ones named after Salvador Allende).

17. Several colonial names have disappeared, such as the Rues d'Aurès and Médéah; the Ruelle Dupleix was appropriately renamed the Rue Pondichéry, and the Square Edouard-Renouard (named after a governor of Indochina) became the Square des Combattants d'Indochine.

18. A few names originated in private initiatives; the name of the Rue du Roi d'Alger was given in 1856 by a local landowner in honour of the infant son of Napoleon III, later to die fighting with the British against the Zulus.

19. R. Posthaus, *Französische Autoren in Strassenverzeichnissen* (thesis, Düsseldorf, 1972), cited by Milo, in Nora, *Les Lieux de mémoire*, p. 1910.

20. A. Fierro, *Histoire et mémoire du nom des rues de Paris* (Parigramme, 1999), an excellent study of Paris street names and their history, unfortunately appeared too late to be used in the preparation of this chapter; it includes a brief section on 'L'Etranger à Paris', pp. 181–9.

Glossary

ancien combattant: war veteran.

Barbouzes (slang word for false beards): a group of about eighty volunteers recruited in the autumn of 1961 for unofficial, extralegal, counter-terrorist action against the OAS under the direction of the Gaullist activist Lucien Bitterlin; ill-trained and undisciplined – unlike the undercover police forming Michel Hacq's Mission C, with whom they worked – they were almost all killed by the OAS within a few months.

chéchia: fez-like woollen headpiece worn by French colonial troops recruited in North Africa and Senegal.

Confédération Générale du Travail Unifié: one of the main French trade unions, established in 1895. Representative of mainstream social-democracy until after World War Two when it became predominantly Communist.

déclassé: was the term used to describe those in the colonial population who had received a French education, but who subsequently were unable to find employment commensurate with their educational qualifications. The fear was that their social marginalisation would make them into a potential source of political discontent if their numbers grew.

direct rule: the system of colonial rule by which colonies were governed directly by the colonial administration, excluding traditional local rulers or institutions.

Ecole Coloniale: often referred to informally as 'Colo', the Ecole Coloniale trained colonial administrators to serve in the colonies of sub-Saharan Africa, the Caribbean, Indochina, Madagascar, the Indian and Pacific Oceans.

Etoile Nord-Africaine: early Algerian militant nationalist party.

évolué: in the colonial vocabulary of the period ('educated natives' is the equivalent term in British colonies), someone who had received education of a European type, often clerks, skilled workers or minor officials. They were therefore, in part at least, acculturated.

Front National: French extreme right party.

Harki: an Algerian who sided with the French side in the Algerian War.

indirect rule: the system of colonial rule by which colonies were administered indirectly by the colonial administration, using traditional local rulers (or their replacements) as intermediaries who retained some measure of competence and authority, e.g. tax-raising powers.

Kanak: name sometimes given to the Melanesians of New Caledonia.

Khedive: the viceroy of the Turkish sultan, and effective ruler of Egypt, from 1867 to 1914.

mise en valeur: a proposed policy for the economic development of the colonies, to the mutual benefit of France and the colonies.

originaires: residents of the Four Communes of Senegal (Dakar, Gorée, Rufisque, Saint-Louis).

le(s) Poilu(s): lit., 'the hairy on(e)s', affectionate nickname given by the civilian population to the French infantry during the First World War, when long periods at the front made regular shaving difficult or unimportant. By extension, brave (virile).

spahis: locally recruited cavalry used in French North African campaigns (the word is of Turkish origin, 'cipaye'; British Indian army derivative, 'Sepoy').

tirailleurs sénégalais: West African infantrymen sometimes deployed as scouts or sharpshooters (snipers).

Select Bibliography

Abd el-Krim et la République du Rif: Actes du colloque international d'études historiques et sociologiques, 18–20 janvier 1973. Paris: Maspéro, 1976 (no editor named; Charles-André Julien chaired the symposium).

Abdel-Jaouad, H., 'Le surréalisme et la question coloniale', *Bulletin of Francophone Africa*, 5, 10, winter 1996–7, pp. 60–73.

Ageron, C.-R., *L'Anticolonialisme en France de 1871 à 1914.* Paris: Presses Universitaires de France, 1973.

Ageron, C.-R., 'L'exposition coloniale de 1931', pp. 561–91, in P. Nora, ed., *Les Lieux de mémoire.* Paris: Gallimard, 1998.

Ageron, C.-R., *France coloniale ou parti colonial.* Paris: Presses Universitaires de France, 1978.

Ageron, C.-R., *Histoire de l'Algérie contemporaine,* 2 vols. Paris: Presses Universitaires de France, 1979.

Alberti J.-B., *Étude sur la colonisation à la Nouvelle-Calédonie, colonisation pénale, colonisation libre.* Paris: Larose, 1909.

Aldrich, R., *Greater France: A History of French Overseas Expansion.* Basingstoke: Macmillan, 1996.

Aldrich, R., 'Vestiges of the Colonial Empire: The Jardin Colonial in Paris', in R. Aldrich and M. Lyons, eds., *The Sphinx in the Tuileries and Other Essays in Modern French History.* Sydney: Department of Economic History, University of Sydney, 1999, pp. 194–204.

Allary, R., *Histoire des rues de ma ville: Rochefort.* Rochefort: no publisher, 1977.

Amselle, J. L. and Sibeud, E., eds, *Maurice Delafosse. Entre Orientalisme et ethnographie: l'itinéraire d'un Africaniste (1870–1926).* Paris: Maisonneuve et Larose, 1998.

Andrew, C. M., Grupp, P. and Kanya-Forstner, A. S.,'Le mouvement colonial français et ses principales personnalités 1890–1914', *Revue Francaise d'Histoire d'Outre-Mer,* 62, 1975, pp. 640–73.

Andrew, C. M. and Kanya-Forstner, A. S., 'The Groupe Colonial in the French Chamber of Deputies, 1892–1932', *Historical Journal,* XVII, 1974, pp. 837–66.

Andrew C. M. and Kanya-Forstner, A. S., 'The French "Colonial Party": Its Composition, Aims and Influence, 1885–1914', *Historical Journal,* 17, 1, 1974, pp. 99–128.

Andrew, C. M. and Kanya-Forstner, A. S., 'Centre and Periphery in the Making of the Second French Colonial Empire, 1815–1920', *Journal of Imperial and Commonwealth History,* 16, 3, 1988, pp. 9–34.

Apollinaire, G., 'Les soupirs du servant de Dakar', in Case d'Armons, 'Calligrammes', Apollinaire, *Oeuvres Poétiques.* Paris: Gallimard, 'Bibliothèque de la Pléiade', 1965.

August, T. G., *The Selling of Empire: British and French Imperialist Propaganda 1890–1940.* Westport, CT: Greenwood, 1985.

Bachollet, R., Delost, J.-B., Lelieur, A.-C., Peyrière, M.-C., *NégriPub (L'Image des noirs dans la publicité).* Paris: Somogy, Editions d'Art, 1987.

Bancel, N., Blanchard, P. and Delabarre, F., *Images d'Empire 1930–1960: trente ans de photographies officielles sur l'Afrique Française.* Paris: Editions de la Martinière/ La Documentation Française, 1997.

Bancel, N., Blanchard, P. and Gervereau, L., eds., *Images et colonies: iconographie et propagande coloniale sur l'Afrique Française de 1880 à 1962*. Paris: BDIC-ACHAC, 1993.

Barcellini, S. and Wieviorka, A., *Passant, souviens-toi! Les Lieux du souvenir de la seconde guerre mondiale en France*. Paris: Plon, 1995.

Barot, Dr., *L'Ame soudanaise. Essai sur la valeur intellectuelle des noirs*. Paris: Pages Libres, 1902.

Beale, H. E., 'Women and First World War memorials in Arles and la Provence mistralienne', *Modern and Contemporary France*, 7, 2, 1999, pp. 209–24.

Ben Fredj, C., *Aux Origines de l'Emigration Nord-Africaine en France*. Paris: University of Paris VII, unpublished doctoral thesis, 1990.

Benoist, A. de, *Europe, Tiers Monde, Même Combat*. Paris: Laffont, 1986.

Benoist d'Azy, A., 'L'expédition française de Cochinchine', *Bulletin de la Société des Etudes Indochinoises (BSEI)*, 1928, 1er trimestre, pp. 25–48.

Benoist-Méchin, J., *Lyautey l'africain ou le rêve immolé*. Paris: Perrin, 1978.

Bernard-Duquenet, N., *Le Sénégal et le Front Populaire*. Paris: Harmattan, 1985.

Berstein, S., 'La peau de chagrin de "l'Algérie française"', in J.-P. Rioux, ed., *La Guerre d'Algérie et les Français*. Paris: Fayard, 1990, pp. 202–17.

Betts, R. F., *Assimilation and Association in French Colonial Theory, 1890–1914*. New York: Columbia University Press, 1961.

Biddiss, M. D., *Father of Racist Ideology. The Social and Political Thought of Count Gobineau*. London: Weidenfeld & Nicolson, 1970.

Biondi, J.-P., and Morin, G., *Les Anticolonialistes (1881–1962)*. Paris: Robert Laffont 1992.

Blanchard, P., Blanchoin, S., Bancel, N., Boëtsch, G. and Gerbeau, H., eds, *L'Autre et nous, 'scènes et types'*. Paris: ACHAC/Syros, 1995.

Blanchard, P. and Chatelier, A., eds, *Images et colonies: nature, discours et influence de l'iconographe coloniale liée à la propagande coloniale et à la représentation des Africains et de l'Afrique en France, de 1920 aux indépendances*. Paris: Syros, 1993.

Blanckaert, C., 'Le système des races', in I. Poutrin, ed., *Le XIXe Siècle*. Paris: Berger-Levrault, 1995, pp. 21–41.

Bonnafont, L., *Trente Ans de Tonkin*. Paris: Figuière, 1924.

Borel, M., *Souvenirs d'un vieux colonialiste*. Six-Fours: Compte d'Auteur, 1963.

Bouche, D., *Histoire de la colonisation française. Vol. 2: Flux et reflux (1815–1962)*. Paris: Fayard, 1991.

Bouguessa, K., 'Emigration et politique. Essai sur la formation et la politique de la communauté algérienne en France à l'entre-deux-guerres mondiales'. Paris: unpublished doctoral thesis, University of Paris V, 1979.

Bourde, P., *De Paris au Tonkin*. Paris: Calmann-Lévy, 1885.

Boverat, F., 'Il faut faire naître', *Revue de l'Alliance Nationale pour l'Accroissement de la Population Française*, 143, 1924, pp. 163–71.

Boyer, A., *L'Institut Musulman de la Mosquée de Paris*. Paris: CHEAM, 1992.

Bresson, G. and C. Lionet, *Le Pen: biographie*. Paris: Seuil, 1994.

Brunschwig, H., *Noirs et blancs dans l'Afrique noire française*. Paris: Presses Universitaires de France, 1983.

Buell, R. L., *The Native Problem in Africa*. New York: Macmillan, 1928.

Camus, A., *Le Premier Homme*. Editions Gallimard, 1994.

Celik, Z., *Displaying the Orient. Architecture of Islam at Nineteenth-Century World's Fairs*. Berkeley: University of California Press, 1992.

Chafer, T. and Sackur, A., *French Colonial Empire and the Popular Front*. Basingstoke: Macmillan, 1999.

Chailley, J., *L'Inde britannique. Société indigène, politique indigène: les idées directrices*. Paris: A. Colin, 1910.

Chailley-Bert, J., *La Colonisation de l'Indochine*. Paris: A. Colin, 1892.

Charles-Roux, J., 'Le général Gallieni', *Bulletin du Comité de Madagascar*, 1899, pp. 7–23.

Chevalier, B., 'Un Essai d'histoire biographique: un grand bourgeois de Marseille, Jules Charles-Roux (1841–1918)'. Aix-en-Provence: unpublished MA dissertation, University of Provence, 1969.

Clancy-Smith, J. and Gouda, F., eds., *Domesticating the Empire: Race, Gender, and Family Life in French and Dutch Colonialism*. Charlottesville: University Press of Virginia, 1998.

Cohen, W. B., 'Literature and Race: Nineteenth-Century French Fiction, Blacks and Africa, 1800–1880', *Race and Class*, 16, 1974, pp. 181–205.

Coloniales 1920–1940, Catalogue de l'exposition tenue au musée municipal de Boulogne-Billancourt du 7 novembre 1989 au 31 janvier 1990.

Comte, G., 'Lyautey l'énigmatique', *Enquête sur l'Histoire*, 8, 1993, pp. 53–8.

Conklin, A. L., *A Mission to Civilize: The Republican Idea of Empire in France and West Africa, 1895–1930*. Stanford University Press, 1997.

Cooper, F. and Stoler, A. L., eds., *Tensions of Empire: Colonial Cultures in a Bourgeois World*. Berkeley: University of California Press, 1997.

Crinson, M., *Empire Building. Orientalism and Victorian Architecture*. London: Routledge, 1995.

Cromer, Lord, 'The government of the subjected races', *Edinburgh Review*, 7, 1908, pp. 127–9.

Crowder, M., 'Indirect Rule. French and British style', *Africa*, 34, 1964, pp. 197–204.

David, P. and Andrault, J.-M., 'Le village noir à l'exposition de Nantes de 1904 en histoire et en images', *Annales de Bretagne et des Pays de l'Ouest*, 4, 1995, pp. 109–25.

David, D., 'France: la puissance contrariée', in *La France en question*. Paris: Gallimard/Limes, 1996.

Debusmann, R. and Riesz, J., eds., *Kolonialausstellungen – Begegnungen mit Afrika?* Frankfurt/M.: IKO-Verlag für Interkulturelle Kommunikation, 1995.

Delafosse, M., *Broussard ou les états d'âme d'un colonial*. Paris: Larose, 1922.

Delafosse, M., 'Pour les indigènes, ceux dont il faut demander l'avis', *Dépêche Coloniale*, 24 September 1924.

Delafosse, M., 'Les libériens et les baoulés. Nègres dits civilisés et nègres dits sauvages', *Les Milieux et les Races*, 2, February 1901.

Deniker, J., *Races et peuples de la terre. Eléments d'anthropologie et d'ethnographie*. Paris: Schleicher Frères, 1900.

Denis, E., *Bordeaux et la Cochinchine sous la Restauration et le Second Empire*, [n.p.], 1965.

Déon, M., *L'Armée d'Algérie et la Pacification*. Paris: Plon, 1959.

Deschamps, H., 'Et maintenant Lord Lugard?', *Africa*, 33, 1963, pp. 294–305.

Dewitte, P., *Les Mouvements nègres en France 1919–1939*. Paris: Harmattan, 1985.

Dias, N., *Le Musée d'Ethnographie du Trocadéro*. Paris: CNRS, 1991.

Dieng, A., *Blaise Diagne, premier député africain*. Paris: Chaka, 1990.

Dine, P., *Images of the Algerian War. French fiction and film, 1954–1992*. Oxford: The Clarendon Press, 1994.

Domergue-Cloarec, D., 'Politique coloniale française et réalités coloniales: l'exemple de la santé en Côte d'Ivoire 1905–1968'. Poitiers: unpublished doctoral thesis, University of Poitiers, 1984.

Dreyfus, C., 'L'Afrique et les Africains vus à Travers les Publicités d'un Journal Strasbourgeois, les *Dernières Nouvelles de Strasbourg*: les coulisses d'un mythe.' Strasbourg: master's dissertation, University of Strasbourg II (UMB), 1996.

Ebihara, M., Ledgerwood, J. and Mortlake, C., eds, *Cambodian Culture, 1970–1990*. Ithaca: Cornell University Press, 1994.

Echenberg, M., *Colonial Conscripts. The Tirailleurs Sénégalais in French West Africa, 1857–1960*. Portsmouth, NH: Heinemann, 1991.

Flood, C. and H. Frey, 'Questions of Decolonisation and Postcolonialism in the Ideology of the French Extreme Right', *Journal of European Studies*, 28, 1/2, 1998, pp. 69–88.

Foort, J., *Glossaire des rues de Dunkerque*. Dunkirk: no publisher, 1976.

Gallieni, General J., *La Pacification de Madagascar (opérations d'octobre 1896 à mars 1899)*. Paris: Librairie Militaire R. Chapelot, 1900.

Gallieni, General J., *Rapport d'ensemble du Général Gallieni sur la situation générale de Madagascar*, 2 vols. Paris: Imprimerie Nationale, 1899.

Galy, R., *Les rues de Bordeaux*. Bordeaux: Les Editions de l'Orée, 1978.

Gannat, P., 'Le nouveau visage du colonialisme', *Identité*, 22, 1994, pp. 18–21.

Gantès, G. de, 'Coloniaux, gouverneurs et ministres. L'influence des français du ViêtNam sur l'évolution du pays à l'époque coloniale, 1902–1914.' Paris: unpublished doctoral thesis, University of Paris, 1994.

Gartner, S., L'exposition coloniale, agricole et industrielles de Strasbourg, 1924. Strasbourg: unpublished master's dissertation, University of Strasbourg, 1994.

Gaspard, F., '"Viollette l'Arabe"', *L'Histoire* special issue, 'Le temps de l'Algérie française', 140, January 1991, pp. 68–72.

Gildea, R., *The Past in French History*. New Haven, CT: Yale University Press, 1994.

Girardet, R., *L'Idée coloniale en France de 1871 à 1962*. Paris: La Table Ronde, 1972.

Goerg, O., 'Exotisme tricolore et imaginaire alsacien. L'exposition coloniale, agricole et industrielle de Strasbourg en 1924', *Revue d'Alsace*, 120, 1994, pp. 239–68.

Gontier Ackermann, S., 'La propagande coloniale à Strasbourg pendant l'entre-deux-guerres à travers les *Dernières Nouvelles de Strasbourg*'. Strasbourg: unpublished master's dissertation, University of Strasbourg II (UMB), 1996.

Greenhalgh, P., *Ephemeral Vistas: the Expositions Universelles, Great Exhibitions and World Fairs, 1851–1939*. Manchester University Press, 1988.

Grégoire, Abbé, *De la Littérature des nègres ou recherches sur leurs facultés intellectu-elles*. Paris: Madan, 1808.

Gutwirth, M., *The Twilight of the Goddesses: Women and Representation in the French Revolutionary Era*. New Brunswick: Rutgers University Press, 1992.

Harmand, J., *Domination et colonisation*. Paris: Flammarion, 1910.

Heckel, E. and Mandine, C., *L'Enseignement colonial en France et à l'Étranger*. Marseille: Balatier, 1907.

Héduy, P., ed., *Algérie française 1942–1962*. Paris: Société de Production Littéraire, 1980.

Heffernan, M., 'The French Right and the Overseas Empire', in N. Atkin and F. Tallett, eds., *The Right in France, 1789–1997*. London: Tauris, 1998, pp. 89–113.

Henrique, L., éd., *Les Colonies françaises: notices illustrées: III. Colonies et protectorats d'Indo-Chine*. Paris: Maison Quantin, 1889.

Hess, J., *L'Ame nègre*. Paris: Calmann-Lévy, 1898.

Hillairet, J., *Dictionnaire historique des rues de Paris*. Paris: Minuit, 1985.

Hodeir, C. and Pierre, M., *L'Exposition Coloniale, 1931*. Brussels: Editions Complexe, 1991.

Hommes et Destins [Biographical Dictionary]. 4 vols. Paris: Académie des Sciences d'Outre-Mer, 1979.

Horne, A., *A Savage War of Peace: Algeria 1954–1962*. London: Macmillan, 1977.

Humbert, J.-M., *L'Egypte à Paris*. Paris: Action Artistique de la Ville de Paris, Paris, 1998.

Hunt, N. R., '"Le Bébé en Brousse": European Women, African Birth-spacing and Colonial Intervention in Breast Feeding in the Belgian Congo', *The International Journal of African Historical Studies*, 21, 3, 1988, pp. 401–33.

Hutton, P. H., ed., *Historical Dictionary of the French Third Republic*, 1870–1940. London: Aldwych Press, 1986.

Hymans, J.-L., *Senghor, an Intellectual Biography*. Edinburgh University Press, 1971.

In, S., *Gatilok ou L'Art de Bien se Conduire*. Phnom Penh: Editions de l'Institut Bouddhique, 1972.

Jauffret, J.-C., 'La loi du 7 juillet 1900 sur l'organisation des troupes coloniales: un accroissement de la Puissance?', in P. Milza and R. Poidevin, *La Puissance Francaise à la 'Belle Epoque', Mythe ou Réalité*. Brussels: Editions Complexes, 1992, pp. 51–62.

Jeaugeon, R., 'Les sociétés d'exploitation au Congo et l'opinion française de 1890 à 1906', *Revue Française d'Histoire d'Outre-Mer*, XLVIII, 1961, pp. 353–437.

Johnson, G. W., ed., *Double Impact: France and Africa in the Age of Imperialism*. Westport, CT: Greenwood Press, 1985.

Kaspi, A. and Marès, A., eds, *Le Paris des Etrangers*. Paris: Imprimerie Nationale, 1989.

Kepel, G., *Les Banlieues de l'Islam: Naissance d'une religion en France*. Paris: Seuil, 1987.

Kharchich, M., 'Left Wing Politics in Lyons and the Rif War', *Journal of North African Studies* 2, 3, 1997, pp. 34–45.

Klein, J.-F., *Un Lyonnais en extrême-orient. Ulysse Pila, vice-roi de l'Indochine, 1837–1909*. Lyon: Editions Lugd, n.d. [1995].

Knibiehler, Y., *Cornettes et blouses blanches. Les Infirmières dans la société française (1880–1980)*. Paris: Hachette, 1984.

Koulakssis, A. and Meynier, G., *L'Emir Khaled premier Za'im? Identité algérienne et colonialisme français*. Paris: Harmattan, 1987.

Koven, S. and Michel, S., eds., *Mothers of a New World: Maternalist Politics and the Origins of Welfare States*. New York and London: Routledge, 1993.

L'Exposition de Hanoi en 1902. Paris: Les actualités diplomatiques et coloniales, 1902.

L'Orient des provençaux novembre 1982 – février 1983. Marseille: Vieille Charité, 1982.

Labouret, H., 'Protectorat ou administration indirecte, direct or indirect rule', *Afrique Française*, 6, May 1934, pp. 289–92.

Labouret, H., 'Question de politique indigène africaine. Protectorat ou administration directe', *Outre Mer*, 1, March 1929, pp. 80–94.

Labouret, H., *A la Recherche d'une nouvelle politique indigène dans l'Ouest Africain*. Paris: Edition du Comité de l'Afrique Française, 1931.

Labouret, H., 'French Colonial Administration', in *Oxford University Summer School on Native Administration*. Oxford: Oxford University Press, 1937.

Labouret, H., 'La colonisation, fait social', *Le Monde Colonial Illustré*, November 1936, p. 242.

Labouret, H., *Paysans d'Afrique occidentale*. Paris: Gallimard 1941.

Lamagat, H., *Souvenirs d'un vieux journaliste indochinois*, III, Saigon, IDEO, 1942.

Lanessan, J.-M. de, *L'Indochine française*. Paris: F. Alcan, 1889.

Lavillé, E., *Guide de l'émigrant en Nouvelle-Calédonie*. Paris: Publication de l'Union Coloniale, 1894.

Lawler, N. E., *Soldiers of Misfortune. Ivoirien Tirailleurs of World War II*. Athens: Ohio University Press, 1992.

Le Roy, Mgr A., 'L'Evolution de l'Esclave dans les Missions Africaines', in *Comptes-rendus des séances du Congrès International Antiesclavagiste de 1900*. Paris: Société Antiesclavagiste de France, 1900.

Le Système des mandats, origines, principes et applications. Genève: Publication SDN, no. 89, 1945.

Lebovics, H., *True France. The Wars of Cultural Identity, 1900–1945*. Ithaca: Cornell University Press, 1992.

Lejeune, D., *Les Sociétes de géographie en France et l'expansion coloniale au XIXe siècle*. Paris: Albin Michel, 1993.

Lemaire S., 'L'Agence économique des colonies. Instrument de propagande ou creuset de l'idéologie coloniale en France (1870–1960)' unpublished PhD thesis, European University Institute, Florence, 2000.

Lemire, C., *La Colonisation et la question sociale en France*. Paris: Challamel Aîné, 1885.

Leprun, S. *Le Théâtre des colonies*. Paris: L'Harmattan, 1986.

Leroy-Beaulieu, P., *De la Colonisation chez les peuples modernes*. Paris: Guillaumin, 1891 (1st edn, 1874).

Liauzu, C., *Aux Origines des tiers-mondismes: colonisés et anticolonialistes en France 1919–1939*. Paris: Harmattan, 1982.

Lugan, B., *Afrique: de la colonisation philanthropique à la recolonisation humanitaire*. Paris: Christian de Bartillat, 1995.

Lugan, B., 'Un empire ruineux', *Enquête sur l'Histoire*, 2, Spring 1992, pp. 72–3.

Lugan, B., *Afrique, bilan de la décolonisation*. Paris: Perrin, 1991.

Lugard, Lord, *The Dual Mandate In British Tropical Africa*. London: Blackwood, 1922.

Lüsebrink, H.-J. and Reichardt, R., *The Bastille: A History of a Symbol of Despotism and Freedom*. Durham, NC: Duke University Press, 1997.

Lyautey, H., *Lettres du Tonkin et de Madagascar*. Paris: A. Colin, 1933.

Lyautey, H., *Paroles d'Action: Madagascar, Sud-Oranais, Oran, Maroc (1900–1926)*. Paris: A. Colin, 1928.

Lyautey, H., 'La colonisation à Madagascar par les soldats', *La Réforme Sociale*, 1 January 1900, pp. 129–39.

Lyautey, H., *Du Rôle colonial de l'armée*. Paris: A. Colin, 1900.

MacKenzie, J.-M., ed., *Imperialism and Popular Culture*. Manchester University Press, 1986.

MacKenzie, J.-M., *Orientalism. History, Theory and the Arts*. Manchester University Press, 1995.

MacKenzie, J.-M., *Propaganda and Empire: The Manipulation of British Public Opinion 1880–1960*. Manchester University Press, 1984.

MacMaster, N., *Colonial Migrants and Racism: Algerians in France, 1900–62.* Basingstoke: Macmillan, 1997.

Marks, S., 'Black Watch on the Rhine: A Study in Propaganda, Prejudice and Prurience', *European Studies Review*, 13, 1983, pp. 297–334.

Marr, D., *Viet-Nam 1945: The Quest for Power.* Berkeley: University of California Press, 1995.

Martial, R., *Les Métis.* Paris: Flammarion, 1942.

Merle, I., *Expériences coloniales. La Nouvelle-Calédonie, 1853–1920.* Paris: Belin, 1995.

Métin, A., *L'Indochine et l'opinion.* Paris: Callamel, 1916.

Meynier, G., *L'Algérie révélée.* Geneva: Droz, 1981.

Michel, M., 'La Colonisation', in J.-F. Sirinelli, ed., *Histoire des Droites en France*, vol. 3. Paris: Gallimard, pp. 125–63.

Michel, M., *La Mission Marchand.* Paris: Mouton et Ecole Pratique des Hautes Etudes, 1972.

Montagnon, P., *La France coloniale I. La Gloire de l'empire.* Paris: Pygmalion, 1988.

Mortimer, E., *France and the Africans.* London: Faber, 1969.

Nederveen Pieterse, J. *White on Black: Images of Africa and Blacks in Western Popular Culture.* New Haven: Yale University Press, 1995.

Nelson, K. L., 'The "Black Horror on the Rhine": Race as a Factor in Post-World War I Diplomacy', *Journal of Modern History*, 42, 1970, pp. 606–27.

Nora, P. *Les Lieux de mémoire*, 3 vols. Paris: Gallimard, 1998.

Nye, R., *Masculinity and Male Codes of Honour in Modern France.* Oxford University Press, 1993.

O'Reilly, P., 'Paul Feillet, Gouverneur de la Nouvelle-Calédonie, 1894–1902', *Revue d'Histoire des Colonies*, t. XL, 1953, pp. 217–48.

Oved, G., *La Gauche française et le nationalisme marocain 1905–1955*, 2 vols. Paris: Harmattan, 1984.

Page, M. E., ed., *Africa and the First World War.* Basingstoke: Macmillan, 1987.

Paillard, Y.-G., *Les Incertitudes du colonialisme. Jean Carol à Madagascar.* Paris: L'Harmattan, 1990.

Payen, E., 'La colonisation libre en Nouvelle-Calédonie', in *Les Annales des Sciences Politiques*, 14, 1899.

Pedersen, S., *Family, Dependence, and the Origins of the Welfare State: Britain and France 1914–1945.* Cambridge, MA: Harvard University Press, 1993.

Perham, M., *Native Administration in Nigeria.* Oxford University Press, 1937.

Perham, M., *West African Passage.* London: Peter Owen, 1983.

Perham, M., *Lugard.* Vol. I: *The Years of Adventure, 1858–1898.* Vol. II: *The Years of Authority.* London: Collins, 1956.

Perham, M., *Colonial Sequence, 1930–1948.* London: Methuen, 1967.

Persell, S. M., 'The Colonial Career of Jules Charles-Roux', *Proceedings of the Western Society for French History*, I, 1974, pp. 306–23.

Persell, S. M., 'Joseph Chailley-Bert and the Importance of the Union Coloniale Francaise', *Historical Journal*, XVII, 1974, pp. 176–85.

Pervillé, G., 'L'Algérie dans la mémoire des droites', in Jean-François Sirinelli, ed., *Histoire des Droites en France*, vol. 2. Paris: Gallimard, 1992, pp. 621–56.

Poinsignon, C., 'La colonisation française dans le Bulletin de la Société de Géographie de l'Est de 1879 à 1914'. Strasbourg: unpublished master's dissertation, Université de Strasbourg II (UMB), 1990.

Poiré, É., *L'Emigration française aux colonies*. Paris: Plon, 1897.

Postel, R., *A Travers la cochinchine*. Paris: Challamel, 1887.

Poupard, C.-A., 'Souvenirs d'un troupier: la prise de Hué, colonnes de police', *Bulletin des Amis du Vieux Hué*, 1939, pp. 237–47.

Pretini, J.-L., 'Saigon-Cyrnos', *Autrement*, série Mémoires, no. 17, pp. 92–106.

Prost, A., *Les Anciens Combattants et la société française, 1914–1939*. Paris: Presses de la Fondation Nationale des Sciences Politiques, 1977.

Raybaud, A., 'Deuil sans travail, travail sans deuil: la France a-t-elle une mémoire coloniale?', *Dédale*, 5–6, pp. 87–104.

Reymond, G., 'Rôle et place des troupes indigènes dans l'est de la France, 1919–1939'. Strasbourg: unpublished master's dissertation, University of Strasbourg II (UMB), 1995.

Reynolds, S., *Gender in Interwar France*. New York and London: Routledge, 1997.

Rich, P. B., *Race and Empire in British Politics*, 2nd edn. Cambridge University Press, 1990.

Riesz, J. and Schultz, J., eds, *Tirailleurs sénégalais*. Frankfurt/M.: Verlag Peter Lang, 1989.

Rivé, P. Becker, A., Pelletier, O., Renoux, D. and Thomas, C., *Monuments de mémoire. Monuments aux morts de la grande guerre*. Paris: La Documentation Française, 1991.

Roberts, M. L., *Civilization without Sexes: Reconstructing Gender in Postwar France, 1917–1927*. University of Chicago Press, 1994.

Ruscio, A., 'L'opinion publique et la guerre d'Indochine. Sondages et témoignages', *Vingtième Siècle*, 1991, pp. 35–46.

Said, E., *Culture and Imperialism*. London: Chatto & Windus, 1993.

Sarraut, A., *Grandeur et servitude coloniales*. Paris: Sagittaire, 1931.

Saussure, L. de, *Psychologie de la colonisation française dans ses rapports avec les sociétés indigènes*. Paris: F. Alcan, 1899.

Schafer, S., *Children in Moral Danger and the Problem of Government in Third Republic France*. Princeton University Press, 1997.

Schneider, W., *Quality and Quantity. The Quest for Biological Regeneration in Twentieth Century France*. New York: Cambridge University Press, 1990.

Schneider, W. H., *An Empire for the Masses. The French Popular Image of Africa, 1870–1900*. Westport, CT: Greenwood Press, 1982.

Schor, R., *L'Opinion française et les étrangers 1919–1939*. Paris: Publications de la Sorbonne, 1985.

Scott, J., *Only Paradoxes to Offer: French Feminists and the Rights of Man*. Cambridge, MA: Harvard University Press, 1996.

Sidos, F., 'Mouvement Jeune Nation', typed statement for national conference of Jeune Nation, 'Peuple de France et d'Outre-mer', Paris, 22 May 1954 (Bibliothèque Nationale).

Sissoko, F. D., 'Les noirs et la culture', in *Congrès International de l'Evolution des Peuples Coloniaux*. Paris: no publisher given, 1938, pp. 119 ff.

Sivan, E., *Communisme et nationalisme en Algérie 1920–1962*. Paris: Presses de la FNSP, 1976.

Spiegler, J. S., *Aspects of Nationalist Thought among French-Speaking West Africans 1921–1939*. Oxford: unpublished DPhil, Oxford University, 1968.

Stéphane, B., *Le Dictionnaire des Noms de Rues*. 2nd edn. Paris: Mengès, 1984.

Stewart, M. L., 'Protecting Infants: The French Campaign for Maternity Leave, 1890–1919', *French Historical Studies*, 13, 1, 1983, pp. 79–105.

Stoler, A. L., *Race and the Education of Desire: Foucault's History of Sexuality and the Colonial Order of Things*. Chapel Hill, NC: Duke University Press, 1995.

Stora, B., *Messali Hadj (1898–1974). Pionnier du Nationalisme Algérien*. Paris: L'Harmattan, 1986.

Stora, B., *Ils venaient d'Algérie. L'immigration algérienne en France 1912–1992*. Paris: Fayard, 1992.

Suret-Canale, J., *L'Afrique noire. L'Ere coloniale 1900–1945*. Paris: Editions Sociales, 1962.

Taguieff, P.-A., 'Doctrines de la race et hantise du métissage. Fragments d'une histoire de la mixophobie savante', *Nouvelle Revue de l'Ethnopsychiatrie*, 17, 1991, pp. 53–100.

Taylor, K. W. and Whitmore, J. K., eds., *Essays into Viet-Namese Pasts*. Ithaca: Cornell University Press, 1993.

Thobie, J., Meynier, G., Coquery-Vidrovitch, C. and Ageron, C.-R., *Histoire de la France coloniale*, vol. 2. Paris: A. Colin, 1992.

Thomas, R., 1960, 'La politique socialiste et le problème colonial de 1905 à 1920', *Revue Française d'Histoire d'Outre-Mer*, XLVII, 1960, pp. 213–45.

Vaillant, J., *Black, French and African: a Life of Léopold Sedar Senghor*. Cambridge, MA: Harvard University Press, 1991.

Van Kley, D. ed., *The French Idea of Freedom: The Old Regime and the Declaration of the Rights of 1789*. Stanford University Press, 1994.

Van Vollenhoven, J., *Une Ame de chef*. Paris: Imprimerie H. Diéval, 1920.

Vaughan, M., *Curing Their Ills. Colonial Power and African Illness*. Stanford University Press, 1993.

Venier, P., 'Le Comité de Madagascar (1894–1911)', *Omaly sy Anio* (Revue d'Histoire, Université de Madagascar), 28, 1988, pp. 43–56.

Venier, P., *Lyautey avant Lyautey*. Paris: L'Harmattan, 1997.

Vial, P., *Nos Premières Années au Tonkin*. Voiron: Baratier et Mollaret, 1889.

Vigné d'Octon, P., *La Gloire du Sabre*. Paris: Flammarion, 1900.

Vignon, L., *Un Programme de politique coloniale. Les Questions indigènes*. Paris: Plon-Nourrit, 1919.

Villaz, M., *Débuts d'un émigrant en Nouvelle-Calédonie*. Paris: Challamel Aîné, 1897.

White, O., *Children of the French Empire. Miscegenation and Colonial Society in French West Africa, 1895–1960*. Oxford University Press, 1999.

Wilson, E. T., *Russia and Black Africa before World War II*. New York: Holmes & Meies, 1974.

Wright, G., *The Politics of Design in French Colonial Urbanism*. University of Chicago Press, 1991.

Zeyons, S., *La Femme en 1900: les années 1900 par la carte postale*. Paris: Larousse, 1994.

Zito, A. and Barlow, T. E., eds., *Body, Subject and Power in China*. University of Chicago Press, 1994.

Index

*Guide de l'Immigrant à
    Madagascar* 35–6
*Guide de l'Emigrant en
    Nouvelle-Calédonie* 43
Guidez, Yvon 192
Guillain, Antoine 29
Guinea 55, 90, 92, 215
Guizot, François 215
Gurkhas 190
Guyana (French) 40, 42, 185, 186,
    187, 217
Guyon, Governor 50

Hadj Ali, Abdelkader 58, 59
Hailey, Lord 177
Haiphong 25
Haiti 217
'Haj Guillaume' 72
Hamy, Ernest-Théodore 157
Hanoi 21, 23, 25, 26, 27, 31, 118,
    125, 126, 218
harkis 195, 202
Harmand, Jules 170
Harvard University 179–80
Haussmann, Baron 212, 213, 217
health 143, 145–51
Héduy, Philippe 203
Hellot, Lieutenant 32
Héloury, Lucien 17
Herriot, Edouard 72, 75, 191
Hervé, Gustave 54
Hess, Jean 162–3
Hirsch, Charles-Henry 134, 135
Hitler, Adolf 135
Ho Chi Minh *see* Nguyen
    Ai Quoc
Holeindre, Roger 196
Hôpital Franco-Musulman 71, 72,
    74–9
Horo Koto 106
Houphouët-Boigny, Félix 219
Humanité, L' 60, 61, 63, 74
Humbert-Hesse 122

Ikdam 58
Ile Bourbon *see* Bourbon Island
Ile-de-France 72
ILO *see* International Labour
    Organisation

immigration to colonies 15–27,
    35–6, 40–50, 85
    to France 57–8, 72, 74, 75, 77, 78,
    79, 90, 97–8, 222
Immigration Bureau *see* Bureau de
    Colonisation
imperialism, popular 1–6, 221
    social 2, 3–4
In, Suttan Prija 122, 123
Indépendants d'Outre-Mer 111
India 125, 170, 215
    French 17, 18, 24, 25
    see also French-Indians
Indian Ocean 17, 18, 20, 213
indirect rule 169, 173–4, 176,
    178, 179
Indochina 1, 7, 15–27, 31, 46, 56, 59,
    60, 62, 85, 88, 89, 90, 92–6, 97,
    102, 104, 105, 106, 112, 113, 118,
    119, 120, 124, 125, 126, 184, 187,
    192, 196, 197, 202, 204, 215, 217,
    218, 219, 220
Institut Musulman de la Mosquée de
    Paris 72
    see also Paris Mosque and Institute
Institute of Colonial Studies 170
'*interlocuteurs valables*' 80, 110–11
International Institute of African
    Languages and Culture 170, 171
International Labour
    Organisation 63, 103, 104–5
International Conference for the
    Cultural Development of Colonial
    Populations 103, 106–7
Isère 25
Islam 62, 63, 72, 73, 75, 76, 79,
    80, 93
    see also Muslims
Istanbul 71
Italy 5, 16, 54, 62, 63

Japan 25
Jaurès, Jean 54, 55
Javanese 45
'Jeanettes' 125
Jeantet, Pierre 17
Jeune Nation 199
Jeunes Algériens 55–6
Jeunes Marocains 62

244 *Index*